Abnormal & Clinical
Psychology

logy Express

The PsychologyExpress series

→ UNDERSTAND QUICKLY
→ REVISE EFFECTIVELY
→ TAKE EXAMS WITH CONFIDENCE

'All of the revision material I need in one place – a must for psychology undergrads.'
Andrea Franklin, Psychology student at Anglia Ruskin University

'Very useful, straight to the point and provides guidance to the student, while helping them to develop independent learning.'
Lindsay Pitcher, Psychology student at Anglia Ruskin University

'Engaging, interesting, comprehensive … it helps to guide understanding and boosts confidence.'
Megan Munro, Forensic Psychology student at Leeds Trinity University College

'Very useful … bridges the gap between Statistics textbooks and Statistics workbooks.'
Chris Lynch, Psychology student at the University of Chester

'The answer guidelines are brilliant, I wish I had had it last year.'
Tony Whalley, Psychology student at the University of Chester

'I definitely would (buy a revision guide) as I like the structure, the assessment advice and practice questions and would feel more confident knowing exactly what to revise and having something to refer to.'
Steff Copestake, Psychology student at the University of Chester

'The clarity is absolutely first rate … These chapters will be an excellent revision guide for students as well as providing a good opportunity for novel forms of assessment in and out of class.'
Dr Deaglan Page, Queen's University, Belfast

'Do you think they will help students when revising/working towards assessment? Unreservedly, yes.'
Dr Mike Cox, Newcastle University

'The revision guide should be very helpful to students preparing for their exams.'
Dr Kun Guo, University of Lincoln

'A brilliant revision guide, very helpful for students of all levels.'
Svetoslav Georgiev, Psychology student at Anglia Ruskin University

'Develops knowledge and understanding in an easy to read manner with details on how to structure the best answers for essays and practical problems – vital for university students.'
Emily Griffiths, Psychology student at Leeds Metropolitan University

'Brilliant! Easy to read and understand – I would recommend this revision guide to every sport psychology student.'
Thomas Platt, Psychology student at Leeds Metropolitan University

Abnormal & Clinical Psychology

Psychology Express

Tim Jones
University of Worcester

Philip Tyson
University of South Wales

Series editor:
Dominic Upton
University of Worcester

PEARSON

Harlow, England • London • New York • Boston • San Francisco • Toronto • Sydney
Auckland • Singapore • Hong Kong • Tokyo • Seoul • Taipei • New Delhi
Cape Town • São Paulo • Mexico City • Madrid • Amsterdam • Munich • Paris • Milan

PEARSON EDUCATION LIMITED
Edinburgh Gate
Harlow CM20 2JE
United Kingdom
Tel: +44 (0)1279 623623

Web: www.pearson.com/uk

First published 2014 (print and electronic)

ISBN: 978-1-4479-2164-6 (print)
       978-1-4479-3100-3 (PDF)
       978-1-4479-3101-0 (ePub)
       978-1-4479-3099-0 (eText)

British Library Cataloguing-in-Publication Data
A catalogue record for the print edition is available from the British Library

Library of Congress Cataloging-in-Publication Data
A catalog record for the print edition is available from the Library of Congress

10 9 8 7 6 5 4 3 2 1
18 17 16 15 14

Cover image © Getty Images

Print edition typeset in 9.5 Avenir LT Std by 73
Print edition printed in Malaysia, CTP-PJB

NOTE THAT ANY PAGE CROSS REFERENCES REFER TO THE PRINT EDITION

Contents

Companion Website

For open-access **student resources** specifically written to complement this textbook and support your learning, please visit **www.pearsoned.co.uk/psychologyexpress**

ON THE WEBSITE

Acknowledgements

Publisher's acknowledgments

We are grateful to the following for permission to reproduce copyright material:

Tables

Table 9.1 adapted from Anorexia nervosa: Definition, epidemiology, and cycle of risk, *International Journal of Eating Disorders*, Vol.37, pp.2–9 (Bulik, C.M., Reba, L., Siega-Riz, A.-M. and Reichborn-Kjennerud, T. 2005), Copyright © 2005 Wiley Periodicals, Inc.

In some instances we have been unable to trace the owners of copyright material, and we would appreciate any information that would enable us to do so.

Introduction

Not only is psychology one of the fastest-growing subjects to study at university worldwide, it is also one of the most exciting and relevant subjects. Over the past decade the scope, breadth and importance of psychology have developed considerably. Important research work from as far afield as the UK, Europe, the USA and Australia has demonstrated the exacting research base of the topic and how this can be applied to all manner of everyday issues and concerns. Being a student of psychology is an exciting experience – the study of mind and behaviour is a fascinating journey of discovery. Studying psychology at degree level brings with it new experiences, new skills and knowledge. As the Quality Assurance Agency (QAA) has stressed:

> psychology is distinctive in the rich and diverse range of attributes it develops – skills which are associated with the humanities (e.g. critical thinking and essay writing) and the sciences (hypotheses-testing and numeracy). (QAA, 2010, p. 5)

Recent evidence suggests that employers appreciate the skills and knowledge of psychology graduates, but in order to reach this pinnacle you need to develop your skills, further your knowledge and most of all successfully complete your degree to your maximum ability. The skills, knowledge and opportunities that you gain during your psychology degree will give you an edge in the employment field. The QAA stresses the high level of employment skills developed during a psychology degree:

> due to the wide range of generic skills, and the rigour with which they are taught, training in psychology is widely accepted as providing an excellent preparation for many careers. In addition to subject skills and knowledge, graduates also develop skills in communication, numeracy, teamwork, critical thinking, computing, independent learning and many others, all of which are highly valued by employers. (QAA, 2010, p. 2)

In 2010, we produced a series of books under the *Psychology Express* title and we are proud to note that both students and tutors have found these books extremely valuable. We appreciated that these books, representing the foundation of the Psychology undergraduate course, covered only one part of a typical course (albeit one of the most important) and that there was a need to build on the success of these and produce a series that covered the application of psychology in applied settings often covered in the latter parts of the Psychology undergraduate programme. This book is part of this new series although written and designed with the positive attributes common to all in the Psychology Express series. It is not a replacement for every single text, journal article, presentation and abstract you will read and review during the course of your degree programme. It is in no way a replacement for your lectures, seminars or additional reading. A top-rated assessment answer is likely to include considerable additional information and wider reading – and you are directed to some of these readings in this text. This revision guide is a conductor: directing you through the maze of your degree by providing an overview of your course, helping you formulate your ideas, and directing your reading.

Each book within Psychology Express presents a summary coverage of the key concepts, theories and research in the field, within an explicit framework of revision. The focus throughout all of the books in the series will be on how you should approach and consider your topics in relation to assessment and exams. Various features have been included to help you build up your skills and knowledge, ready for your assessments. More detail of the features can be found in the guided tour for this book on page xii.

By reading and engaging with this book, you will develop your skills and knowledge base and in this way you should excel in your studies and your associated assessments.

Psychology Express: Abnormal & Clinical Psychology is divided into ten chapters and your course has probably been divided up into similar sections. However we, the series authors and editor, must stress a key point: do not let the purchase, reading and engagement with the material in this text restrict your reading or your thinking. In psychology, you need to be aware of the wider literature and how it interrelates and how authors and thinkers have criticised and developed the arguments of others. So even if an essay asks you about one particular topic, you need to draw on similar issues raised in other areas of psychology. There are, of course, some similar themes that run throughout the material covered in this text, but you can learn from the other areas of psychology covered in the other texts in this series as well as from material presented elsewhere.

We hope you enjoy this text and the others in the Psychology Express series, which cover the complete knowledge base of psychology:

- *Health Psychology* (Angel Chater and Erica Cook);
- *Sport Psychology* (Mark Allen and Paul McCarthy);
- *Educational Psychology* (Penney Upton and Charlotte Taylor);
- *Occupational Psychology* (Catherine Steele, Kazia Solowiej, Holly Sands and Ann Bicknell);
- *Forensic Psychology* (Laura Caulfield and Dean Wilkinson);

This book, and the other companion volumes in this series, should cover all your study needs (there will also be further guidance on the website). It will, obviously, need to be supplemented with further reading and this text directs you towards suitable sources. Hopefully, quite a bit of what you read here you will already have come across and the text will act as a jolt to set your mind at rest – you do know the material in depth. Overall, we hope that you find this book useful and informative as a guide both for your study now and in your future as a successful psychology graduate.

Revision note

- *Use evidence based on your reading, not on anecdotes or your 'common sense'.*
- *Show the examiner you know your material in depth – use your additional reading wisely.*
- *Remember to draw on a number of different sources: there is rarely one 'correct' answer to any psychological problem.*
- *Base your conclusions on research-based evidence.*

Explore the accompanying website at www.pearsoned.co.uk/psychologyexpress
- → Prepare more effectively for exams and assignments using the answer guidelines for questions from this book.
- → Test your knowledge using multiple choice questions and flashcards.
- → Improve your essay skills by exploring the You be the marker exercises.

Guided tour

→ ## Understand key concepts quickly

Start to plan your revision using the **Topic maps.**

Grasp **Key terms** quickly using the handy definitions. Use the flashcards online to test yourself.

Across both sides of the Atlantic, treatments were historic, experimental and without a clear psychological or physiological rationale. In short, no one really knew what caused mental illness with any degree of certainty. This situation began to change with the discovery that a particular feature of certain mental health problems, grandiose delusions, was found to be related to the syphilis bacteria. Grandiose delusions are when individuals believe that they have a special purpose in life, such as to save the world or that they are very famous. The significance of this finding was that it provided a clear indication that some

→ ## Revise effectively

KEY STUDY

Jack had been a quiet child and did not take an interest in the outdoor activities that most other boys did. He would often prefer to stay inside by himself, watch TV and play video games. On trips to the beach with the family he would prefer to sit and read rather than swim in the sea or play. For these reasons Jack was considered a little different from other children. During adolescence his behaviour became very odd. He would lock himself in his room throughout the day and his mother would leave his meals outside the door for Jack to take when no one was around. At night he would sneak downstairs and hide behind the sofa, peering at the TV. His appearance became very unkempt and he refused to shower or brush his teeth. He wore the same clothes for weeks at a time and would always roll one trouser leg up to his knee, and whenever he was seen he was carrying a can of shaving cream in one hand and a teddy bear in another. When mental health services assessed Jack he said that he was a secret agent and that he had to be very careful with what he said as there were a network of spies observing who could access his thoughts using their 'mind machine'. He was in constant contact with his 'handlers', who communicated with him with messages sent directly into his head. Their voices told him of things he must do to avoid being caught by the British mafia.

Quickly remind yourself of the **Key studies** using the special boxes in the text.

xi

Test your knowledge

5.8   How do we know that schizophrenia has a genetic component?
5.9   What do the effects of L-DOPA tell us about the causes of schizophrenia?
5.10 Describe some of the childhood factors associated with the development of schizophrenia.

Answers to the questions can be found on the companion website at:
www.pearsoned.co.uk/psychologyexpress

Prepare for upcoming exams and tests using the **Test your knowledge** and **Sample question** features.

Compare your responses with the **Answer guidelines** in the text and on the website.

Answer guidelines

✱ *Sample question*   *Essay*

Consider whether schizophrenia is primarily a *psychological* or *biological* disorder.

Approaching the question

It is important that you recognise that the question requires you to adopt a critical perspective on psychological and biological explanations of schizophrenia. This means that an awareness of both the strengths and

---

→ # Make your answers stand out

Use the **Critical focus** boxes to impress your examiner with your deep and critical understanding.

CRITICAL FOCUS

Legal and clinical definitions

There is some overlap, as well as clear distinctions, between the clinical diagnosis of antisocial personality disorder, which is a clinical disorder featured in the DSM (APA, 2000), and the legal and sometimes more globally used term psychopathy, a concept developed by Hare (1993). Psychopathy is often associated with criminal or antisocial behaviours, and it is highly likely that individuals considered to be a psychopath could also be classified as having antisocial personality disorder. However, the majority of individuals with antisocial personality disorder are not psychopaths. The clinical classification of antisocial personality disorder is much more diverse, whereas the assessment of psychopathy is much more precise and indepth.

Make your answer standout

A strong answer to this question would incorporate contemporary thinking and research on the proposed causes of schizophrenia. So, for example, when you consider the biological explanations you should refer to the most recent or most renowned research on genetic, neuroanatomical or neurochemical factors associated with the disorder. Remember that schizophrenia is likely to be caused by a complex interplay between biological, environmental and psychological factors and this should be emphasised in your conclusion.

Go into the exam with confidence using the handy tips to **make your answer stand out**.

1

History of mental health perspectives and treatment approaches

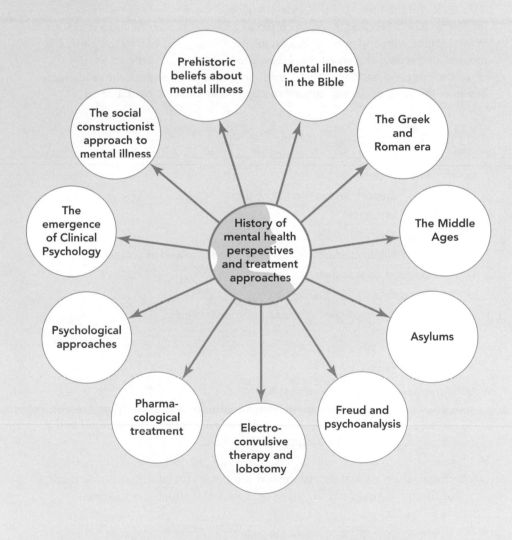

Introduction

Today, mental illness is considered to be caused by several interrelating factors. These may include biological factors such as a genetic predisposition or brain abnormality, psychological factors such as might stem from a disturbed childhood or dysfunctional thinking patterns, and social factors such as environmental stressors or relationship difficulties. This is called the *biopsychosocial* approach and is adopted by most mainstream practitioners involved in the treatment or care of someone with mental health problems. However, the recognition that mental illness stems from a combination of contributory factors is a relatively new one. If we look into the history of the understanding and treatment of mental health problems we will see that there was often a unitary approach to understanding mental illness, with one overarching explanation which was tied to the pervasive thought of the day. This chapter will consider the historical approaches to understanding and treating mental health problems and consider the relationship between religious, social and cultural thoughts and ideas of mental illness.

> ### → *Revision checklist*
>
> *Essential points to revise are:*
> - ❏ Historical perspectives on mental health
> - ❏ The use of asylums
> - ❏ Freud and psychoanalysis
> - ❏ The use of Electroconvulsive Therapy, lobotomy and pharmacology
> - ❏ Psychological approaches
> - ❏ The emergence of Clinical Psychology
> - ❏ The social constructionist approach to mental illness

Assessment advice

- When answering a question about the history of mental health it is important that you discuss how ideas about what constitutes a mental illness are tied in to social, cultural, religious and individual factors. This is represented in the social constructionist approach to mental illness.

- Over time there have been demonic, religious, biological and psychological perspectives on mental illness and it is important that you can briefly discuss these using examples of how these perspectives influenced treatment approaches.

- When answering a question about the history of Clinical Psychology, a strong answer would consider the historical underpinnings of some of the treatments used within Clinical Psychology. For example, Cognitive Behavioural Therapy (CBT) is heavily based on behaviourist principles and the work of Skinner and Watson.

Sample question

Could you answer this question? Below is a typical essay question that could arise on this topic.

> ✳ *Sample question*   *Essay*
>
> Using historical examples, critically discuss the social constructionist approach to mental illness.

Guidelines on answering this question are included at the end of this chapter, whilst guidelines on tackling other exam questions can be found on the companion website at: www.pearsoned.co.uk/psychologyexpress

Prehistoric beliefs about mental illness

Within communities there have always been individuals who behaved, thought or spoke in an unusual way which made them stand out from those around them. These individuals may have rushed around in a chaotic manner, sat unmoving for long periods of time, spoke in an unintelligible way or heard voices that no one else could hear. Prehistorically, such individuals were not considered to have a mental health problem, but were considered to be possessed by demons who were to blame for the bizarre behaviour, thought and speech. The evidence for this assertion comes from two main sources: the discovery of ancient trepanned skulls and also from what we know about the ancient belief systems from the communities who still practise them today. Trepanning describes a form of surgery involving a hole being made in the skull of living individuals. These holes could be made by scraping, grooving, cutting or boring (Gross, 1999). Archaeologists have uncovered trepanned skulls over 8000 years old, which dates them at the time of the Stone Age (Lillie, 1998), and thousands of skulls have been uncovered over the last two hundred years with neat, man-made holes in them. One of the reasons for this surgery was conjectured to be to allow evil spirits to escape from within the skull, a suggestion first proffered by the renowned neurologist Paul Broca. Broca examined many trepanned skulls and noted that some skulls had been trepanned before *and* after death and reasoned that during life the individual would have been trepanned to allow evil spirits to escape. On cessation of the symptoms that the individual displayed after trepanning, they became a figure of reverence in their community and then after their death, pieces of the skull were removed to act as amulets to protect others from spirit possession.

3

Trepanning: the practice of making holes in the skull for supposed therapeutic purposes.

Taken by itself, the discovery of trepanned skulls does not provide convincing evidence of the belief systems of ancient cultures. However, we know that the belief that spirits or demons can infest the body and cause abnormal behaviour or illness has been widespread throughout history and still exists in some communities. For example, Norbeck (1961) reported the beliefs of members of a rural Japanese community who stated the following: 'The Spirits . . . wander about in the world of human beings searching for a host, and are capable of entering bodies and causing sickness until [an] appropriate ceremony is held to send them off to the other world' (p. 215–216). In addition, Kidd (1946) reported that an Indian chief in British Columbia asked a missionary to bore a hole in his skull to release an evil spirit trapped there, which had been giving him headaches. There is also documented evidence from the Middle Ages of trepanning being used to relieve behavioural abnormality, thought to be caused by demons trapped in the skull (Finger & Clower, 2003). Certainly it is easy to imagine how some of the behavioural characteristics associated with mental illness could be interpreted as evidence of demonic possession especially when the behaviour is bizarre or involves hearing voices which are not perceptible to other members of the community.

Test your knowledge

1.1 What is the main evidence to suggest that ancient cultures believed mental illness was caused by demons or spirits being trapped in the skull?

An answer to this question can be found on the companion website at: www.pearsoned.co.uk/psychologyexpress

Further reading Trepanning

Key reading

Gross, C. G. (1999). A hole in the head. *The Neuroscientist, 5*(4), 263–269.

Mental illness in the Bible

Whereas prehistoric ideas of madness appeared to relate to demonic possession, the Bible predominantly portrays madness as an affliction bestowed on individuals by God as a punishment for sin. Indeed, the Book of Deuteronomy contains a warning from Moses that if people do not follow the commandments from God then 'the Lord will smite you with madness' (Deuteronomy 28:28).

Two key figures are portrayed as suffering from madness in the Bible as a consequence of displeasing God: King Saul and King Nebuchadnezzar II. King Saul ruled Israel 3,000 years ago and was punished with madness after disobeying the orders of the prophet Samuel. He was said to be tormented by an evil spirit sent from God. His torment appeared to involve depression, paranoia and violent jealous rages. He also lost his capacity for leadership, which ultimately led to his suicide on the battle field.

King Nebuchadnezzar II ruled ancient Babylon around 600 years before the birth of Christ (BC) and is said to have displeased God by becoming too powerful and prideful. A voice came from Heaven one day proclaiming 'You, King Nebuchadnezzar, are now informed: Kingship is taken away from you. You will be driven away from other humans and will live with the wild animals. You will eat grass like cattle, and seven periods of time will pass over you until you acknowledge that the Most High dominates human kingship, giving it to anyone he wants' (Daniel 4:31, 32). King Nebuchadnezzar was indeed driven away from his kingdom and lived a wild existence for a period of years during which he grew 'hair like eagle feathers and claws like a bird'(Daniel, 4:33). Some authors have suggested that a literal transformation into an ox had taken place (e.g. Pusey, 1865), but a more likely explanation is a psychological transformation where King Nebuchadnezzar believed he had been changed into an animal. The condition where an individual believes that they have become an animal is called lycanthropy (derived from the Greek words for 'wolf-human') and, although rare, cases exist up to the modern day where individuals believe that they are wolves, werewolves, dogs, gerbils, rabbits, horses, tigers, cats, birds, frogs, bees, hyenas, crocodiles and sharks (Garlipp, Gödecke-Koch, Dietrich, & Haltenhof, 2004). The association between lycanthropy and other mental health problems such as schizophrenia, affective disorders and substance misuse has been noted in the psychiatric literature (Garlipp et al., 2004). Psychodynamic interpretations on the other hand have suggested that the transformation represents the manifestation of primitive id instincts (e.g. for sex or aggression), such as in the case of a women who acted like a wild dog after sexual activity for which there was guilt attached. The transformation allowed her conscious mind to escape these guilty feelings (Jackson, 1978).

Another biblical figure of interest to us is the Prophet Ezekiel who was a Jewish priest living around 600 years BC. The case of Ezekiel is slightly different from that of King Saul and King Nebuchadnezzar because his behaviour during his life, although regarded as possibly psychopathological today, was mostly considered appropriate for a prophet under divine inspiration during the time of his existence. Examples of his behaviour include prophesying the fate of Jerusalem by drawing a picture of the besieged city on a brick, and lying on his left side for 390 days and his right side for 40 days to represent the years of punishment that Israel and Judah respectively would suffer for disobeying God's wishes. Seemingly bizarre behaviour such as this has led to some contemporary authors suggesting that he suffered from schizophrenia (Jaspers, 1951; Stein, 2010). In support of this suggestion are the stories of Ezekiel regularly hearing the voice of God inside his head, hearing voices being one of the core symptoms of schizophrenia. However, Cook (2012) disagrees with these ideas and generally cautions against the examination of biblical figures using modern diagnostic criteria because contemporary authors will not have a full appreciation of the cultural context within which these individuals, and stories about them, derive.

The Greek and Roman era

With Greek and Roman society we see a move away from conceptions of madness in terms of gods and spirits, with the adoption of a more rational and systematic approach (Conrad & Schneider, 1992). The renowned philosopher Plato (427–347 BC) was very influential in this era and his conception of madness started with his supposition that humans possessed both a rational and an irrational soul. The rational soul was located in the brain, whilst the irrational soul was located in the chest. Although these souls were interlinked, on occasions when the irrational soul became disconnected from the rational soul, madness could result (Stone, 1998). Plato is also credited with being one of the first to suggest a distinction between different forms of madness, and he identified: melancholia (sadness/depression), mania (mental excitement) and dementia (declining mental faculties) (Zilboorg, 1941). Plato's categorisations are still recognised today and there are also clear parallels between his ideas of a rational and an irrational soul with psychodynamic ideas of the ego and id in conflict.

A contemporary of Plato, the physician Hippocrates (460–370 BC) was another influential figure of the time. Hippocrates promoted a pre-existing idea that related madness to varying quantities of bodily fluids present in the body (Rosen, 1968). These fluids were called humours and there were thought to be four different types, an imbalance of each triggering a particular type of madness (Conrad & Schneider, 1992). An excess of 'Black Bile' was considered to cause melancholia (depression), and an excess of 'Yellow Bile' brought on symptoms of anxiety and impulsiveness. The other two humours, 'Blood' and 'Phlegm', were considered to lead to mania and emotional indifference respectively (Davison, 2006). Notably, Hippocrates was the first physician to describe the psychosis that sometimes occurs after childbirth, now termed *puerperal psychosis*, although he was mistaken in his assumption that madness affecting women was caused by the womb travelling to the brain (Stone, 1998).

Key term

Humours: fluids which were thought to be present in the body in differing quantities: Black Bile, Yellow Bile, Blood and Phlegm. An imbalance of humours was thought to cause madness.

The therapeutic approaches adopted in the Greek and Roman era utilised both psychological and physiological methods. Plato was an advocate of persuasion or a reward-based approach for individuals behaving in an irrational or worrying manner. Physiological methods used by others had an emphasis on relaxation (e.g. massage) but at the more extreme end might have involved forced cold baths, blood-letting, physical constraint, whipping or beating (Conrad & Schneider, 1992). Such treatments, however, would have been restricted to either the mad from wealthy families or those considered a danger to society. In the main, madness was considered to be a family problem where the emphasis would have been on caring for the individual without the need to consult external agencies such as physicians. Some individuals took to wandering the towns and countryside, which they were permitted to do as long as they did not cause a nuisance.

Test your knowledge

1.2 What is the main cause of madness according to biblical stories?

1.3 What treatments did the ancient Greeks use to treat madness?

Answers to these questions can be found on the companion website at:
www.pearsoned.co.uk/psychologyexpress

Further reading Using contemporary diagnostic methods on historical figures

Key reading

Cook, C. C. H. (2012). Psychiatry in scripture: Sacred texts and psychopathology. *The Psychiatrist, 36*(6), 225–229.

The Middle Ages

The end of the Greek and Roman civilisations around the 5th century AD resulted in a move away from a rational and systematic approach to understanding mental illness. In its place came the revival of superstitious and theological thinking with an emphasis on faith rather than logic and reason (Stone, 1998). Madness was considered to be a punishment from God for sin, a test of faith or the result of a witch's curse. However, by the 15th century there was a reinterpretation of madness as providing a clear indication that a mad individual was a willing agent of the devil. In these terms, the mission of the Catholic Church in Europe was simply to identify and execute all of those found guilty of diabolical consort. In reality, this meant that any individual who acted in an unusual way, who looked a little different or who did not conform to strict religious guidance was at risk of being denounced a witch. Execution by burning, drowning or hanging was the usual method of punishment for those erroneously found guilty of witchcraft (Rosen, 1968).

A highly influential book was written to provide guidance on methods of identifying witches and how to conduct their trial and execution. This book was called the the *Malleus Maleficarum* (or *Witches' hammer* in English) and within its pages it stated that anyone who did not believe in the reality of witchcraft and the existence of the devil was a heretic and thereby at risk of trial and execution themselves (Zilboorg, 1941). With this in mind it is no wonder that rational and physiological explanations of mental illness were not championed by the physicians of the day. Occasionally, however, naturalistic explanations were considered and a Dutch physician, Johann Weyer, published a book in 1563 which argued that although witchcraft and the devil existed, sometimes those accused of witchcraft actually had a mental illness. This book, *The Deception of Demons*, is considered to be a key starting point for a resurgence of non-supernatural explanations of madness (Zilboorg, 1941). The approach of Weyer was to consider a wealth of supposed cases of witchcraft and offer more rational explanations to the occurrences. The European Renaissance was occurring around the time of Weyer's writings and within this there came a rediscovery of the Greek and Roman approach to madness. The Humoural theory became popular again as well as the systematic approach to madness originally practised by Plato and Hippocrates 2000 years earlier. The mad became less and less likely to be accused of witchcraft and were either looked after within the community or allowed to roam freely. However, some were considered troublesome and this led to an era of confinement with asylums springing up all over Europe to house the most disruptive individuals.

Asylums

The first asylums were not exclusively for the mad: others who caused a nuisance to society would also be contained therein. Such people included criminals, prostitutes, beggars, the poor and the unemployed (Conrad & Schneider, 1992). Essentially any individual who was not considered to be a useful member of society might have found themselves in such an institution. Forced labour was also a reality to many who were confined. The incarceration of such a diverse group of people created a chaotic environment where it was difficult to determine those who were fit for work from those who were not. This led to an institutional diversification with prisons, workhouses, almshouse and madhouses being created. Dedicated confinement for the mad, however, was not without its own problems as indicated in a report from a French Inspector of madhouses in 1785: 'thousands of lunatics are locked up in prison without anyone even thinking of administering the slightest remedy. The half mad are mingled with those who are totally deranged, those with rage with those who are quiet; some are in chains, while others are free' (Semelaigne, 1930; quoted in Rosen, 1968, p. 151).

Treatment for those in asylums was often based on methods introduced by the ancient Greeks and included blood-letting, forced vomiting, bathing or herbal remedies (Cox, 1813). More experimental methods were also introduced such as the spinning chair where patients were rotated at speed for supposed tranquilisation purposes, although there were reports that some patients were spun until blood came out of their mouths, ears and noses. Nevertheless, it was thought an effective method for some patients at that time, and could be considered an early form of 'shock' therapy (Conrad & Schneider, 1992).

In contrast to these mainly European attempts to treat madness by physical and biological means, the American approach of the 19th century had a focus on social explanations of mental illness. Here, madness was considered to be due to a combination of social factors at a familial level (e.g. lack of discipline growing up) and/or social level (e.g. poor economic conditions). This approach necessitated a social approach to treatment which largely involved restoring order on the supposedly chaotic lifestyle that the individual was thought to have led prior to the onset of madness. For example, in American asylums there was a focus on order, punctuality and precision. Based on this method, some asylums reported impressive recovery rates, as high as 100% in some cases. However, the figures reported were, to say the least, statistically naïve, and in some cases asylums reported figures only for individuals who had been discharged, not for those who remained or were readmitted. Clearly every patient who was discharged had been cured to some extent. Furthermore, some patients had been reported cured, and then readmitted, and one in particular had been discharged as cured 48 times. Nevertheless, such social cures of insanity prompted the building of many new asylums. However, within America in the latter half of the 19th century, such institutions became overpopulated, sometimes with immigrants, which warranted social cures and the imposition of 'curative' rules and regulations impossible. As a consequence the purpose of the institutions reverted once again to one of containment, restraint and general subjugation (Conrad & Schneider, 1992).

Key term

Social approach: this approach to madness was prominent in the USA in the 19th century and considered madness to derive from a range of social factors such as poor parenting and social deprivation. Treatment using this approach focused on promoting order, structure and responsibility.

Across both sides of the Atlantic, treatments were historic, experimental and without a clear psychological or physiological rationale. In short, no one really knew what caused mental illness with any degree of certainty. This situation began to change with the discovery that a particular feature of certain mental health problems, grandiose delusions, was found to be related to the syphilis bacteria. Grandiose delusions are when individuals believe that they have a special purpose in life, such as to save the world or that they are very famous. The significance of this finding was that it provided a clear indication that some mental health problems were of biological origin, rather than social or spiritual. This served to place the understanding and treatment of mental health problems firmly within the medical domain.

Test your knowledge

1.4 What was the *Malleus Maleficarum*?

1.5 What was the main reason for the development of dedicated places to house the mad?

Answers to these questions can be found on the companion website at: **www.pearsoned.co.uk/psychologyexpress**

Further reading The medicalisation of mental illness

Key reading

Conrad, P., & Schneider, J. W. (1992). Medical model of madness. In P. Conrad & J. W. Schneider (Eds.), *Deviance and medicalization: From badness to sickness*. Philadelphia: Temple University Press.

Freud and psychoanalysis

A revolution in the understanding of mental health problems occurred in the late 19th and early years of the 20th centuries with the work of Sigmund Freud. Building on the ideas of the renowned French neurologist Jean-Martin Charcot, Freud set up a clinic to see clients with *hysteria*. This term was coined by Charcot to describe individuals whose emotional trauma appeared to result in physical symptoms. For example, someone who narrowly escaped their leg being run over by a carriage may walk with a limp as if they had been run over. Freud saw patients and developed his ideas over 20 years, culminating in his theory of the mind and mental disorder.

At the centre of this theory was the idea that the human mind contains competing drives which are shaped by childhood experiences. The *id* was conceptualised as the instinctual drive which operated on a pleasure-seeking principle (e.g. for food or warmth), and is the part of the personality which dominates in early infancy. The *ego* is the part of the personality which operates on the reality principle. It still seeks gratification, like the id, but recognises that there are social constraints which impede this gratification. For example, crying for food is not going to work if there is not a food source around. This part of the personality develops in later infancy. The third part of Freud's personality structure, and last to develop, is the *superego* or conscience. This represents the internalisation of parental or societal values and might be considered as a type of moral compass. For example, if your parents had very strong opinions against sex before marriage then this attitude might be internalised. The superego and the id are in constant conflict, with the ego playing a reconciliation role between the primitive instincts of the id with the moral concerns of the superego (Stevens, 1983).

According to Freudian theory, hysteria and other types of mental disorder may result as a consequence of the unconscious interplay between these different facets of the personality. For example, in *Studies in Hysteria* (Breuer & Freud, 1895) there is consideration of the case of a woman named Anna O, who presented with a phobia for drinking. To quench her thirst Anna ate large quantities of moist fruit such as melons. Under hypnosis, where unconscious thoughts and desires were uncovered, Anna recalled the story of seeing a female companion's dog drinking out of a glass reserved for human use only. This disgusted Anna, who at the time did not say anything to her companion so as not to appear impolite. However, the disgust felt at this event stayed with Anna at an unconscious level and manifested itself as a phobia for drinking water. Once Anna recalled this story under hypnosis her phobia disappeared: this is also a key aspect of psychodynamic therapy. Once an individual gains recognition of their unconscious thoughts and feelings which are causing hysteria or other types of mental health problems, then the problem would dissipate. Recognition leads to recovery.

Another important aspect of Freud's psychoanalytic theory is that of psychosexual development where individuals need to successfully go through a series of stages during childhood in order to become a psychologically healthy adult (i.e. oral, anal, psychosexual). These stages are described in Chapter 2.

Freudian psychodynamic theory attracted a lot of interest in the mental health arena, and in particular the theories and treatments became a substantial part of mainstream North American psychiatry. For the first time, psychiatrists were presented with a theoretical model of how the human mind works and what might cause mental disorder. In addition, with Freudian theory they also had a clear guide as to what therapeutic techniques they should use in order to help patients, and such talking therapy was a welcome alternative to the experimental physical type treatments that were still being used in institutions (Conrad & Schneider, 1992). However, psychoanalysis was not suited to every type of mental disorder and in particular it was considered to be unsuitable for severe mental illness such as psychosis or schizophrenia (Stevens, 1983).

Test your knowledge

1.6 What is hysteria?

1.7 Who was Anna O?

Answers to these questions can be found on the companion website at: www.pearsoned.co.uk/psychologyexpress

Electroconvulsive Therapy and lobotomy

Despite the impact of psychoanalysis on the understanding and treatment of mental disorder, some within the medical community still favoured biologically based treatments, particularly for those with severe and enduring mental illness. The starting point for the use of Electroconvulsive Therapy (ECT) to treat mental disorder came in 1929 when a Berlin physician, Manfred Sakel, accidentally gave an overdose of insulin to a patient with schizophrenia. The patient went into convulsions and then coma, but on regaining consciousness Sakel noted that his symptoms had improved. Sakel continued to practise the technique on his most disturbed patients and the improvements reported prompted other physicians to adopt the technique, so much so that it became a common treatment for schizophrenia over the course of two decades (Conrad & Schneider, 1992). However, concerns about the dangers, cost and time associated with this technique led to it being superseded by ECT, where an electric current is passed through the brain. This method was seen as less dangerous and more controllable than insulin shock treatment, and is still used today, mainly to treat depression in cases where it does not respond to other interventions.

Around the same time that insulin shock therapy was being used, a Portuguese neurologist was experimenting with damaging the frontal lobe of the brain as a potential treatment for mental disorder. Egas Moniz believed that recurrent depressive or obsessive thoughts were caused by abnormal neural circuits within the frontal lobes of the brain and that by damaging these circuits the disturbed thought patterns could be stopped (Stone, 1998). Initially Moniz would damage patients' brains by injecting alcohol through holes he had drilled in their skulls. However, later he abandoned the alcohol technique in favour of using a special cutting device which was inserted through the hole in the skull. It was reported that many patients with schizophrenia, depression and anxiety were helped by having a prefrontal lobotomy, and the work of Moniz was perceived in such a positive light that he received the Nobel Prize for Medicine (Conrad & Schneider, 1992).

Key term

Prefrontal lobotomy: a neurosurgical technique where the frontal area of the brain is deliberately damaged in order to produce changes in thought and behaviour.

The use of lobotomy was also championed in the USA by the physician Walter Freeman who advocated its use for even mild psychological problems and the procedure was carried out on an estimated 50,000 people up to the 1950s. However, the procedure went disastrously wrong at times. The sister of President John F. Kennedy, Rosemary, was given a lobotomy at the age of 23.

Her father had requested the procedure after becoming concerned about her mood swings and he complained to doctors about the 23-year-old's moodiness and attraction towards young men. Dr Freeman performed the lobotomy and it had devastating consequences. Rosemary regressed to an infantile state. She was incontinent, could barely speak and would spend hours staring at the wall. Her condition was hidden from the world for years in order to avoid political scandal.

Pharmacological treatment

The 1950s was a decade of two contrasting approaches to the treatment of mental health problems. On one side there were advocates of the psychodynamic approach where the focus was on talking therapy in order to uncover unconscious conflicts within the personality. On the other side were the advocates of the physiological approach to madness, as typified by the use of ECT and lobotomy. However, the decade also saw the development of psychoactive agents which were to revolutionise the care of the mentally ill. In the case of patients who would have previously be institutionalised, these drugs permitted many to be well enough to live in the community. Antidepressants, mood stabilisers, neuroleptics (for schizophrenia) and anxiolytics (for anxiety disorders) were all discovered during the 1950s and all worked by affecting neurotransmitter systems (Stone, 1998). With these new medications came the widespread assumption in the medical and psychiatric community that mental illness could be treated by biological means alone.

Key term

Psychodynamic approach: explaining mental health problems as being due to dysfunctional childhood experiences and conflicts between different aspects of the personality.

Test your knowledge

1.8   Why did ECT replace insulin-induced coma as a treatment for schizophrenia?

1.9   What does the case of Rosemary Kennedy tell us about the use of lobotomy?

1.10 Why was the development of pharmacological agents important for those with mental health problems?

Answers to these questions can be found on the companion website at: www.pearsoned.co.uk/psychologyexpress

Psychological approaches

Aside from pharmacological and psychodynamic means of treating mental illness, from the 1950s onwards behavioural and cognitive approaches were also being pursued. Based upon the work of the behaviourists such as Pavlov, Thorndike, Skinner and Watson, the focus on these methods was to alter the dysfunctional learnt behaviour of an individual. For example, the technique of systematic desensitisation was first used in the late 1950s and involved treating phobias by gradually exposing the individual to the feared stimulus until their fear dissipated. Someone with a phobia for a spider may initially be shown a drawing of a spider's leg, then a spider's body, then a drawing of a whole spider, then a picture of a spider, then a dead spider in a jar, until they are ready to be exposed to a live spider (Bennett, 2006). During this graded exposure the phobic person would be taught relaxation techniques.

Cognitive approaches became popular in the 1970s and these involved altering the dysfunctional thought patterns of an individual through cognitive retraining. For example, negative emotions such as those experienced in depression may be the result of faulty assumptions. Someone might interpret being passed over for promotion as a sign that they are worthless or that there is a conspiracy in the organisation against them. This might result in depression. The cognitive approach would be focused on challenging these assumptions so that they do not lead to negative emotions (Bennett, 2006). A combination of behavioural and cognitive approaches are widely used today under the term Cognitive Behavioural Therapy (CBT) for a range of psychological problems.

Key term

Cognitive Behavioural Therapy (CBT): a therapeutic technique widely used in Clinical Psychology where there is a focus on changing maladaptive behaviour and dysfunctional thought patterns.

The emergence of Clinical Psychology

The modern-day discipline of Clinical Psychology has its origins in the work of a psychology graduate from the University of Pennsylvania. After completing his degree in 1888, Lightner Witmer (1867–1956) studied for a doctorate under Wilhelm Wundt, and then found work lecturing to teachers in child psychology.

One of the teachers asked his advice about a pupil who appeared to have a language deficiency affecting both oral and written communication although his intellect appeared to be normal. Witmer conducted a detailed assessment and discovered that the child had a deficiency in his ability to recognise and distinguish between word sounds, and this was the cause of his problems with spoken and written language (Witmer, 1907). Taking responsibility for tutoring this pupil, Witmer observed improvements and the subsequent write-up of the assessment and treatment of this pupil is considered to be the first Clinical Psychology case study. More children with educational difficulties were referred to Witmer after this initial success, and in response he set up a specialist psychological clinic and the first Clinical Psychology journal *The Psychological Clinic* in 1907. The term Clinical Psychology was coined by Witmer to reflect the close allegiance he felt this new discipline had to medicine, in that they shared the same broad purpose involving the assessment and treatment of individuals with problems. Other psychological clinics were set up to mirror and extend the work of Witmer, both in the USA and the UK, but there was initial reluctance for the new branch of psychology to be taken seriously by the wider community of psychologists. In the first decades of the 20th century, psychology was perceived to be a strictly scientific discipline in the experimental tradition and Clinical Psychology was viewed as far too removed from this (Brysbaert & Rastle, 2009). Suspicion was also levelled at the newly emerging discipline from those in psychiatry and neurology who were concerned that clinical psychologists might interfere with their well-established therapeutic traditions.

The opportunity for Clinical Psychology to find a role where it could be clearly distinguished from psychiatry and neurology came with the advent of World War I. These were the pioneering days of intelligence testing and clinical psychologists were tasked with assessing recruits for their suitability for different military roles (Tyson, 2011). They also found a very important role in investigating the effects of a newly recognised phenomenon, 'shellshock', and helping the servicemen who presented with this acute anxiety response. The psychiatric profession was simply overwhelmed with the number of personnel suffering from this disorder and Clinical Psychology provided much-needed assistance (Brysbaert & Rastle, 2009). However, it was not until after World War II that training programmes in Clinical Psychology were set up in universities, and, recognising the important work that those in the profession did for military personnel, the Veterans' Association in the USA became the main employer for clinical psychologists. A conference in Boulder, Colorado, in 1949 finally clarified the identity of the profession and in so doing made it distinct from that of psychiatry.

Clinical Psychology was to follow a scientist-practitioner model where clinical psychologists were to be both researchers and practitioners. The model ensured that high standards of both scholarly and clinical practice were met; this became the template for Clinical Psychology training programmes all over the world.

Further reading The birth of Clinical Psychology

Key reading

Witmer, L. (1907). Clinical psychology, *Psychological Clinic*, 1, 1–9.

The social constructionist approach to mental illness

The preceding summary of the history of mental health perceptions and treatment indicates how ideas about mental illness change over time. Throughout different periods of history, explanations of the causes of mental illness have included: demonic possession, punishment from God, irregular levels of humours, being an ally of the devil, unconscious conflicts and problems with the neural circuitry or neurotransmitter systems. Treatments for mental illness have also been varied, at various times involving opening the skull, penitence to God, blood-letting, containment, psychodynamic therapy, ECT, lobotomy, psychopharmacology, behavioural and cognitive methods. These differing perceptions and methods of treatment indicate that ideas of mental illness are not stable and do indeed change over time as a result of religious, social, cultural and individual factors (Tyson, 2011). For example, when the Christian Church was the predominant cultural force across Europe, ideas of mental illness were consistent with Christian theology. In addition to perceptions of the causes of mental illness and treatments being culturally relative, so were ideas of what behaviour constitutes a mental illness. See Critical Focus for five mental disorders of the past.

The idea that mental illness stems from a combination of biological, psychological and social factors is referred to by the term biopsychosocial. The model is an attempt to provide a more holistic approach to understanding mental disorder and addresses the disadvantages of considering a disorder from just one perspective. The model also recognises the interrelationship between the multitude of factors which contribute to mental health and ill health. For example, schizophrenia is now understood to stem from a combination of biological factors (e.g. genetics), psychological factors (e.g. problems with thoughts/cognition) and social factors (e.g. living in a deprived environment).

Key term

Biopsychosocial: the idea that mental illness stems from a combination of biological, psychological and social factors.

CRITICAL FOCUS

Five mental disorders of the past

1 **Drapetomania** (1851) – This term described a mental disorder which was thought to cause Negro slaves on plantations to run away from their captors.

2 **Nostalgia** (1688) – This described a condition whereby soldiers and sailors in faraway lands were preoccupied with their home and family.

3 **Onanism** (1710 +) – This is another term for masturbation of which the consequences were considered to be poor sight, memory problems and death in extreme cases.

4 **Tarantism** (Middle Ages) – This 'disorder' centred around the bite of the tarantula spider which caused victims to dance until exhausted.

5 **Homosexuality** (1800s to 1980) – This was considered to be a mental disorder up until 1980 when it was removed from the Diagnostic and Statistical Manual for Mental Disorders.

Source: adapted from Tyson (2011).

✳ *Sample question*   *Essay*

The 20th century saw the application of several new treatment approaches to mental illness. Critically consider the relative importance of biological-based treatments (e.g. pharmacological treatment) and psychological treatments (e.g. psychoanalysis).

Chapter summary – pulling it all together

→ Can you tick all the points from the revision checklist at the beginning of this chapter?

→ Attempt the sample question from the beginning of this chapter using the answer guidelines below.

→ Go to the companion website at www.pearsoned.co.uk/psychologyexpress to access more revision support online, including interactive quizzes, flashcards, You be the marker exercises as well as answer guidance for the Test your knowledge and Sample questions from this chapter.

Answer guidelines

❋ Sample question

Using historical examples, critically discuss the social constructionist approach to mental illness.

Approaching the question

It is important that you have a clear understanding of what the social constructionist perspective is before you attempt to answer this question. Within the history of mental health approaches there are many examples of the social constructionist approach, so be sure to use some of these to illustrate your answer.

Important points to include

A clear description of the social constructionist approach to mental illness is necessary early on in this essay.

The history of mental health approaches includes many examples of where predominant world views of mental illness influenced the way the mentally ill were treated. Remember to include several of these as examples of changing perspectives over different time periods.

What we consider to be a mental illness has changed over time – remember to include examples of historic mental illnesses.

You should also present a reasoned argument as to whether current perspectives on mental illness reflect the social constructionist approach.

Make your answer standout

A strong answer to this question would include an explicit recognition that all ideas about the causes of mental health problems are reflections of the social constructionist approach, even the predominant biopsychosocial explanations popular today. Focus on the cultural relativism of ideas of mental illness, with contemporary examples, would further strengthen your essay.

Explore the accompanying website at www.pearsoned.co.uk/psychologyexpress
→ Prepare more effectively for exams and assignments using the answer guidelines for questions from this chapter.
→ Test your knowledge using multiple choice questions and flashcards.
→ Improve your essay skills by exploring the You be the marker exercises

Notes

Notes

Theoretical perspectives

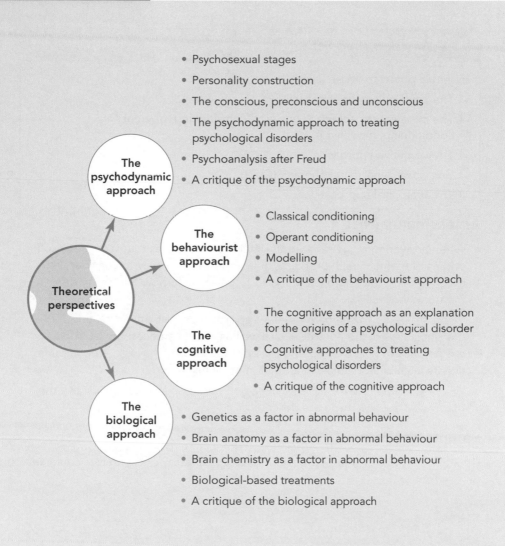

- Psychosexual stages
- Personality construction
- The conscious, preconscious and unconscious
- The psychodynamic approach to treating psychological disorders
- Psychoanalysis after Freud
- A critique of the psychodynamic approach

The psychodynamic approach

The behaviourist approach

- Classical conditioning
- Operant conditioning
- Modelling
- A critique of the behaviourist approach

Theoretical perspectives

The cognitive approach

- The cognitive approach as an explanation for the origins of a psychological disorder
- Cognitive approaches to treating psychological disorders
- A critique of the cognitive approach

The biological approach

- Genetics as a factor in abnormal behaviour
- Brain anatomy as a factor in abnormal behaviour
- Brain chemistry as a factor in abnormal behaviour
- Biological-based treatments
- A critique of the biological approach

A printable version of this topic map is available from
www.pearsoned.co.uk/psychologyexpress

Introduction

As we have seen from the previous chapter, perspectives on mental health have changed over time and been dependent on many cultural, social and individual factors. This long history has, however, not led to a unitary approach to understanding mental illness today. Rather, there are several different approaches which coexist and have alternative perspectives on the origins of, and treatment for, mental health problems. The following chapter discusses the key elements of the psychodynamic, behaviourist, cognitive and biological perspectives.

→ Revision checklist

Essential points to revise are:
- ❏ The psychodynamic approach
- ❏ The behaviourist approach (classical conditioning, operant conditioning, modelling)
- ❏ The cognitive approach
- ❏ Cognitive Behavioural Therapy (CBT)
- ❏ The biological approach

Assessment advice

- When answering a question about different approaches to understanding the origins of mental health problems, it is important not only to consider the theory behind the approach, but also to understand how the theory guides the treatments used.

- If you are asked to compare different approaches, remember to consider the similarities of the approaches as well as the differences. For example, the psychodynamic and behavioural approaches both have an emphasis on events in childhood influencing adult mental health.

- Where possible, use examples of research and case studies to illustrate the theoretical approach you are describing.

Sample question

Could you answer this question? Below is a typical essay question that could arise on this topic.

✱ Sample question   Essay

Compare and contrast any two theoretical approaches to understanding the causes of mental health problems.

The psychodynamic approach

Sigmund Freud (1856–1939) is the originator of the psychodynamic approach which incorporates very influential theories of personality construction, psychological development and psychopathology. Originally a neurologist, Freud became interested in *hysteria*, which was a term used to describe a condition where there were physical reactions to emotional trauma. For example, Fräulein Elizabeth von R. suffered from leg pains which were thought by Freud to be a physical manifestation of guilty feelings. The Fräulein's father had recently died but during his illness he used to rest his legs on those of his daughter for his bandages to be changed. The pain she felt in her legs was at the same place where her father's legs had rested. During therapy, it emerged that the Fräulein thought that tending to her dying father hindered the development of a relationship with a young man. After her father's death she repressed her guilty feelings about these thoughts but they became manifest as physical symptoms (Breuer & Freud, 1895). The culmination of two decades of work with hysteric patients led to Freud's highly influential theory of the mind and mental disorder: psychoanalysis. The focus of this approach is on the investigation of the role that childhood experiences and competing drives within our personality play in mental health.

Psychosexual stages

A key aspect of Freudian psychoanalytic theory is that of the psychosexual stages that children must pass through in order to become balanced and mentally healthy adults. If a child does not successfully navigate each stage, perhaps because they are over- or under-indulged at each stage, then they become fixated at that stage and mental health problems may result as adults. Table 2.1 illustrates the psychosexual stages proposed in classic psychoanalytical theory and the psychological consequences of the child being over- or under-satisfied at each stage.

Table 2.1 Psychosexual stages

Psychosexual stage	Typical behaviour	Consequence of over-satisfaction at this stage	Consequence of under-satisfaction at this stage
Oral stage (0–18 months)	The infant gets primary pleasure from sucking and licking and when teeth develop, biting.	Dependency on others may result and with the loss of others, a pathological reaction such as depression.	Compensatory behaviours as an adult might include thumb sucking, eating, smoking or any other oral behaviour.

Table 2.1 Continued

Psychosexual stage	Typical behaviour	Consequence of over-satisfaction at this stage	Consequence of under-satisfaction at this stage
Anal stage (1–3 years)	The infant becomes focused on either the retention or expulsion of faeces.	If the child, unhindered by their parents, gets pleasure in being messy with their toilet habits, then an anally expulsive personality may result in adulthood. This is typified by a lack of self-control, including untidiness and aggression.	If the child is chastised by the parents during this stage, e.g. if they have an accident, then an anally retentive personality may result in adulthood. Here, there is an obsession with orderliness and cleanliness.
Phallic stage (4–5 years)	Here the focus of attention is on the penis in boys and the clitoris in girls. The *Oedipal conflict* describes the process whereby boys desire their mothers sexually and see their fathers as competitors for their mother's love. The boy believes the father knows these thoughts and so will punish him for them. To resolve this anxiety the boy identifies with the father, adopting his gender-specific behaviour. Girls go through the *Electra complex*. This involves the girl being envious of her father's penis (penis envy) and as a consequence desires him. She recognises she is in conflict with her mother for his attention, and to relieve this conflict identifies with the mother, adopting her gender-specific behaviour.	If the child is not discouraged from masturbatory behaviour at this stage, then as an adult they become promiscuous, an exhibitionist and impulsive. Fixation at the phallic stage may result in problems with gender role behaviour. Freud argued that boys' failure to resolve their Oedipus complex and identify with their father may result in homosexuality, whilst girls who do not resolve their Electra complex may act in a masculine way. In general, relationship difficulties are considered to be a consequence of fixation at the phallic stage.	Chastisement for taking an interest in their genital regions may result in guilt and anxiety about sex and might also impede sexual satisfaction.
Latency stage (5–12)	This is considered to be a stable stage where sexual energy lies dormant. Any residual energy is channelled into other life pursuits such as school and sport.		
Genital stage (adolescence)	Here there is a resurgence of a sexual drive which is now focused on the genitalia of the opposite sex. Any problems arising from a lack of resolution of previous stages will re-emerge here.		

Personality construction

According to Freud, there are three fundamental elements to our personality: the *id*, *ego* and *superego*.

- *The id.* This part of the personality is the first to develop and dominates in infancy. It is only concerned with pleasure-seeking behaviour such as for food, drink or comfort. In adulthood this is the part of the personality concerned with the immediate gratification of desires for sex or outbursts of temper. The id operates on the *pleasure principle*.

- *The ego.* Developing out of the id, the ego recognises that sometimes circumstances do not allow for the immediate gratification of id desires. Therefore a key role of the ego is to employ reason to judge when it is appropriate for the id impulse to be expressed. The ego operates on the *reality principle*.

- *The superego.* Extending from the ego, the superego represents the values instilled in us from our parents, teachers and role models. The focus of the superego is on making sure we act in a morally and socially acceptable manner at all times. The superego represents our *conscience*.

The id, ego and superego are often in conflict because the id seeks pleasure, the superego seeks to uphold moral values and the ego tries to mediate between the two. If id impulses were allowed to be expressed unhindered, then problematic behaviour would emerge. Therefore, according to Freud, the ego has developed a number of strategies which have the purpose of restraining undesirable id impulses and reducing the anxiety they cause. These are called *defence mechanisms*. Three ego defence mechanisms are:

- *Repression.* Anxiety-producing thoughts are kept from the conscious mind, such as having aggressive feelings towards a same sex parent.

- *Denial.* There is a refusal to recognise an external anxiety producing stimuli, for example a smoker may be in denial about the health consequences of smoking.

- *Projection.* This is the projection of your own anxiety-producing thoughts on to others: for example if you desire a married work colleague you may convince yourself that the attraction is the other way around.

The conscious, preconscious and unconscious

Freud made a distinction between our conscious mind, our preconscious mind and our unconscious. The conscious mind represents our current sensory, emotional and cognitive awareness whilst our preconscious mind is the repository for memories and ideas which can be effortlessly brought to conscious awareness. The unconscious, however, is the repository for anxiety-producing thoughts and feelings which could stem from a fixation during psychosexual development and/or uncomfortable id impulses (such as sexual desires or the *libido*). The content of the unconscious mind is not available for conscious awareness. It can still influence behaviour but in a way that is disguised so that anxiety associated with these thoughts and feelings is reduced. For example, the anxiety produced by under-satisfaction at the oral stage of psychosexual development will be hidden in the unconscious. However it will still be expressed through oral type behaviour as an adult.

> **Key term**
>
> **The unconscious**: according to Freud, the unconscious mind is the place where all our hidden desires are held, and if these desires were allowed into our conscious minds then they would cause us anxiety and distress. For example, Freud said boys have an aggressive impulse towards their fathers which is held within the unconscious.

The psychodynamic approach to treating psychological disorders

The purpose of psychodynamic therapy is threefold: 1) to gain access to repressed thoughts and feelings, 2) to resolve conflicts which arose during childhood, and 3) to assist clients to gain an awareness of their hidden desires and motivations (Sue, Sue, Sue, & Sue, 2010).

Traditional psychodynamic therapy adopts the assumption that once a client has gained insight into their unconscious emotional conflicts then positive effects will be observed, for example in being able to relate to family members in a healthier way. There are four main techniques which are used in order to access these unconscious emotional conflicts: *free association, resistance, transference* and *dream analysis* (Table 2.2).

Table 2.2 Techniques used in psychodynamic therapy

Technique	Description	Example
Free association	The client is asked to talk openly about anything that comes to mind and eventually uncomfortable topics and emotionally laden memories will surface which can be explored further.	*I really don't like my boss. He wears an expensive suit as if to say he is better than us, and he talks in a patronising way. It's as if he is some kind of guru and we are his disciples. My father used to wear expensive suits.*
Analysis of resistance	This is where the client obstructs the analysis in order to prevent the uncovering of repressed material. This resistance can take several forms, from the client becoming silent during therapy, changing the topic of conversation or stopping the session altogether.	Messer (2002) reports the case of Brian who was never happy in his work and moved from one job to another without finding satisfaction. He blamed his dissatisfaction on the working environment rather than on his own reaction to the demands of the job. As soon as the therapist started exploring Brian's dysfunctional attitude, he quit therapy.

Table 2.2 Continued

Technique	Description	Example
Transference	Here, the client transfers their feelings towards significant others, such as parents, onto the therapist. These feelings can then be explored to uncover unconscious conflicts.	Levy and Scala (2012) report the case of a client who became angry with the therapist in response to a question. The client felt that the therapist was trying to undermine and provoke them, which was what their father used to do.
Dream analysis	The client is asked to describe their dreams in great detail and these are interpreted by the therapist. According to Freud, dreams are the 'royal road to the unconscious' and therefore can provide important clues about unconscious emotional conflicts.	Freud (1913) reported the dream of a lady with agoraphobia: 'I am walking in the street in the summer. I am wearing a straw hat of peculiar shape, the middle piece of which is bent upwards, while the side pieces hang downwards…I am cheerful and in a confident mood, and as I pass a number of young officers I think to myself, you can't do anything to me'. Freud said her agoraphobia stemmed from her unconscious desire for sexual union with other men as represented by the officers in her dream. The hat represented her husband's genitalia which provided protection from her unconscious sexual desires.

Psychoanalysis after Freud

Psychodynamic therapy today is a little different from that practised by Freud. There is less emphasis on sexual drive as the primary motivating factor in client's endeavours and an increased emphasis on clients having freedom of choice rather than being purely at the mercy of past experiences and conflicts within their personality. There is also a focus on motivating clients to achieve future goals rather than purely being concerned with past experiences. Short-term psychodynamic therapy, where there is a focus on resolving one particular issue over a restricted time period, is a recent development within this approach.

A critique of the psychodynamic approach

Positives

The psychodynamic approach had a tremendous impact on our understanding of the mind, of the role that childhood experiences play in the development of the adult personality, and of the origins of psychological problems. The approach was the first to propose that psychological factors could account for mental health problems, which was in contrast to biological-based explanations which were widespread at the time. In addition, psychodynamic therapy was the first 'talking therapy' for psychological problems and therefore acted as the precursor to later psychological treatments.

Negatives

Criticisms of this approach stem from Freud's reliance on a limited number of case studies and his own analysis in order to formulate his theories. In addition, many of Freud's central concepts, such as the id or repression, are unobservable and untestable as they operate at an unconscious level. Therefore it is uncertain whether these concepts exist at all. Freud's focus on sexuality as a primary drive has also been criticised, particularly his theory of female sexuality involving penis envy. The assumption here is that women are incomplete beings because they do not possess the male appendage. Finally, psychodynamic therapy is not suited to everyone. The reliance on solid skills in verbal expression, self-reflection, honesty and openness has meant that the therapy is not suited to individuals with thought disorder or those who are not psychologically minded.

Test your knowledge

2.1 What factors led Freud to develop his theory of the mind and mental disorder?

2.2 What problems can develop with under-satisfaction of the oral stage of development?

2.3 Why is psychodynamic therapy not suited to everyone?

Answers to these questions can be found on the companion website at: www.pearsoned.co.uk/psychologyexpress

Further reading Transference within psychodynamic therapy

Key reading

Levy, K. N., & Scala, J. W. (2012). Transference, transference interpretations, and transference-focused psychotherapies. *Psychotherapy*, 49 (3), 391–403.

The behaviourist approach

The behaviourist approach to mental health problems places the emphasis on the role of learning in the development of psychopathology. There are three sub-divisions of this approach: classical conditioning, operant conditioning and modelling.

Classical conditioning

Classical conditioning was first defined by the Russian physiologist Ivan Pavlov in the early 20th century. Pavlov was conducting research on the salivary systems of dogs, which involved measuring the amount of saliva they produced. He noted that the dogs would begin to salivate when they heard the footsteps of the assistant who regularly fed them, or heard their food dishes rattling. This was in contrast to the accepted idea that salivation was a physiological response which was only elicited when food entered the mouth. Pavlov's observations suggested that the dogs had *learnt* to associate other events (such as the footsteps of the feeder) to being fed and this triggered salivation. Pavlov experimented with pairing other events with the food, most famously ringing a bell to signal the arrival of food, and he used the term classical conditioning to describe the process whereby physiological reflexes are associated with previously unrelated events through a process of repeated pairings.

In terms of psychopathology, the principles of classical conditioning were first used in an infamous study by Watson and Rayner in 1920. They were interested to see if a phobia could be learnt and their methodology involved training a young child, Little Albert, to be scared of a white rat. Every time Albert touched the rat a steel bar was struck by a hammer to create a loud and distressing noise. After only two presentations of the rat with the sound, Albert became very frightened at the sight of the rat and tried to avoid proximity to it. Albert's fear even extended to other objects which resembled the rat, including a Santa Claus mask and a fur coat.

Another early example of a phobia which was learnt through the process of classical conditioning was described by Bagby (1922). A seven-year-old girl was exploring the woods when she became stuck between rocks by a stream which had a waterfall overhead. The girl became terrified at not being able to escape, and to compound her fear, water poured down over her from the waterfall. After a while she was rescued by her aunt, but after this event the girl had a phobia of water. This was so extreme that she could not bear to be near the sound of running water, and it took several family members to get her into the bath.The phobia stemmed from the girl associating the fear of being trapped with the sound of running water. The principles for all learning according to the classical conditioning paradigm are the same. In the first instance there is a stimulus in the environment (called the Unconditioned Stimulus or US) which produces a natural, reflexive response (called the Unconditioned Response or UR). In the examples we have used these are food (US) causing salivation (UR), a loud noise or being trapped (US) causing fear (UR). See Figure 2.1.

When the US is presented at the same time as another event or item (such as the bell, white rat or water) then an association is learnt between the two. The paired item or event is called the Conditioned Stimulus. See Figure 2.2.

After repeated pairings the CS on its own is sufficient to produce the response, but this is now termed the Conditioned Response as it has been learnt rather than being one that would be naturally observed. See Figure 2.3.

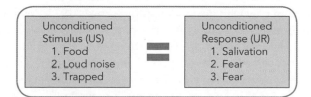

Figure 2.1 Before training

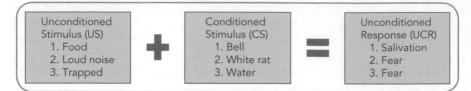

Figure 2.2 During training

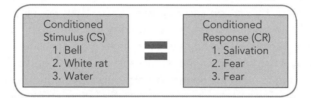

Figure 2.3 After training

The process of classical conditioning has also been used as a therapeutic aid for some mental health problems. For example, Cannon and Baker (1981) used repeated pairing of an emetic (a substance that causes nausea and vomiting) with alcohol in order to treat individuals with an addiction to alcohol. Here, the learnt association between alcohol and vomiting made the participants avoid alcohol. This is termed *aversion therapy*.

Another therapeutic technique which uses the principles of classical conditioning is that of *systematic desensitisation*. This describes the process whereby phobias are treated by the pairing of relaxing feelings with the feared stimulus. For example, someone with a fear of spiders would be taught a relaxation response to spider-related items and after training this relaxation response would replace the fear response. This technique has been successful in a wide variety of phobias such as that for snakes (Lang & Lazovik, 1963), dentists (Shaw & Thoresen, 1974) and school (Houlihan & Jones, 1989). The techniques of *flooding* and *implosion therapy* are also used as treatments for phobias and are based on repeated exposure of the individual to the feared object or situation so that they learn that they are not harmful and the fear response is lost. In flooding the client is made to come into contact with the feared stimulus directly such as in the case of a woman who had a fear of contracting 'cancer germs' from raw meat and other objects. Gradual exposure to raw meat extinguished this fear to the extent that the women could play with raw pork (Baum & Poser, 1971). With implosion therapy the client is asked to imagine a frightening scenario involving their feared object or situation. The therapist tries to maintain their fear with imagery and the theory is that since the fear response cannot be sustained indefinitely, it will dissipate. For example, Hogan and Kirchner (1968) asked snake phobics to imagine being bitten by a snake and also having a snake tightly wrapped around their necks, slowly choking them.

Operant conditioning

When a behaviour has pleasant consequences, it is more likely to be repeated, whilst a behaviour with negative consequences is less likely to be repeated. This simple maxim is the basis of operant conditioning. The theory originated from the work of Edward Thorndike who explored the behaviour of cats by putting them in boxes where the only means of escape would be to press a button or pull a string. After trial and error the cats would learn the behaviour which freed them, and when placed in the same situation again would reproduce the successful behaviour. Thorndike explained his findings in terms of the *law of effect* which proposes that any behaviour which is followed by rewarding consequences will be repeated and any behaviour which is followed by negative consequences would not be repeated. In the example of the cat in a box, all behaviours which did not result in release (such as scratching in the corner, turning in circles) had negative consequences as they did not permit release, whilst pressing a button had positive consequences and so this behaviour was repeated. B.F. Skinner extended Thorndike's work and for more rigorous testing of operant conditioning he designed a specialised piece of equipment which came to be known as the *Skinner box*. This was essentially an adapted rodent cage which contained a lever and a food-dispensing device. Rats and pigeons were placed in the box and Skinner observed and recorded their behaviour in response to different types and different frequencies of reinforcement. By reinforcing simple behaviours sequentially, Skinner was able to train animals to perform highly complex patterns of behaviour, such as pigeons playing table tennis. This is termed behavioural *shaping*.

Methods used in operant conditioning

- *Positive reinforcement*. A reward is given on the exhibition of a particular behaviour.
- *Negative reinforcement*. A behaviour allows an organism to escape from unpleasant circumstances.
- *Punishment*. An unpleasant consequence follows from a particular behaviour.
- *Behavioural shaping*. Complex behaviours are built up from the reinforcing of consecutive simple behaviours.

Operant conditioning as an explanation for the origins of a psychological disorder

The principles of operant conditioning have been used as explanations for the development of some abnormal behaviours. For example, Kurtz et al. (2003) reported that positive reinforcement explained 87.5% of problem behaviour in a sample of young children. This reinforcement included picking up and holding the child or allowing the child to watch television when problem behaviour was exhibited.

In terms of negative reinforcement, any behaviour that allows someone to escape unpleasant events will be reinforced. For example, a child who fears school and is able to stay off school by relating this fear to their parents is using the principle of negative reinforcement. The unpleasant event is attending school and by relaying a fear of school the unpleasant event is avoided.

Operant conditioning as treatment for a psychological disorder

- *Positive reinforcement.* Patients with schizophrenia in a psychiatric hospital were given a sweet, cigarette, cup of coffee or milk if they used the correct cutlery at mealtimes (Ayllon & Azrin, 1964). Individuals undergoing treatment for opioid dependence were given vouchers to exchange for goods contingent on opioid-free urine specimens (Chopra et al., 2009).

- *Negative reinforcement.* Young men who had a tendency for self-injury were able to avoid participation in a learning task if they desisted from self-injury (Vollmer, Marcus, & Ringdahl, 1995). Fazio and Erck (1973) attempted to treat an insect phobia by emphasising that participants would be able to avoid the unpleasant social consequences of their fear (e.g. embarrassment, ridicule) if they stopped their phobic-related behaviour.

Modelling

Modelling describes the process whereby learning occurs through the observation and imitation of others' behaviour. As such, it is also termed social learning or vicarious conditioning. The classic study often cited to illustrate this type of learning is that of Bandura, Roth and Ross (1963) who showed children a video of adults either acting aggressively or playing calmly with a large doll. Children who saw the adults acting aggressively towards the doll acted in the same way when presented with the doll, and those in the 'calm' condition imitated this style of interaction. Clearly the behaviour of others is an important influencing factor in our own behaviour, and this has been used in a psychopathological context. For example, Burstein and Ginsburg (2010) found that children imitated the anxious behaviour of parents prior to a spelling test, and Brown, Tate, Vik, Haas and Aarons (1999) reported that exposure to an alcohol-abusing family member was an important determinant of an adolescent's involvement with alcohol. In addition to modelling providing an explanation for the development of some abnormal behaviours, it has also been used as a therapeutic technique. For example, Blanchard (1970) used it successfully to help snake phobics, and the technique can be used whenever the observation of particular behaviours is deemed therapeutically useful.

Key term

Vicarious conditioning: learning which occurs through the observation of others. For example, a child who sees his mother panicking at the sight of a spider may learn to be afraid of spiders.

A critique of the behaviourist approach

Positives

The behavioural model has proved enduring and popular both as an explanation for the origin of some mental health problems and particularly as a treatment option. The attraction of this approach is that it deals with observable and testable phenomena, so that, for example, a behavioural treatment can be implemented and effects observed. Indeed, there is much empirical support for the efficacy of behavioural approaches within a mental health setting. In contrast, some other approaches, such as the psychodynamic one, do not deal with observable phenomena and therefore their theories are not open to empirical investigation.

Negatives

There is limited evidence of the role that conditioning plays in the development of many psychological disorders. Although behavioural explanations of the origins of anxiety disorders such as phobias can be quite persuasive, they are much less convincing with disorders such as schizophrenia or anorexia nervosa. Secondly, behavioural therapies have been criticised for having limited generalisability outside the therapist's office. For example, Fairburn et al. (1995) found that patients with eating disorders fared worse in the long term after behaviour therapy compared with those who had cognitive behavioural therapy or focal interpersonal therapy. Thirdly, the focus on observable behaviour within this approach neglects the cognitive determinants of behaviours. Humans rarely just react to environmental events based on previously conditioned experiences as the behavioural approach might suggest. Rather, there is a cognitive dimension which helps guide our actions and this allows us to judge, anticipate and interpret events in order to guide our actions and experiences. The cognitive aspect of human experience is neglected within the pure behaviourist tradition.

Test your knowledge

2.4 Outline Watson and Rayner's famous study with Little Albert.

2.5 Think of one example of the classical conditioning of a phobia.

2.6 How could positive reinforcement help some with a fear of heights?

Answers to these questions can be found on the companion website at: www.pearsoned.co.uk/psychologyexpress

---

Further reading Aversion therapy for alcohol dependence

Key reading

Cannon, D. S., & Baker, T. B. (1981). Emetic and electric shock alcohol aversion therapy: Assessment of conditioning. *Journal of Consulting and Clinical Psychology, 49*(1), 20–33.

The cognitive approach

Whereas the behavioural approach has a focus on learnt behaviour as an explanation of psychological disorders, the cognitive approach is focused on the role of thought processes. For example, the old adage about whether a glass is half full or half empty indicates that certain events could be thought of in either a positive (half full) or negative (half empty) light and this is one of the fundamental principles of the cognitive approach to mental health problems.

The cognitive approach as an explanation for the origins of a psychological disorder

The cognitive approach to understanding and treating mental health problems stems from the work of the clinical psychologist Albert Ellis (1913–2007). Ellis was concerned with irrational beliefs which he believed played a major role in the development and persistence of mental health problems, and he devised the ABC model as an explanation of the role that thinking patterns played in mental health and ill health. The A stands for Activating event and can be any event that we experience. The B stands for Beliefs about the event and the C stands for the Consequences of the beliefs about the event. For example, an Activating event could be a young man being rejected when asking a girl out on a date. The Belief held by the man as a consequence of this could be that the girl hates him and that he is worthless because the girl hates him. This emotional reaction can lead to anxiety, depression and other psychological disorders (Ellis, 1993). Stemming from the work of Ellis, the core aspect of the cognitive approach is that it is not events in the environment that cause emotional problems, but the interpretation and belief attributed to the events. Since the work of Ellis, other therapists such as Aaron Beck have identified and classified specific types of thinking patterns that play a role in the development and persistence of mental health problems (see Table 2.3).

Key term

ABC model: describes how our beliefs about particular events can influence our emotional reactions to them. For example, someone who sees a friend in the street but is ignored (A = Activating event) may believe (B = Belief about the event) that their friend no longer likes them and may become depressed as a result (C = Consequence of the belief).

Cognitive approaches to treating psychological disorders

The form of therapy that was originally devised by Ellis to address irrational beliefs was termed Rational Emotive Therapy (RET). Here, clients were trained to look at their beliefs about the activating events and to replace irrational thoughts with more rational ones. This would then diminish the emotional consequences

Table 2.3 Faulty thinking processes

Type of faulty thinking	Description	Example
Overgeneralising	Making sweeping generalisations from single incidents.	Someone who has a bad time at a party may start to think that all social occasions are distressing events and avoid them.
Selective abstraction	Focussing on negative events and ignoring positive ones.	A football player who has a great game but makes one mistake may focus on the one mistake afterwards.
Dichotomous thinking	Categorising all things as either extremely positive or extremely negative.	A depressed individual would use an extremely negative categorisation to describe themselves, e.g. believe that they are worthless.
Personalisation	Relating external events to themselves with no rational basis for doing so.	An individual whose usual bus does not stop for them may believe they had done something to upset the driver.
Catastrophising	Worrying that the worst will always happen.	An anxious individual may think that because their friend is late for lunch that they may have died in a car crash.

Source: adapted from Beck, Rush, Shaw, & Emery (1987).

(e.g. anxiety or depression) of the irrational beliefs. For example, the young man who was turned down for a date may be taught to replace the idea that he is worthless with other ideas about why she may not have been able to go on the date, or to look for confirmatory evidence that he has worth. The cognitive therapy developed by Beck was also concerned with challenging irrational beliefs, although Beck had a particular focus on cognitive biases in thought patterns. The techniques to address these cognitive biases were suggested by Beck (Beck & Weishaar, 2010) and involved training the client to:

- keep track of any negative thoughts (cognitions) they have;
- understand the relationship between their thoughts, their emotion and their behaviour;
- take a critical stance with regard to their distorted cognitions – explore evidence for and against these thoughts;
- replace biased cognitions with more reality-based thoughts;
- acquire the skills to recognise and change the beliefs which lead to their distorted cognitions.

A critique of the cognitive approach

Positives

The cognitive model of mental disorder has become the principal therapeutic model used in Clinical Psychology in the UK today (Beinart, Kennedy, & Llewelyn, 2009). It has been successfully used to treat a wide range of psychiatric disorders and psychological problems including depression (Dobson, 1989), social phobia (Ougrin, 2011) and anorexia nervosa (Serfaty, Turkington, Heap, Ledsham, & Jolley, 1999). Furthermore, it has been claimed that cognitive therapy could be successfully used in other disorders such as substance misuse, and schizophrenia (for a review of the application of cognitive therapy to a wide range of psychological problems, see Leahy, 2004).

Negatives

Not all research has supported the efficacy of this treatment. For example, Ougrin (2011) reviewed the literature and found that cognitive therapy was not superior to exposure therapy (e.g. systematic desensitisation) for a range of anxiety disorders including post-traumatic stress disorder, obsessive compulsive disorder and panic disorder. In addition, several criticisms have been made of the cognitive approach and its use in a therapeutic environment. Firstly, the cognitive approach is reductionist because the complex nature of psychological problems are perceived to be primarily caused by faulty cognition. There is no regard for other factors (physiological, behavioural, social, developmental) which may play a role in psychological problems. Nor is there recognition of the complex interplay between a variety of factors affecting our psychological state. Secondly, there is confusion between symptoms and causes of psychological problems within the cognitive approach. It is just as feasible that faulty cognitions are a *symptom* of the problem rather than the cause and that addressing faulty cognition will not address this cause. For example, there may be an underlying physiological, behavioural, social or developmental cause for an anxious individual to engage in catastrophic thinking. Therefore reframing the faulty cognition will not address the origin of this psychological problem. Thirdly, Skinner (1990) criticised the cognitive approach on the grounds that cognitions are not observable phenomena and therefore should not be part of the scientific approach which psychology claims to adopt. Thoughts cannot be observed or tested and therefore the cognitive approach is not suited to the empirical identity of psychology. Fourthly, cognitive therapy has been criticised for adopting a direct and confrontation approach particularly when cognitions are being challenged. This may be perceived as intimidatory by the client and have a detrimental effect on the therapeutic relationship (Sue et al., 2010).

✳ Sample question   *Essay*

Describe and evaluate the cognitive approach to treating mental health problems.

CRITICAL FOCUS

Cognitive Behavioural Therapy (CBT)

The behavioural and cognitive approaches to therapy have been combined to create a very successful model of treatment called Cognitive Behavioural Therapy (CBT). This approach has a focus both on identifying and modifying faulty cognitions *and* on changing problematic behaviours. This therapy has the potential to indirectly change emotional and physical states leading to positive outcomes for the client. For example, Fennell (1998) outlines the CBT treatment of depression which involves the following strategies:

- **Cognitive strategies.** This might include the use of distraction techniques to avoid painful memories, e.g. recalling pleasant memories.
- **Behavioural strategies.** Clients may be encouraged to keep a diary of their daily activities to note which ones they find most pleasurable to encourage an increase in these activities.
- **Cognitive behavioural strategies.** The identification of negative thoughts and questioning them is the cognitive component here. The behavioural component involves testing faulty assumptions. For example, a client who believes everyone dislikes them may be asked to keep a record of all the pleasant things which are said to them on daily basis.
- **Preventative strategies.** This involves the client learning to identify and challenge mistaken assumptions which contribute to their depressed mood.

CBT has proved effective at treating a variety of psychological problems, although whether it is superior to other psychotherapies is still in question (Lynch, Laws, & McKenna, 2010; Roth & Fonagy, 2005).

Test your knowledge

2.7 What does 'dichotomous thinking' mean?

2.8 How might cognitive biases be addressed?

2.9 What is CBT?

Answers to these questions can be found on the companion website at: www.pearsoned.co.uk/psychologyexpress

Further reading The use of CBT in treating a variety of mental health problems

Key reading

Lynch, D., Laws, K. R., & McKenna, P. J. (2010) Cognitive behavioural treatment for major psychiatric disorder: Does it really work? A meta-analytical review of well-controlled trials. *Psychological Medicine, 40*(1), 9–24.

The biological approach

The assumption of the biological approach is that mental disorders are the result of problems at a biological level, predominantly involving brain anatomy and chemistry and with some disorders a genetic component has also been identified.

Genetics as a factor in abnormal behaviour

Genes are responsible for inherited characteristics and traits of an individual including eye colour and height, but there is also a growing body of evidence to suggest that our genes play a role in susceptibility to mental health problems. A prominent example of this is in schizophrenia. Population-based studies indicated that the risk of any one person developing the disorder is 1%, but later research has shown that if you had a close biological relative with schizophrenia then your risk of developing it is 10%. However the most convincing evidence for the role of genes in schizophrenia came from studies which showed that the chance of having the disorder is much higher, at 48%, if you have an identical twin with the disorder than if you have an affected non-identical twin (17%: Gottesman, 1991). These findings are supported by adoption studies where environmental factors can be largely ruled out as contributing to the development of the disorder (e.g. Tienari et al., 2000). So far efforts to identify specific genes which are linked with schizophrenia have been disappointing (Sanders et al., 2008), and this has led to suggestions that perhaps there are abnormalities across multiple genes.

Aside from schizophrenia, twin studies in other mental disorders have also shown higher concordance rates amongst monozygotic twins compared to dizygotic twins. Shih, Belmonte and Zandi (2004) reviewed these studies and the range of concordance rates found across different studies are reported in Table 2.4.

Table 2.4 **Range of concordance rates for mental disorders for dizygotic and monozygotic twins**

Type of disorder	Prevalence in general population[1]	Range of concordance rates Dizygotic twins	Monozygotic twins
Major depressive disorder	6.7%	0–45%	12–67%
Bipolar disorder	2.6%	0–8%	20–75%
Obsessive compulsive disorder	1%	0–47%	0–87%
Panic disorder	2.7%	0–17%	24–73%
Schizophrenia	1%	0–17%	41–79%

[1]Figures from the US National Institute of Mental Health.

Brain anatomy as a factor in abnormal behaviour

Abnormalities in the anatomy of the brain have been consistently found in schizophrenia and a recent meta-analysis of 42 magnetic resonance imaging (MRI) studies involving over 2000 patients has shown a consistent pattern of grey matter deficits in frontal and temporal brain regions, as well as in the cingulate and insular cortex and the thalamus (Ellison-Wright & Bullmore, 2010). Microscopic studies have indicated that these deficits are the result of cell bodies being abnormally small rather than absent in number (Goldman-Rakic & Selemon, 1997). One of the consequences of these abnormalities is that patients perform poorly on tasks which are mediated by these brain regions. For example, the prefrontal cortex is involved in many tasks involving memory and attention and patients with schizophrenia have difficulty performing these tasks (Spindler, Sullivan, Menon, Lim, & Pfefferbaum, 1997). Brain abnormalities in schizophrenia have been found soon after the onset of the disorder (Lieberman et al., 2001), suggesting a neuro-developmental cause rather than an effect of antipsychotic medication. It is unclear at this stage whether there is a progressive deterioration of neurons during the course of the disorder.

Anatomical abnormalities have also been found in mood disorders. Mood disorders consist primarily of major depression and bipolar disorder. Within major depression a decrease in the volume of the prefrontal cortex has been consistently found, as have disturbances of cognitive functions (e.g. attention) mediated by this area (Sharpley, 2010). It has been suggested that the emotional features of depression (i.e. low mood) are caused by the prefrontal cortex having inadequate control of fear responses, including withdrawal and anxiety, which originate in the amygdala (Arnsten, 2009). The amygdala plays a role in emotional reactivity and given the high and low emotions displayed in bipolar disorder, it is perhaps not surprising that this area appears to be structurally and functionally irregular in this disorder (Malhi & Lagopoulos, 2008).

Brain chemistry as a factor in abnormal behaviour

Neurotransmitters are the chemical messengers of the brain and a disturbance in the amount of specific neurotransmitters has been associated with several psychological disorders. A prominent theory of one of the causes of schizophrenia is an increase in the activity of the neurotransmitter *dopamine*. The evidence for this comes from research indicating that drugs which block dopamine receptors are successful at alleviating the symptoms of schizophrenia, and drugs such as amphetamine, met-amphetamine and cocaine increase the amount of dopamine in the brain and prolonged use of these drugs produces psychotic symptoms like those seen in schizophrenia (see Chapter 5 for further details). There is also evidence for the role of neurotransmitter systems in the symptoms of depression. Medications which increase the amount of monoamines (a class of neurotransmitter which includes serotonin, dopamine and norepinephrine) in the system are successful at alleviating depressive symptomology. Conversely, depression can be caused by medication that disrupts the functioning of monoamines, such as reserpine (Slattery, Hudson, & Nutt, 2004). Problems with neurotransmitter systems are also implicated in other psychological disorders such as anxiety and mania.

Biological-based treatments

The assumption of biological-based treatments for mental health problems is that by altering a patient's underlying physiological state, their psychological state can be improved. Biological-based treatments predominantly involve psychopharmacology, i.e. medication, which influence neurotransmitter systems in an attempt to decrease the symptomology and distress of the individual affected. Table 2.5 shows the main classes of medication used in mental health today.

Table 2.5 Pharmacological treatments for mental health problems

Class of medication	Examples	Used to treat	Reported side effects
Antianxiety drugs (or minor tranquillisers)	Diazepam, Lorazepam	Anxiety disorders	Drowsiness, loss of energy, dependency
Antipsychotic drugs (or major tranquillisers)	Risperidone, Olanzapine	Schizophrenia and psychotic disorders	Drowsiness, weight gain
Antidepressant drugs	Fluoxetine, Venlafaxine	Depression	Nausea, insomnia
Antimanic drugs	Lithium	Bipolar disorder	Thirst, increased urination

Key term

Psychopharmacology: describes the use of prescribed drugs to alter neurotransmitter systems in order to treat mental health problems. These include antidepressant, antianxiety and antipsychotic medications.

Besides pharmacological therapy, biological-based treatments can also involve Electroconvulsive Therapy (ECT) to treat depression. ECT involves an electric current being passed through the brain whilst the patient is sedated in order to induce a seizure. Although it is not understood how ECT works, numerous studies have shown it to be efficacious at relieving depressive symptoms (Pagnin, de Queiroz, Pini, & Cassano, 2004). However, it still remains a controversial treatment and is therefore reserved for patients with depression which does not respond to antidepressant medication and where there is suicidal intent (Bradvik & Bergland, 2006).

A critique of the biological approach

Positives

Biological approaches to understanding mental disorder are very popular today. There is no doubt that considerable success in helping individuals with mental health problems have stemmed from biological-based approaches, and in particular the discovery of antipsychotic medication facilitated the move away from institutionalised care to supported living in the community. Another advantage of the biological approach is that theories and treatments are open to empirical investigation. Because the assumption is that there are physiological changes associated with mental health problems, these can be observed as can the proposed effects of biological-based treatments. This is in contrast to some other approaches, such as the psychodynamic and cognitive ones, which are much less open to study.

Negatives

Firstly, the biological approach takes a *reductionist approach* whereby all human thought, emotion and behaviour are understood at a genetic, cellular, chemical or neuroanatomical level. Many would argue that humans are much more than the sum of their biological parts and some aspects of abnormal behaviour (e.g. delusions or faulty cognition) may never be explainable with reference to biological elements. Secondly, there is often a lack of appreciation within the biological approach of the role that the environment plays in the development of mental health problems. Rather than biological factors (e.g. genes) being the sole explanation for a disorder we now know that mental health problems result from the complex interplay of biological and environmental factors. This is exemplified by the diatheses stress theory which proposes that individuals have a predisposition to developing a disorder but this is only expressed under certain environmental conditions (e.g. stress). Finally, there are many psychological disorders which cannot be explained with reference to underlying biology.

Test your knowledge

2.10 What do twin studies tell us about the genetic basis of mental disorders?

2.11 What brain abnormalities are seen in schizophrenia?

2.12 Why might someone be prescribed lithium?

Answers to these questions can be found on the companion website at: www.pearsoned.co.uk/psychologyexpress

---

Further reading   Evidence for anatomical irregularities in a range of psychiatric disorders

Key reading

Malhi, G. S., & Lagopoulos, J. (2008). Making sense of neuroimaging in psychiatry. *Acta Psychiatrica Scandinavica, 117*, 100–117.

Chapter summary – pulling it all together

→ Can you tick all the points from the revision checklist at the beginning of this chapter?

→ Attempt the sample question from the beginning of this chapter using the answer guidelines below.

→ Go to the companion website at www.pearsoned.co.uk/psychologyexpress to access more revision support online, including interactive quizzes, flashcards, You be the marker exercises as well as answer guidance for the Test your knowledge and Sample questions from this chapter.

Answer guidelines

✱ Sample question

Compare and contrast any two theoretical approaches to understanding the causes of mental health problems.

Approaching the question

When you are given a choice of particular theoretical perspectives to cover in your answer, it is best to choose the ones you are most familiar with. When comparing and contrasting two approaches, it is a good idea to choose two of them where there are clear differences in assumptions, perspectives on mental health and treatments as this provides more material to cover in your answer.

Important points to include

● Each theoretical approach is based on key assumptions and it is important these are outlined initially, e.g. the cognitive approach focuses on the role of cognitive processes.

● Each approach interprets the origins of mental illness from a different perspective and it is important to not only outline this perspective but also to use case examples to illustrate the theory.

● Remember to include research, where possible, which supports or contradicts a particular perspective.

● The consideration of the treatment of mental health problems from different perspectives provides a good opportunity to compare and contrast different approaches.

● The essay is asking you to compare and contrast two approaches, so remember to focus as much on the similarities between these approaches as the differences.

Make your answer standout

A strong answer to this question would incorporate contemporary thinking and research on the different perspectives. Therefore you should refer to the most recent or most renowned research within a particular perspective. Remember that no one particular perspective is the 'correct' one and therefore you should acknowledge that although each perspective does have value, none can provide an all-encompassing explanation for a particular disorder.

Explore the accompanying website at www.pearsoned.co.uk/psychologyexpress
→ Prepare more effectively for exams and assignments using the answer guidelines for questions from this chapter.
→ Test your knowledge using multiple choice questions and flashcards.
→ Improve your essay skills by exploring the You be the marker exercises.

Notes

Notes

3

Mood disorders

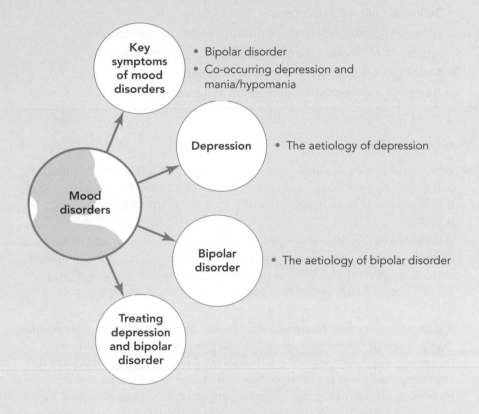

- Key symptoms of mood disorders
  - Bipolar disorder
  - Co-occurring depression and mania/hypomania
- Depression
  - The aetiology of depression
- Mood disorders
- Bipolar disorder
  - The aetiology of bipolar disorder
- Treating depression and bipolar disorder

A printable version of this topic map is available from
www.pearsoned.co.uk/psychologyexpress

Introduction

Mood or *affective* disorders are so called because they primarily affect our emotional functioning. We all experience periods in our lives when we feel happy, excited and energised or conversely unhappy, bored and lethargic. Within mood disorders the emotions we experience are more extreme than usual and often have a profound effect on an individual's ability to function.

→ *Revision checklist*

Essential points to revise are:
- ❏ Definitions of mood disorders
- ❏ Symptoms of major depressive disorder and dysthymic disorder
- ❏ Symptoms of bipolar I, bipolar II and cyclothymic disorder
- ❏ Aetiology of depression and bipolar disorder
- ❏ Treatment approaches for depression and bipolar disorder

Assessment advice

- When answering a question about mood disorders it is important that you clearly define the different types of mood disorders so that it is clear that there are several types, each with its own symptoms, causes and treatments.
- If asked to discuss the causes (aetiology) of a mood disorder you should describe one or two studies to support your arguments. So, for example, if you are suggesting that brain abnormalities are a factor in depression, you would need to briefly summarise some of the research which supports this idea.
- If evaluating different treatment approaches for mood disorders, remember that you would need to firstly outline the theoretical position of the treatment, e.g. biological vs. psychological. Criticisms of the theoretical approach could also be used in the context of critiquing a particular treatment. For example, the biological approach has been criticised for not taking into consideration psychological and social factors in treating these disorders.

Sample question

Could you answer this question? Below is a typical essay question that could arise on this topic.

❋ *Sample question*   *Essay*

Critically consider biological approaches to understanding the causes of major depression.

Key symptoms of mood disorders

In general, mood disorders are classified as involving a depressive episode or a manic episode with key symptoms associated with both (Table 3.1).

Table 3.1 **Key symptoms of mood disorders**

Major depressive episode	Manic episode
Depressed mood consistently over a period of time	Extremely elevated mood.
Lack of interest in usual activities	Grandiose ideas
Change in body weight of more than 5% in a month	Diminished need for sleep
Insomnia or hypersomnia (increased sleep)	Over-talkative
Loss of energy	Flight of ideas
Problems in concentration	Distractibility
Recurrent thoughts of death	Psychomotor agitation

Importantly, both depressive episodes and manic episodes must be severe enough to cause significant impairment in social or occupational function. In addition, episodes should not be explainable as being due to the effect of substance or medication usage. With depressive episodes, the symptoms must not stem from bereavement.

As well as outlining the distinction between major depressive episodes and manic episodes within mood disorders, the DSM-5 (APA, 2013) categories the following subdivisions of depressive disorders:

- *Major depressive disorder.* This describes either a single or recurrent episode of depression where symptoms last for more than two months.
- *Dysthymic disorder (persistent depressive disorder).* Symptoms here are similar to those in major depressive disorder but are considered to be less serious and fewer in number. However they also last much longer, at least two years.
- *Disruptive mood dysregulation disorder.* This describes severe recurring temper tantrums of a verbal and/or behavioural nature.
- *Premenstrual dysphoric disorder.* Here, mood swings are associated with phases of the menstrual cycle.

Bipolar disorder

Bipolar disorders (formerly known as manic depression) describe extreme fluctuations in mood whereby someone may alternate between depression and mania. The term bipolar reflects the contrasting emotions experienced, i.e. they are at different ends (or poles) of the spectrum of mood disorders. Bipolar disorders are split into three subtypes, *bipolar I disorder, bipolar II disorder* and *cylcothymic disorder.*

- *Bipolar I disorder.* Patients diagnosed with bipolar I disorder present with a manic episode, a hypomanic episode or a depressive episode. In addition there may have previously been manic or depressive episodes. Psychosis may also be present (e.g. delusions).

CASE STUDY

Nathalie was a PhD student at a British university and her friends became concerned when she started acting out of character. She had always been a quiet person and had suffered from periods of depression, but recently she had begun acting in a very energised and extroverted manner. At lunch one time, she had difficulty sitting still and would pace up and down the canteen, relating grandiose ideas about how her PhD thesis had ground-breaking implications for the future of humanity and that she was certain to receive the Nobel Prize for science. She felt compelled to contact her local MP to arrange a meeting with the Prime Minister to discuss her ideas. The previous night she had not had any sleep as she had been writing a pamphlet explaining her ideas which she handed out to students in the canteen. The pamphlets explained her proposal to start a World Wide Feminist Parliament where all the injustices to women would be resolved and she was promoting herself as the leader. At one stage during the morning, she stood on a chair to outline her ideas to the students in the canteen. Nathalie's friends were so concerned about her behaviour that they persuaded her to see someone from student services. Eventually she was assessed by a psychiatrist who diagnosed her as suffering from bipolar I disorder.

- *Bipolar II disorder.* Patients here present with a major depressive or hypomanic episode and have a history of at least one episode of major depression or **hypomania** (but not mania).
- *Cyclothymic disorder.* Within a two-year period there is a cycle of hypomanic episodes alternating with depressive symptoms. The depressive symptoms are not severe enough to warrant classification as a major depressive episode. There is no history of major depression or mania.

Key term

Hypomania: symptoms are similar to those in mania, i.e. elevated mood, grandiose ideas and decreased need for sleep. However, unlike during a manic episode, these symptoms are not severe enough to impair functioning. Hypomania can therefore be described as a less severe form of mania.

Distinguishing between bipolar I and bipolar II

- *Severity of the manic symptoms.* In bipolar I there is the presence of manic symptoms which may be severe enough to cause an impairment in social and occupational function. In contrast, patients with bipolar II experience hypomania and although these symptoms are similar to those in mania, they are not severe enough to cause social and occupational impairment.

- *Presence of psychosis.* Symptoms in bipolar I may include psychosis but this is not the case in bipolar II.

CRITICAL FOCUS

The cyclical nature of bipolar disorders

Patients with bipolar disorders experience alternating symptoms of major depression and mania or hypomania, and the length of each of these episodes has been reported to be between two and seven months, with a median of three (Angst & Sellaro, 2000). There may also be periods of mood stability between episodes. However, between 12 and 24% of patients experience four or more episodes of manic/hypomanic and depressive symptoms within one year and this is known as *rapid-cycling*. In addition, some patients experience extreme fluctuations in mood over a period of days (ultra-rapid cycling) or even within the same day (ultradian cycling: Bauer, Beaulieu, Dunner, Lafer, & Kupka, 2008). Seasonal affective disorder (SAD) has recently been recognised as a distinct condition in which the onset and remission from depression regularly coincides with particular times of year (APA, 2000). The usual pattern is depression in autumn and winter with recovery in spring and summer (Westrin & Lam, 2007).

✱ Sample question   Essay

Outline the symptoms seen in bipolar 1 and bipolar 2 and consider the treatment options for both.

Co-occurring depression and mania/hypomania

Some patients show features of both depression and mania/hypomania at the same time, for example by having flight of ideas as well as a depressed mood (Benazzi, 2004). One of the dangers of having both manic and depressive symptoms is that there is an increased risk of suicide as patients may have recurring thoughts of death combined with impulsivity (Swann et al., 2007).

In the next section we will consider the epidemiology, proposed causes and treatments for depression and bipolar disorders separately.

Test your knowledge

3.1 What is another name for mood disorders?

3.2 Give an example of the symptoms someone may exhibit if they were having a major depressive episode.

3.3 Give an example of the symptoms someone may exhibit if they were having a manic episode.

3.4 According to the DSM-5, how are depressive disorders classified?

Answers to the questions can be found on the companion website at: www.pearsoned.co.uk/psychologyexpress

---

Further reading Historical and contemporary overview of bipolar disorders

Key reading

Angst, J., & Sellaro, R. (2000). Historical perspectives and natural history of bipolar disorder. *Biological Psychiatry, 48*(6), 445–457.

Depression

The lifetime prevalence rate of depression in the general population has been estimated to be 16.2% based on a census sample of 9000 American adults (Kessler et al., 2003), equivalent to 35 million Americans with the disorder. An even larger study of 43,000 adults found a lifetime prevalence of approximately 13.23% (Hasin, Goodwin, Stinson, & Grabt, 2005). From both studies there was elevated risk of depression in women, the unemployed, the single, and those with low income and limited education. Age of onset is usually around 30. Preventative factors relate to being retired or from an Asian, Hispanic or black population. Those who reported depressive symptoms lost an average of 35 days a year when they were unable to carry out their usual daily activities or work due to the condition (Kessler et al., 2003). Half of those who have a single incidence of depression will go onto experience another episode, whilst 80% of those who have had two episodes will experience another (Burcusa & Iacono, 2007). Approximately 9% of individuals with depression attempt suicide although 36% have felt that they wanted to die (Hasin et al., 2005).

The aetiology of depression

As with all mental health problems, explanations have been multidimensional and involve biological, psychological and environmental factors as proposed causes for the disorder.

Biological factors

Genetic predisposition

Evidence indicates that depression has a genetic component to it. Studies comparing the incidence of depression in first-degree relatives of those with the disorder have shown an almost three-fold increased risk compared with the general population (Hettema, 2010). Twin studies have reported a concordance rate for dizygotic twins of 16–35% whilst this is much higher in monozygotic twins at between 70 and 90% (Sadock & Sadock, 2007), again indicting a genetic component. The search for candidate genes which may play a role in the development of depression have implicated an abnormality of the serotonin transporter gene (5-HTTLPR). This gene plays a key role in the availability of serotonin, and furthermore there is strong evidence that this genetic abnormality increases the risk of people developing depression when under stress (Karg, Burmeister, Shedden, & Sen, 2011). Other candidate genes have been suggested (e.g. DRD4: the gene encoding the dopamine D4 receptor) but genetic studies in general are limited by low subject numbers and an incomplete understanding of the precise pathophysiology of depression (Hettema, 2010).

Neurotransmitter systems

The first evidence for the role of neurotransmitter systems in depression came when it was discovered that reserpine, a pharmacological treatment for hypertension, caused depressive side effects. Reserpine depletes the amount of monoamine neurotransmitters in the system, including serotonin and norepinephrine. Conversely a compound which increased the amount of neurotransmitters in the system, iproniazid, was found to elevate the mood of depressed patients (Slattery, Hudson, & Nutt, 2004). These findings led to the monoamine hypothesis in depression which proposes that depression results from insufficient quantities of serotonin and norepinephrine. There is still considerable support for the monoamine hypothesis today and most antidepressant medications work by increasing the availability of serotonin and norepinephrine in the brain. However, there are some problems with this approach as summarised by Hirschfield (2000):

- Monoamine levels are increased rapidly on antidepressant medication, yet their therapeutic effect takes at least two weeks.

- Antidepressants are also effective at treating some anxiety disorders yet these effects are not explained by the monoamine hypothesis.

- Some other compounds increase serotonin or norepinephrine yet do not have antidepressant effects.

Key term

Monoamine neurotransmitters: this class of neurotransmitter appears to play a role in emotional regulation, arousal and cognition. A depletion of monoamine neurotransmitters is one of the biological explanations for depression, as medications which increase these neurotransmitter levels also improve mood. They include serotonin, dopamine and norepinephrine.

Cortisol levels

When an individual is under stress their body releases the hormone cortisol which forms part of the fight or flight response and causes physiological arousal and anxiety. There is evidence to suggest that individuals with depression have higher than usual levels of cortisol (Young, 2004) and it has been proposed that this increased and prolonged reactivity to stressors may deplete neurotransmitter systems, particularly serotonin (Leonard, 2010).

Circadian rhythms

Circadian rhythms describe the cyclical physiological changes that occur within an organism over a repeated time period, with one example being our 24-hour sleep and waking cycle. Disturbances in circadian rhythms have been observed in depression with the majority of depressed patients having trouble falling asleep, staying asleep and waking early in the morning. Once asleep, depressed patients have increased rapid eye movement (REM) sleep (where dreaming occurs) and decreased slow-wave sleep. It has been postulated that the central regulator which controls circadian rhythms is dysfunctional in depression and this contributes to the symptoms experienced (Germain & Kupfer, 2008).

Neuroanatomical factors

One of the most consistent anatomical findings in depression is that of reduced activity in the prefrontal cortex which may be due to a reduced volume of this brain area (Davidson, Pizzagalli, Nitschke, & Putnam, 2002). Interestingly, diminished activity in this area can be restored with successful treatment (Malhi & Lagopoulos, 2008). It is suggested that one of the roles of the prefrontal cortex is to control fear responses originating in the limbic system, particularly the amygdala. If this control is not exercised fully, then fear responses which are a feature of depression (e.g. anxiety) will be manifest (Arnsten, 2009). There is also evidence of reduced hippocampus size in depression (Malhi & Lagopoulos, 2008). The hippocampus plays a role in learning and memory and studies have found that aspects of memory impaired in depression, i.e. recollection memory, are mediated by the hippocampus (Campbell & MacQueen, 2004). However, drawing firm conclusions of neuroanatomical irregularities in depression is difficult because it is impossible to tease apart any effect of medication from an effect of the disorder itself. It is also difficult to distinguish between irregularities which may be symptom related and transient, or those which may provide a stable biological marker of the illness (Malhi & Lagopoulos, 2008).

Psychological factors

Psychodynamic explanation

Freud drew similarities between the feelings engendered when one is mourning the death of a loved one and the feelings often seen in melancholia or depression. For Freud, depression resulted from a symbolic or actual loss of a loved individual, but rather than the loss being due to their death, it is a loss of a relationship with the loved figure. This could be the end of a romantic relationship, or a falling out with a friend or sibling. The loss has a profoundly negative effect on self-esteem, as well as engendering feelings of hurt, rejection, disappointment and subsequent anger at the individual who is now absent. These feelings of anger result in guilt and self-criticism at having hostile feelings and these trigger depression (Freud, 1971/1917). Although not wholeheartedly accepted within psychoanalytic circles, some have supported Freud's idea that low self-esteem is a key feature in depression. Others have emphasised the role that guilt plays in depressive feelings, with McWilliams (1994) even suggesting that children of depressed parents may themselves develop depression due to their guilty feelings at their imagined role in the parents' depressive state. Critics of this theory have pointed out that depression does not inevitably lead on from the loss of a loved relationship and that Freud's theory stems from the analysis of a small number of Viennese women (Dozois, 2000).

Behavioural explanation
Behavioural explanations of the causes of depression emphasise the role that social reinforcement, or lack of it, plays in the development of the disorder. Everyone becomes accustomed to various social reinforcers, such as feeling good when we see a friend, having our work praised by our employer or being in a satisfying relationship. If something happens which removes this reinforcement, e.g. losing a job or finishing a relationship, then depression will result as the positive reinforcement we were accustomed to has been withdrawn. A very influential behavioural explanation of depression was developed by Lewinsohn (1974; Lewinsohn, Munoz, Youngren, & Zeiss, 1994) who emphasised the role that the social environment and the behaviour of the individual played in the development of depression. In terms of the social environment, if someone loses their job and has difficulty finding another one, then the whole potential for employment-related positive reinforcement is gone. The behaviour of the individual may also contribute to the development of depression if they lack the social skills in order to engage in potentially reinforcing activities. For example, a shy individual may not be comfortable attempting to make new friends and therefore this potential source of positive reinforcement is lost. Criticisms of Lewinsohn's theory have emphasised the paucity of solid empirical research to support the model and the lack of consideration of emotional and cognitive factors which play a role in the disorder (Blaney 1977; Eastman, 1976).

Cognitive explanation
The cognitive explanation for depression focuses on the role of thought processes in the development of the disorder. According to Ellis (1993) people with depression interpret events in a negative way and this leads to a depressive

emotional reaction. For example, someone who is unsuccessful at a job interview may blame themselves for their situation and believe that they will fail at any attempt to find work. They may also feel that any initiative to do with work, social life or romance may be destined to fail. Indeed, it is well established that individuals with depression focus on negative events (Gotlib & Joormann, 2010) and that their pessimistic outlook stems from childhood experiences which are characterised by negative parental interactions (Renner, Lobbestael, Peeters, Arntz, & Huibers, 2012). Beck, Rush, Shaw and Emery (1987) identified several types of faulty thinking that are present in depression. These include *catastrophic thinking* where someone believes that the worst will always happen, and *overgeneralising* whereby negative generalisations are made from isolated incidents (see Chapter 2).

Learned helplessness

This theory has its origins in behavioural experiments where dogs were given unavoidable electric shocks. Once the dogs had learnt that there was no escape, they passively accepted the electric shocks despite their discomfort. They became accustomed to the fact that they could not change their environment for the better. Applied to humans, this theory suggests that depression arises when individuals believe that they have no control over their physical or social environment (Seligman, 1975). This leads to a key feature of depression, hopelessness, where someone believes that everything will always turn out for the worse and they are to blame for the situation (Abramson, Seligman, & Teasdale, 1978).

Environmental factors

Environmental stressors have been frequently linked to the onset, prolongation and reoccurrence of depression (Hammen, Kim, Eberhart, & Brennan, 2009). This is the case both for acute stress (e.g. sudden loss of a job) and chronic stress (e.g. long-term relationship difficulties). Other evidence suggests that stress experienced during childhood leads to more severe depression (Lara, Klein, & Kasch, 2000). However, not all types of stress lead to depression. For example, stress involving loss, social rejection or humiliation are more likely to lead to depression than stress stemming from exposure to dangerous situations (Kendler, Hettema, Butera, Gardner, & Prescott, 2003; Slavich, Way, Eisenberger, & Taylor, 2010). Furthermore, recent research has started to focus on the role that genetic factors play in our vulnerability to stress. There is now evidence that a polymorphism on the serotonin transporter gene mediates the relationship between stress and depression (Karg et al., 2011), so that someone born with this particular genetic abnormality is much more likely to suffer from depression as a consequence of stress than those born without the abnormality. There are environmental factors which appear to offer some protection against depression being triggered by stress. These include familial support, financial support and participation in sport (Babiss & Gangwisch, 2009; Knowlton & Latkin, 2007; Moos, Cronkite, & Moos, 1998).

Test your knowledge

3.5 What does SAD stand for?

3.6 Why might co-occurring symptoms of depression and mania be of particular concern?

3.7 Is there an increased risk of depression after having a single episode?

3.8 Name two factors which are preventative against depression.

3.9 What do twin studies tell us about depression?

Answers to the questions can be found on the companion website at: www.pearsoned.co.uk/psychologyexpress

---

Further reading Monoamine hypothesis of depression

Key reading

Hirschfield, R. M. (2000). History and evolution of the monoamine hypothesis of depression. *Journal of Clinical Psychiatry*, 61(6), 4–6.

Bipolar disorder

Bipolar disorders are less frequent in the general population than depression, with bipolar I (BPI) having a lifetime incidence rate of 0.6%, bipolar II (BPII) of 0.4% and cyclothymia between 0.4 and 1.0% (APA, 2000; Merikangas et al., 2011). There is, however, evidence that prevalence rates differ between countries, with the USA having the highest incidence rates of all bipolar disorders including milder, subclinical forms (4.4%) whilst India had the lowest (0.1%: Merikangas et al., 2011). Impairment of function at home, work, or in social or close relationships is greater during depressive phases than manic phases and suicide attempts are also a feature of the disorder. Merikangas et al. (2011) found that 25% of individuals with BP1 and 20% of those with BPII had a history of suicide attempts.

The aetiology of bipolar disorder

Biological factors

Genetic predisposition

Twin studies have indicated a higher concordance rate between monozygotic twins (range between 20–75%) compared to dizygotic twins (0–8%), strongly indicating a genetic component (Shih, Belmonte, & Zandi, 2004). The focus for the past few years has been to identify candidate genes which may contribute to the development of the disorder, but this is proving to be a very difficult task with much inconsistency in the literature (Kato, 2007). However there is now evidence that genes responsible for the regulation of circadian rhythms may play a role in the disorder (Soria et al., 2010).

Brain abnormalities

There is evidence of altered dopaminergic and serotonergic systems in bipolar disorder with different patterns being seen depending on whether the individual is in a depressed or a manic phase. For example, Nikolaus, Hautzel, Heinzel, & Müller (2012) reported increased serotonin levels in the limbic system in depression but a decrease in these levels in mania. Importantly, two brain areas which play an important role in emotion have been found to be abnormal in bipolar disorders. Firstly. the brain area responsible for the generation of emotional responses, the amygdala, has been shown to be enlarged (Arnone et al., 2009) whilst one of the brain areas involved in emotional regulation, the cerebellum, has a decreased volume (Baldaçara et al., 2011).

Psychological factors

Psychological explanations for bipolar disorder have tended to focus on the depressive states as described above, although there is an increasing body of research looking at behavioural and cognitive aspects of manic states. Freud and others in the psychodynamic tradition firstly described mania as a symbolic liberation from the depression (melancholia) caused by the loss of a loved one, whilst Melanie Klein considered mania to be a defence mechanism triggered by guilt for the hostile feelings that are harboured for the loved individual (Freud, 1917/1957: Klein, 1940). Within the behavioural tradition, there is evidence suggesting that individuals with mania or at risk of mania have heightened sensitivity to reward, i.e. they get more pleasure from a positive event than other people (for a review, see Johnson & Jones, 2009). Cognitive models of mania are underdeveloped, although there is some recent evidence that certain thinking styles may be risk factors for mania, including a tendency to act before thinking and over confidence (Johnson & Jones, 2009). Furthermore, familial emphases on achievement and ambition have also been found to be related to manic symptoms (Chen & Johnson, 2012).

Test your knowledge

3.10 Which country has the highest incidence rate of bipolar disorder?

3.11 Is the amygdala reduced or enlarged in bipolar disorder?

Answers to the questions can be found on the companion website at: www.pearsoned.co.uk/psychologyexpress

---

Further reading Familial influences on manic states

Key reading

Chen, S. H., & Johnson, S. L. (2012). Family influences on mania-relevant cognitions and beliefs: A cognitive model of mania and reward. *Journal of Clinical Psychology, 68*(7), 829–842.

Treating depression and bipolar disorder

The following tables (Tables 3.2 and 3.3) detail the main types of treatments currently used for major depression and bipolar disorder.

Table 3.2 Main treatments for major depression

Type of treatment	Description of treatment
Biological	
Antidepressants	These medications generally work by preventing the depletion of neurotransmitters in the brain. There are three main classes: 1) Tricyclics (e.g. Amitriptyline): prevent the absorption of serotonin and norepinephrine. Side effects include dry mouth, increased heartbeat and constipation. 2) Selective serotonin reuptake inhibitors (SSRIs, e.g. Fluoxetine): stop the reuptake of serotonin. Side effects include nausea, anxiety and indigestion. 3) Serotonin and noradrenaline reuptake inhibitors (SNRI, e.g. Venlafaxine): obstruct the absorption of norepinephrine and serotonin. Side effects comparable to SSRIs but should not be used in people with pre-existing heart problems.
Electroconvulsive Therapy (ECT)	This involves producing a seizure by the application of an electric current to the brain. Mainly used for depression when other approaches have failed or there is serious risk to life. Short-term side effects include headaches and muscle ache. Long-term side effects include memory problems.
Psychological	
Cognitive Behavioural Therapy (CBT)	The identification and modification of faulty cognitions and problematic behaviours is the goal of CBT. For example, catastrophic thinking patterns could be challenged and the individual trained to use more reality-based assessment of events. The behavioural component might include amending behavioural patterns which precipitate or prolong depressive episodes, e.g. an inactive individual may be encouraged to go for walks.
Behavioural activation therapy	This therapeutic approach adopts the standpoint that depression results from a lack of positive reinforcement and therefore the main goal is to increase the number of enjoyable activities an individual engages in.

Key term

Selective Serotonin Reuptake Inhibitors (SSRIs): a class of antidepressant medication which increase the availability of serotonin by inhibiting its absorption. A depletion of serotonin is one of the biological theories of depression, and thereby by increasing the availability of this neurotransmitter it is believed that depression can be treated.

Table 3.3 Main treatments for bipolar disorder

Type of treatment	Description of treatment
Biological	
Mood-stabilising drugs	The main medication used to treat bipolar disorder is lithium which is effective at treating both depressive and manic symptoms. It is not well understood how Lithium works, and there are side effects associated with this treatment which can include thirstiness, weight gain and blurred vision. Sodium valproate is another mood-stabilising drug which is sometimes used.
Antipsychotic drugs	Psychotic symptoms may be present in bipolar 1, and if so, treatment with an antipsychotic may be appropriate. There are several different types of antipsychotics (e.g. Olanzapine, Risperidone) which work by altering levels of neurotransmitters, commonly dopamine and serotonin.
Psychological	
CBT	CBT for bipolar disorder will focus on addressing the irrational thoughts and maladaptive behaviour patterns that occur during depressive and manic phases. For example, grandiose ideas may be challenged during a manic phase as well as behavioural strategies to reduce psychomotor agitation.
Psychoeducation	The purpose of psychoeducation is to facilitate an understanding of bipolar disorder both for individual sufferer, but also for their family and friends. This will include learning about the symptoms, treatments, precipitating factors and coping strategies. Importantly, educating family and friends about the disorder can create a more caring and understanding environment which will reduce environmental stressors and likelihood of relapse.
Family-focused therapy (FFT)	As well as incorporating psychoeducation, FFT aims to enhance positive communication patterns within the family as well as providing problem-solving strategies to help everyone cope with the symptoms of the disorder.

Test your knowledge

3.12 Name two types of antidepressants.

3.13 What does ECT stand for?

3.14 Aside from Lithium, what other mood-stabilising medication might be used in bipolar disorder?

Answers to the questions can be found on the companion website at: www.pearsoned.co.uk/psychologyexpress

> **Further reading** Stress and depression
>
> *Key reading*
>
> Hammen, C., Kim, E. Y., Eberhart, N. K., & Brennan, P. A. (2009). Chronic and acute stress and the prediction of major depression in women. *Depression and Anxiety, 26*, 718–723.

Chapter summary – pulling it all together

→ Can you tick all the points from the revision checklist at the beginning of this chapter?

→ Attempt the sample question from the beginning of this chapter using the answer guidelines below.

→ Go to the companion website at **www.pearsoned.co.uk/psychologyexpress** to access more revision support online, including interactive quizzes, flashcards, You be the marker exercises as well as answer guidance for the Test your knowledge and Sample questions from this chapter.

Answer guidelines

✳ *Sample question*

Critically consider biological approaches to understanding the causes of major depression.

Approaching the question

When asked to critically consider a particular approach it is necessary for you to be aware of the strengths and weaknesses of the approach, plus key research and theory in support of, and contradicting, the particular perspective. You should also give a reasoned opinion based on the evidence provided.

Important points to include

● You will need to demonstrate an understanding of the main symptoms of major depression so be sure you can briefly describe them. Incorporating case examples of particular symptoms would be useful in demonstrating your understanding of the disorder.

● Biological explanations of major depression include genes, neurotransmitter systems, cortisol levels, circadian rhythms and neuroanatomical factors. You will need to describe each of these explanations.

● In providing a critique of the biological approach, remember to contrast this approach with the psychological and environmental perspective.

Make your answer stand out

A strong answer to this question would incorporate contemporary thinking and research on the proposed causes of major depression. Therefore you should refer to the most recent or most renowned research on genes, neurotransmitter systems, cortisol levels, circadian rhythms and neuroanatomical factors associated with the disorder. Remember that major depression is likely to be caused by a complex interplay between biological, environmental and psychological factors and this should be emphasised in your conclusion.

Explore the accompanying website at www.pearsoned.co.uk/psychologyexpress

→ Prepare more effectively for exams and assignments using the answer guidelines for questions from this chapter.
→ Test your knowledge using multiple choice questions and flashcards.
→ Improve your essay skills by exploring the You be the marker exercises.

Notes

4

Anxiety disorders

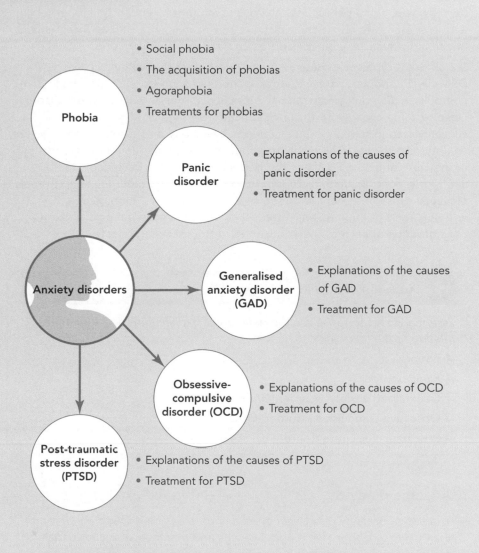

- Social phobia
- The acquisition of phobias
- Agoraphobia
- Treatments for phobias

Phobia

Panic disorder

- Explanations of the causes of panic disorder
- Treatment for panic disorder

Anxiety disorders

Generalised anxiety disorder (GAD)

- Explanations of the causes of GAD
- Treatment for GAD

Obsessive-compulsive disorder (OCD)

- Explanations of the causes of OCD
- Treatment for OCD

Post-traumatic stress disorder (PTSD)

- Explanations of the causes of PTSD
- Treatment for PTSD

A printable version of this topic map is available from
www.pearsoned.co.uk/psychologyexpress

Introduction

We all become anxious at various points in our lives: first day at school, taking exams, driving test, leaving home, job interviews, to name a few. Therefore it is true to say that anxiety is a fundamental part of our emotional lives. In addition, anxiety appears to serve the purpose of making us physiologically and mentally prepared for potentially threatening situations as the bodily changes we undergo during an anxious state are part of the 'fight or flight' response. Therefore anxiety has an important survival function for us. However, some people feel anxious much more frequently than others, and in response to situations which are not usually regarded as threatening. These individuals may be considered to have an anxiety disorder.

Six different types of anxiety disorders were classified within the DSM-IV-TR: phobias, panic disorder, generalised anxiety disorder, obsessive-compulsive disorder, post-traumatic stress disorder and acute stress disorder. Despite some changes to these classifications in the DSM-5, they remain clinically recognised as distinct subtypes of anxiety disorders. Taken together, anxiety disorders are the most frequently occurring of all mental disorders in the USA, affecting 28.8% of the population (Kessler, Berglund, Demler, Jin, Merikangas, & Walters, 2005). Although their key feature is an extremely elevated sense of anxiety and fear, their onset triggers, time course, aetiology and treatments are often very different necessitating a separate consideration of each of these subtypes in the following chapter.

→ Revision checklist

Essential points to revise are the definitions, explanations and treatments relating to the following:
❏ Phobias
❏ Panic disorder
❏ Generalised anxiety disorder (GAD)
❏ Obsessive-compulsive disorder (OCD)
❏ Post-traumatic stress disorder (PTSD)

Assessment advice

● The topic of anxiety disorders covers a large area. It is advisable that rather than trying to learn or write about causes and treatments for all five main types of anxiety disorders, you should focus on two or three of them and cover these in depth.

- If you are writing an essay on phobias, it is important that you have a clear description of the different types of phobias and how there are potentially different explanations for different types of phobias. For example, a phobia for animals may be explainable using the principles of classical conditioning, but agoraphobia may be better explained using neurobiological models.

- It is crucial with any piece of work in this area that you provide case examples of people suffering from a particular problem. This will not only serve to illustrate an understanding of the interpersonal aspects of a particular disorder, but will also show that you have a clear understanding of symptoms. In OCD, remember to cover both the obsessions and related compulsions, and in PTSD it is advisable to use more than one case example to illustrate different traumatic experiences which could cause the disorder.

Sample question

Could you answer this question? Below is a typical essay question that could arise on this topic.

> **✳ *Sample question***   *Essay*
>
> Critically consider psychological explanations for the acquisition of phobias.

Phobia

Phobias are classified into two separate categories by the DSM-5: specific phobia and social phobia (also termed Social Anxiety Disorder). A specific phobia is where there is a persistent and excessive fear of a particular object or situation and the lifetime prevalence of this type of anxiety disorder is estimated to be between 12 and 20% (Fredrikson, Annas, Fischer, & Wik, 1996; Kessler et al., 2005). Five separate subtypes of specific phobias have been identified:

- animals (e.g. spiders, snakes, dogs);
- natural environments (e.g. water, heights, storms);
- blood–injection–injuries (e.g. receiving injections, seeing blood);
- situational type (e.g. enclosed spaces, flying, elevators);
- other types (e.g. loud noises, choking, costumed characters).

Many of these specific phobias have been given their own names which usually derive from the Greek or Latin word for the fear-inducing object or situation followed by the suffix 'phobia'. So, for example, the Greek word for spider is *arachne* and therefore a phobia for spiders is called *arachnophobia*. *Claustrophobia* derives from the Latin word for an enclosed space *claustrum* and describes a fear of confined spaces. Other examples of phobia names are presented in Table 4.1.

Table 4.1 Five phobias

Fear of	Name
Blood	Haematophobia
Germs	Microphobia
Heights	Acrophobia
Snakes	Ophidiophobia
Water	Aquaphobia

There is inconsistency in the literature as to which is the most common specific phobia. Depla, ten Have, van Balkom and de Graaf (2008) reported that fear of heights was the most prevalent, affecting 4.9% of the general population, whilst Oosterink, de Jongh and Hoogstraten (2009) found dental phobia to be the most common (3.7%), with phobia of heights the second most prevalent (3.1%) and spider phobia third (2.7%). Females appear to be at greater risk of specific phobia than men (21% vs. 11%), with women having greater prevalence of animal phobia (12% vs. 3%) and situational phobia (17% vs. 8%) than males although no gender difference was evident for the blood–injection–injuries subtype (Fredrikson et al., 1996).

Social phobia

Sometimes termed *social anxiety disorder*, social phobia is a condition where an individual has an intense and persistent fear of being under scrutiny or embarrassing themselves in social situations. For example, a middle-aged lady may hate going shopping because she fears everyone will be looking at her and if she is engaged in conversation in a shop or at the checkout she worries that she will stutter and make a fool of herself. This fear prevents her from going shopping. Social phobia has a lifetime prevalence of 12.1% (Kessler et al., 2005) with fears relating to meeting new people, speaking in public or using public bathrooms being most common (APA, 2011). Individuals with social phobia have negative opinions about themselves and the possible outcomes of social situations. For example, Wells et al. (1995) report the case of a lady who was afraid of walking into crowded shops because she thought she would collapse and people would stare at her. In order to relieve her anxiety about collapsing, this lady would lean on things in the shop, sing to herself and avoid the eye contact of others. These anxiety-relieving strategies are called *safety behaviours*.

Social phobias and safety behaviours

Situation	Fear	Safety behaviour
Talking to strangers	Babbling	Speak quickly, take deep breaths, rehearse sentences
Drinking in front of others	Losing control	Use both hands, grip cup tightly, move slowly
Reading to a group	Shake uncontrollably	Try to avoid holding the book, turn pages slowly, take deep breaths
Eating in public	Vomiting	Eat small amounts, nibble, drink water

Adapted from Wells et al. (1995).

The acquisition of phobias

Biological perspectives

Twin studies have suggested a heritability of between 35 and 45% for phobias overall (Hettema, Annas, Neale, Kendler, & Fredrikson, 2003). Other biological theories have emphasised the heightened sensitivity of brain regions involved in the fear network, such as the amygdala, medial prefrontal cortex and thalamus. For example, these areas have been found to be highly active when spider phobics have been shown pictures of spiders (Schweckendiek et al., 2011). Several neurotransmitter systems are also thought to be involved in phobias, particularly serotonin (Stein & Stahl, 2000).

An interesting evolutionary perspective suggests that we all have an innate tendency to be afraid of certain animals and situations which stems from the danger that these things have held for us in the past. For example, our fear of snakes and heights has been evolutionarily advantageous as our fear prevents us being exposed to potentially harmful situations (Öhman & Mineka, 2001). This preparedness theory has some support as both humans and monkeys do appear to have a very quick visual detection system for potentially threatening animals in the environment such as snakes and spiders (Shibasaki & Kawai, 2009; Soares, Esteves, Lundqvist, & Öhman, 2009). However, this theory would have great difficulty explaining some of the phobias associated with modern living, such as fear of elevators or costumed characters.

Key term

Preparedness theory: suggests that humans have an innate tendency to be afraid of certain objects or situations that could potentially cause us harm, e.g. snakes or heights. By avoiding these things, we have a better chance of survival. This theory is one explanation for the acquisition of phobias and contrasts with other theories which suggest phobias can be learnt.

Psychological perspectives

Some phobias appear to be acquired through the process of classical conditioning where the phobic stimulus has been paired with a frightening event (Öst, 1987). This theory was illustrated in the classic study by Watson & Rayner (1920) where they conditioned Little Albert to be scared of a white rat and also in the case study of Bagby (1922) where a girl developed a phobia for water after having a terrifying experience in a waterfall (see Chapter 2). More recently, Jacobson et al. (1995) was able to condition fear and nausea in response to a beverage in a distinctive container (lemon-lime Kool-Aid) after repeated pairings of the beverage to the chemotherapy treatment that a group of women were undergoing.

However, not all phobias stem from classical conditioning and some people develop phobias after seeing someone else show a fear of an object or situation (e.g. a child observers her mother panic when a wasp is close). This type of learning is called *modelling* or *observational learning* and there is some empirical support for phobias originating in this way. For example, one study found that children copied the anxious behaviour of their parents prior to a spelling test (Burstein, Ginsburg, & Tein, 2010) whilst Broeren et al. (2011) reported that children imitated the calm or anxious behaviours shown towards animals by their peers. Rhesus monkeys have also been found to acquire fears by observing fearful behaviours in other monkeys (Mineka & Cook, 1986).

From an informational perspective there is the suggestion that phobias can originate when individuals are given *negative information* about an object or situation (Rachman, 2002), such as in the study by Muris, van Zwol, Huijding and Mayer (2010) where children who were given frightening information about an animal ('it can jump at your throat') were more fearful of it than those who were given neutral or positive information. Studies have also emphasised the important role that parents play in creating fear in their children through passing on negative information about animals (Remmerswaal, Muris, Mayer, & Smeets, 2010).

Several studies have considered the key competing psychological explanations for the development of phobias by asking phobics about the origins of their fears (e.g. Ollendick & King, 1991). Explanations relating to *classical conditioning*, *modelling* and the influence of *negative information* have all been reported in these studies but it appears that the three possible routes of phobia acquisition may interact with each other and that different types of fears may have distinct origins (Coelho & Purkis, 2009). However, each of the main theories of the acquisition of phobias have been criticised (see Coelho & Purkis, 2009 for a review).

Agoraphobia

Agoraphobia literally means fear of the market place but in contemporary clinical terms it describes a fear of being in places including: outside of the home alone, in small crowded places or wide open spaces, shops, cinemas, and on public transport. However, the fear is not about these places per se; rather, the fear is of the individual having a panic attack in these situations and there being no escape route or there would be no-one to help if this happened. Agoraphobia is considered to be related to panic disorder because the overriding fear is of having a panic attack in specific situations (for a review see Perugi, Frare, & Toni, 2007). The lifetime prevalence of agoraphobia with panic attacks is 8% (Kessler et al., 2006) but agoraphobia alone is much less frequent at 1.4% (Kessler et al., 2005). This disorder is more frequent in women than in men and it usually begins between the ages of 15 and 35 years and it can persist for years if left untreated.

Treatments for phobias

Biological-based treatments

Biological-based treatments for phobias almost exclusively involve the use of pharmacological agents to alter neurotransmitter systems. Antianxiety medication (also known as anxiolytics) such as the benzodiazepines (e.g. Lorazepam, Diazepam) have been found to reduce anxiety in social phobia (Davidson, Tuppler, & Potts, 1994) and specific phobia (Thom, Sartory, & Jöhren, 2000). Antidepressant medication, particularly the selective serotonin reuptake inhibitors (SSRIs), have shown considerable success in treating social phobia (Schneier, 2001) but not specific phobia.

Psychological-based treatments

Psychological techniques to treat phobias tend to focus on the emotion, cognition and behaviour associated with phobias.

Emotion

Being afraid can be an unpleasant experience during which we may sweat, tremble, have shortness of breath, increased heartbeat and sometimes nausea. Individuals with phobias will experience such symptoms in the presence of the feared stimulus and one of the goals of psychological treatment for phobias would be to reduce this physiological reactivity using somatic control exercises. These primarily include techniques to help the phobic relax and regulate their breathing as outlined by Kearney and Trull (2012):

- *Relaxation training.* Here the phobic is taught how to relax, such as in progressive muscle relaxation techniques where the client is asked to tense, and then relax, different muscle groups (e.g. shoulders, stomach) sequentially. The purpose of this is to assist the client in recognising when they are tense and anxious and also teach them how they can control their physical tension. This technique has proved successful at reducing reactivity to phobic stimuli, such as in the study by Lundgren, Carlsson and Berggren (2006) who used it to reduce dental fear.

- *Breathing retraining.* When exposed to a phobic stimulus some individuals will hyperventilate (breathing becomes quicker and deeper) and this will contribute to their physiological reaction and state of fear. The purpose of breathing retraining is to reduce these irregular breathing patterns and this technique has been shown to reduce phobic reactivity (e.g. Bonn, Redhead, & Timmons, 1984).

Cognition
Faulty thinking patterns are a well-established feature of phobias, with individuals tending to have an attentional focus on fear-related stimuli. For example, spider phobics have been shown to be exceptionally quick at identifying spider-related images compared with images of other animals (Mogg & Bradley, 2006). In addition, phobic individuals tend to overestimate the chances of the phobic stimulus causing them harm, such as in the study by Jones & Menzies (2000) who found that spider phobics think they have a high likelihood of being bitten by spiders, and that injuries received will be very serious. Similarly, Coelho and Purkis (2009) suggest that someone with acrophobia may believe there is a high likelihood of them having a fatal fall if they are at the top of a staircase.

Cognitive therapy for phobias will involve identifying and challenging these faulty cognitions so that the individual can think more rationally about the phobic stimulus and potential outcomes of coming into contact with it (see Chapter 2 for further details of the cognitive approach). Cognitive therapy has been found to successfully amend phobic beliefs such as in the study by Kamphuis and Telch (2000) where claustrophobic individuals were enclosed in a dark chamber and asked to cognitively appraise their likelihood of harm. However, it appears that cognitive therapy alone may not be superior to exposure based, or combined therapy (Wolitzky-Taylor, Horowitz, Powers, & Telch, 2008).

Behaviour
Several therapeutic techniques exist to alter the maladaptive behavioural patterns seen in phobia:

- *Exposure-based treatment.* Here the phobic is repeatedly exposed to the feared object or situation until they learn that there is nothing to fear and the phobia is extinguished. An important element of this treatment is that there is a graded exposure to the feared object or situation with very limited exposure at the beginning of therapy which increases as treatment progresses. Recently, exposure-based treatment has taken advantage of technological advances to create virtual reality exposure therapy where phobics are exposed to a virtual reality representation of the feared stimulus. For example, fear of flying has been found to be successfully treated using a head mounted display which gave the phobics a visual and auditory recreation of flying (e.g. Maltby, Kirsch, Mayers, & Allen, 2002).

- *Systematic desensitisation.* This technique is a form of exposure-based treatment although here the phobic is taught relaxation techniques to pair with the presentation of the feared stimulus or environment. For example, Lang and Lazovik (1963) successfully treated snake phobia by gradual exposure to a live snake combined with learning relaxation techniques when exposed to the feared stimulus. Phobia for dentists and school has also been treated in a similar way (Houlihan & Jones, 1989; Shaw & Thoresen, 1974).

- *Flooding and implosion therapy.* These techniques are also forms of exposure-based treatments which are based on the presentation of the feared stimulus. In flooding the presentation of the feared stimulus is done without relaxation training and with little preparation. The idea here is that the client would quickly learn that the phobic stimulus is not harmful. This therapy might involve someone with a phobia for dogs being introduced to a dog, or in the case of a women with a phobia for uncooked meat, exposed to a piece of raw pork (Baum & Poser, 1971). In *implosion therapy* the client is asked to visualise fear-provoking situations involving the phobic stimulus. As the fear response cannot be sustained indefinitely, after repeated fearful imaginings the phobic will habituate to the phobic stimulus and no longer feel fear. This technique was used successfully with a school-phobic 13-year-old boy who was asked to imagine many frightening scenarios at school (e.g. he is dragged onto the stage in the main hall by the headmaster with all pupils and teachers laughing at him: Smith & Sharpe, 1970).

Cognitive Behavioural Therapy (CBT), which involves the identification and modification of problematic thoughts and behaviours and utilises elements of the cognitive and behavioural approaches above, may also be used as a treatment for phobias. Furthermore, another important part of therapy may also involve psychoeducation which involves educating the individual about their phobia so they understand the link between their irrational thoughts, behaviours and emotions. For example, someone with a fear of spiders may be taught about all the different species and how very few are harmful to people.

Key term

Psychoeducation: the provision of knowledge and training about a particular disorder in order to facilitate better understanding and recovery. For example, clients may be taught to recognise symptoms indicative of a reoccurrence of an illness, or how to reduce stress.

Test your knowledge

4.1 What are the most common types of phobias?

4.2 Why might a middle-aged lady with social phobia dislike going shopping?

4.3 Give an example of how a phobia might be acquired through observational learning.

4.4 What happens during relaxation training?

Answers to the questions can be found on the companion website at: www.pearsoned.co.uk/psychologyexpress

Further reading Phobias

Key reading

Coelho, C. M., & Purkis, H. (2009). The origins of specific phobias: Influential theories and current perspectives. *Review of General Psychology, 13*(4), 335–348.

Panic disorder

A panic attack is where an individual becomes extremely anxious, experiences physical discomfort and has heart palpitations, trembling, sweating and shortness of breath; they may even feel that they are dying. Panic disorder is where these panic attacks are recurrent and unexpected, and there is a continuing fear of having additional attacks which may lead to a change in behaviour associated with this fear (e.g. the individual may avoid places where the attacks have occurred before). If the individual begins to associate particular situations or places with having a panic attack, then they might develop agoraphobia as described above. The lifetime prevalence of panic disorder is 4.7% (Kessler et al., 2005), is twice as prevalent in women than in men and affects Caucasians much more than other racial groups (Sheikh, Leskin, & Klein, 2002).

Explanations of the causes of panic disorder

There are both biological and psychological explanations for panic disorder.

Biological explanations

Biological explanations for panic disorder focus on a genetic predisposition, brain structure abnormalities and neurochemical imbalances. Studies of the concordance rate of panic disorder amongst twins and other family members suggest a heritability estimate of 43% (Hettema, Neale, & Kendler, 2001). However, the identification of specific genes which play a key role in the disorder has proved difficult (e.g. Gratacòs et al., 2007), which has led to consideration of gene and environment interactions. Klauke, Deckert, Reif, Pauli and Domschke (2010) reported that stressful life events (e.g. separation and interpersonal conflicts) and personality factors (e.g. neuroticism) may interact with genetic vulnerability to cause the development of panic disorder. A disturbance of the neurotransmitter serotonin has been found in panic disorder, although it is still a matter of contention whether there is an excess or deficit (Maron & Shlik, 2006). Neuroanatomically, the brain regions involved in the fear response such as the amygdala, hippocampus and thalamus are considered to be highly sensitive in panic disorder (Gorman, Kent, Sullivan, & Coplan, 2000).

Psychological explanations

There is evidence that individuals with panic disorder have anxiety sensitivity (AS) where they are hypersensitive to changes in bodily sensations (e.g. increase in heartbeat) and attribute these changes to imminent harm such as having a heart attack (Schmidt et al., 2010). Research has found that this anxiety sensitivity not only is a feature of panic disorder, but that it can predict the future development of panic disorder and other anxiety disorders (Schmidt et al., 2010). A related cognitive feature of panic disorder is catastrophic thinking, where individuals fear that they will be socially embarrassed ('People will laugh at me'), have a mental breakdown ('I will go crazy') or die, when they detect changes in bodily sensations (Hicks et al., 2005). These catastrophic thoughts only serve to increase the bodily sensations associated with fear (e.g. a further increase in heart rate), leading to more catastrophic thoughts so that the individual is trapped in a vicious cycle. This can lead to a classically conditioned association between any change in bodily sensations and fear and panic, termed interoceptive conditioning (Roy-Byrne, Craske, & Stein, 2006).

Key terms

Catastrophic thinking: the belief that the worst will always happen. It typifies the thinking patterns in several anxiety disorders. For example, if someone is late for work they may believe that as a consequence they will get fired and end up living on the street.

Interoceptive conditioning: a type of classical conditioning where changes in bodily state, such as an increase in heart rate, result in feelings of fear and panic so that someone may think they are about to have a heart attack. The change in bodily sensation becomes the conditioned stimulus leading to fear and panic which are the conditioned response.

Treatment for panic disorder

The most widely used and successful psychological treatment for panic disorder is CBT (Roy-Byrne et al., 2006). This treatment follows the usual approach within CBT where psychoeducation, cognitive restructuring, exposure to changes in bodily sensations (e.g. heart palpitations) and exposure to the feared stimulus are all used to minimise anxiety and fear. Biological-based treatments involve the use of antidepressant or antianxiety medication such as the SSRIs or the benzodiazepines. However, it appears that treatment involving a combination of medication and psychological treatment is the most successful at alleviating the symptoms of panic disorder (Furukawa, Watanabe, & Churchill, 2006).

Test your knowledge

4.5 What is the heritability estimate for panic disorder?

4.6 What types of thinking patterns are common to all anxiety disorders?

4.7 Which treatment is most successful in panic disorder?

Answers to the questions can be found on the companion website at: www.pearsoned.co.uk/psychologyexpress

Further reading Panic disorder

Key reading

Klauke, B., Deckert, J., Reif, A., Pauli, P., & Domschke, K. (2010). Life events in panic disorder – an update on 'candidate stressors'. *Depression and Anxiety, 27*, 716–730.

Generalised anxiety disorder (GAD)

With a lifetime prevalence of 5.7% (Kessler et al., 2005), GAD is a condition where there is excessive anxiety and worry which is difficult to control and has lasted for at least six months (DSM-5). The worry is not specific to individual situations or events but extends more generally to many different aspects of life such as relationships, money, religion, politics, the environment and minor daily issues (Hoyer, Becker, & Roth, 2001). Symptoms including feeling on edge, fatigue, difficulty concentrating, irritability and sleep disturbance also need to be present for a DSM-5 diagnosis of GAD.

Explanations of the causes of GAD

Biological explanations

Genetic factors do a play a role in GAD but not a prominent one, as heritability estimates are only of the magnitude of approximately 32% (Hettema et al., 2001). There are indications that neurotransmitter systems involving gamma-aminobutyric acid (GABA), serotonin and noradrenaline may be faulty although the precise genetic and neurochemical basis for the disorder is still not known (Tyrer & Baldwin, 2006). Neuroanatomically, there does appear to be an increased sensitivity of the fear circuit in GAD, particularly involving the amygdala (e.g. McClure et al., 2007).

Psychological explanations

On a psychological level, cognitive factors appear to play an important role in the aetiology of the disorder. For example, Reinecke, Becker, Hoyer and Rinck (2010) demonstrated that individuals with GAD are prone to associating neutral words with negative attributes (e.g. bank, relationships), indicating an underlying negative cognitive schema. Indeed, all individuals with anxiety disorders including GAD are prone to negative thinking patterns such as catastrophising (the worst will always happen) and selective abstraction (focusing on the negative and ignoring the positive; Beck, Emery, & Greenberg, 1985).

Wells (2005, 2009) developed the metacognitive model of GAD where he proposed that the disorder stemmed from individuals having negative beliefs about the controllability and consequences of worrying. Worrying can be a productive experience if it allows an individual to consider ways of coping with unpleasant circumstances (e.g. 'what would I do if my house caught fire?'). However, with GAD, the individual becomes concerned that their worrying is out of control and that serious health consequences might result from excessive worry. Therefore the process of worrying becomes the main cause of anxiety for the individual (e.g. this worrying is driving me crazy) and results in a self-perpetuating cycle of 'worrying about worrying'.

A slightly different cognitive perspective is suggested by Dugas and Robichaud (2007) where the focus is on an intolerance of uncertainty in the thinking patterns of those with GAD. For example someone with GAD may know that there is a miniscule chance that the plane they are about to board is going to crash but they cannot be 100% sure that the plane is not going to crash and therefore they worry. Individuals with GAD need absolute certainty that a particular event will not occur (e.g. plan crash, getting fired) in order to prevent their worry and anxiety.

Treatment for GAD

Biological-based treatments involve the administration of either antidepressant or antianxiety medications. Both classes of medication have been shown to be effective in the short term, but only antidepressants are recommended for long-term treatment because of the risks of dependency with antianxiety medication (Tyrer & Baldwin, 2006). It has been recommended that initial pharmacological treatment comprises both an antidepressant and an antianxiety drug for maximum efficacy over the short term (Rickels & Rynn, 2002).

Of the psychological therapies, applied relaxation and CBT have both been found to be effective (e.g. Arntz, 2003; Öst & Breitholtz, 2000). In applied relaxation the individual is trained to identify the physiological changes they undergo as a result of worry and anxiety and apply physical relaxation techniques (e.g. regulate breathing) to reduce these. In CBT, the approach is to educate the individual about GAD, identify and challenge worrisome beliefs, train the individual to develop self-control and coping skills, and to use techniques of muscle relaxation to deal with the physiological symptoms. CBT has been found to be as effective at treating GAD as drug treatment (Tyrer & Baldwin, 2006).

Test your knowledge

4.8 What types of things might cause worry in GAD?
4.9 What does it mean to say that individuals with GAD have an underlying negative cognitive schema?
4.10 What does the technique of applied relaxation involve?

Answers to the questions can be found on the companion website at: www.pearsoned.co.uk/psychologyexpress

Further reading Generalised anxiety disorder

Key reading

Tyrer, P., & Baldwin, D. (2006). Generalised anxiety disorder. *Lancet, 368*, 2156–2166.

Obsessive-compulsive disorder (OCD)

OCD is defined by the presence of obsessions and compulsions. Obsessions are reoccurring and persistent thoughts, images and impulses which cause distress and anxiety. Compulsions are behaviours which individuals feel the need to perform in order to relieve the distress caused by their obsession, and evidence suggests that obsessions and compulsions always occur together (Williams et al., 2011) (Table 4.2). The lifetime prevalence of OCD is estimated to be 1.6% (Kessler et al., 2005), although both obsessions and compulsions individually occur in 13% of the general population at a subclinical level. For example, nearly 8% of individuals have recurrent impulses to check things such as locks and cookers, and 4.6% obsess about either themselves or someone close to them having a serious illness (Fullana et al., 2010).

Table 4.2 Obsessions and related compulsions in OCD

Type of obsession	Related compulsive behaviour
Contamination from germs when touching things that others have touched, e.g. money, door handles	Wearing gloves or handwashing repeatedly
Need for order and symmetry, e.g. furniture in a room needs to be in exactly the 'right' place	Not allowing people into the room or rearranging items to achieve order and symmetry
Aggressive impulses, such as deliberately knocking down a pedestrian whilst driving	Only driving at times when there are few pedestrians about and checking the newspapers for reports of hit and run accidents
Obsessions that violate religious beliefs, such as swearing in church	Putting something in the mouth which prevents talking whilst in church, excessive praying
Sexual obsessions, such as the belief that they are gay	Repeatedly checking the body for signs of arousal to homosexual imagery or praying excessively

Source: adapted from Fenske and Schwenk (2009), Radomsky and Rachman (2004) and Purdon (2004).

Explanations of the causes of OCD

Biological explanations

Twin and familial studies have indicated a clear genetic component to OCD with heritability estimates in the region of 50% (Pauls, 2010). However, studies which have tried to identify the candidate genes within the serotonergic, dopaminergic and glutamatergic systems have not yielded consistent results so the precise genetic loci remains unknown (Pauls, 2010). Neuroanatomically, strong evidence from neuroimaging studies suggests that areas of the orbitofrontal cortex, caudate nucleus and thalamus have increased metabolism in the disorder (Whiteside, Port, & Abramowitz, 2004) which may lead to excessive worry and repetitive behaviours (Markarian et al., 2010). There is evidence that abnormalities in neurochemistry also play a role in the disorder as medications which increase the amount of serotonin in the brain (SSRIs) have been found to be successful treatments (Simpson, 2010).

Psychological explanations

Behavioural explanations for OCD emphasise the repeated pairing of the obsessive thought and the anxiety-relieving compulsion. For example, if anxiety about leaving the cooker turned on is relieved by checking that the cooker is turned off, then the compulsive behaviour is being negatively reinforced. There also appear to be cognitive factors involved in the development and continuation of OCD symptoms. As indicated previously, many individuals without OCD have obsessional thoughts. However, in OCD these thoughts take on added significance and the individual may believe that negative or even catastrophic events may occur if the obsessional thought is not acted upon (Markarian et al., 2010). Indeed, an exaggerated fear of the threat of harm is considered to be one of the cognitive characteristics of OCD ('If I don't wash my hands I will contract AIDS and die': Clark & Beck, 2009). The key cognitive features of OCD were summarised by the Obsessive Compulsive Cognitions Working Group (1997):

- Over-importance of thoughts – thoughts necessarily lead to actions and so a thought about committing a violent act means that the individual will become violent.
- Inflated responsibility – the belief that the individual has the responsibility for preventing negative events occurring.
- Intolerance of uncertainty – the need for certainty to be demonstrated, e.g. 'I need to be certain that I have locked the door'.

Treatment for OCD

The front-line biological treatment for OCD are antidepressants of the SSRI class due to their effective action on the serotonergic system. Evidence shows that between 60 and 70% of clients with the disorder respond to this treatment (Fenske & Schwenk, 2009). However, these medications can take a month to start working and sometimes dosages need to be high to be effective, which brings the risk of serotonin syndrome with side effects including sweating, tremor and anxiety (Fenske & Schwenk, 2009).

Psychological treatment for OCD most often comprises CBT where exposure to the fear arousing situation (e.g. dirt on hands) is used in conjunction with response prevention (not being allowed to wash hands). Psychoeducation, cognitive restricting to address dysfunctional attitudes and negative thoughts, plus strategies for relapse prevention are also used within CBT for this disorder (Jónsson, Hougaard, & Bennedsen, 2011). CBT has been found to be very effective in OCD (Olatunji, Davis, Powers, & Smits, 2011) and there is evidence that the beneficial effects of this treatment are more long lasting, and relapse rates lower, than pharmacological treatment (Simpson, Hubbert, Petkova, Foa, & Liebowitz, 2006).

Test your knowledge

4.11 What types of thinking patterns are common in OCD?

4.12 Give an example of an obsession and related compulsion.

4.13 Which treatment is more effective in the long term for OCD, pharmacological or psychological?

Answers to the questions can be found on the companion website at: www.pearsoned.co.uk/psychologyexpress

---

Further reading Obsessive-compulsive disorder

Key reading

Markarian, Y., Larson, M. J., Aldea, M. A., Baldwin, S. A., Good, D., Berkeljon, A., Murphey, T. K., Storch, E. A., & McKay, D. (2010). Multiple pathways to functional impairment in obsessive-compulsive disorder. *Clinical Psychology Review, 30*, 78–88.

Post-traumatic stress disorder (PTSD)

PTSD is sometimes the consequence of an individual experiencing a frightening event where there is the risk of themselves or those around them suffering serious injury or death. The symptoms of the disorder involve:

- reliving the trauma via intrusive memories, flashbacks, dreams, thoughts and perceptions which cause psychological distress and a physiological reaction;
- efforts to try to avoid all things that might remind them of the trauma, including people, places, activities, thoughts, conversations;
- increased physical arousal and reactivity so that the individual may have difficulty falling asleep and outbursts of anger.

Key term

Flashback: the sudden reoccurrence of a vivid memory where the individual may believe they are reliving a past event. In PTSD these flashbacks relate to a traumatic experience and involve extreme feelings of fear.

Individuals who have been caught up in a whole range of unfortunate circumstances have developed PTSD, including the victims of terrorism, violent assault, sexual assault, car accidents and natural disasters (Sue, Sue, Sue, & Sue,

2010). In addition, those involved in armed combat appear to have particularly high rates of PTSD, with up to 20% of soldiers who served in Iraq or Afghanistan meeting the diagnostic criteria (Ramchand et al., 2010). This compares to the incidence rate in the general population of 6.8% (Kessler et al., 2005).

Explanations of the causes of PTSD

Biological explanations

Identifying a genetic vulnerability to PTSD has not been easy since the disorder is expressed only when the individual is exposed to a traumatic event. Therefore twin or familial studies are only of worth when related individuals have been exposed to a traumatic event because it is only then that the disorder is expressed (Koenen, Nugent, & Amstadter, 2008). However, of the limited number of studies that have been conducted, a genetic contribution to the disorder has been implicated. For example, Yehuda, Halligan and Bierer (2001) found that the children of holocaust survivors with PTSD were more likely to have PTSD after experiencing a traumatic event than the children of holocaust survivors without PTSD. In addition, True et al. (1993) completed a very large twin study (4042 twin pairs) and reported that genes accounted for approximately 30% of PTSD symptoms. The converging evidence does implicate a genetic vulnerability to PTSD, but the specific gene or genes remain unknown at present (Koenen et al., 2008). Neuroanatomically, the amygdala is a key brain region involved in the fear response and this appears to have heightened sensitivity in those with PTSD which may have stemmed from chronic stress (Ressler, 2010).

Psychological explanations

The physiological response of those with PTSD to things that remind them of the traumatic event have been considered to reflect the process of classical conditioning. The traumatic event is the unconditioned stimulus leading to the unconditioned response (i.e. fear), and the conditioned stimuli are cues which remind the individual of the event, e.g. sights, sounds, smells. Therefore through the process of classical conditioning any cue which reminds the individual of the traumatic event is sufficient to induce a physiological response (Peri, Ben-Shakhar, Orr, & Shalev, 2000). Psychological explanations of PTSD which focus on cognition have also been proposed. Ehlers and Clark (2000) suggest that individuals with PTSD develop a negative pattern of thinking where threat is continually perceived in the environment and there may be an element of self-blame about the traumatic event. For example, the individual may feel that they attract disasters or that they will perpetually be a victim because the traumatic event happened to them. In addition, Ehlers and Clark (2000) suggest that there is also a problem with the trauma memory being integrated into autobiographical memory. This may be due to the fact that people experience confusion and detachment during a traumatic event and therefore the usual memory integration processes will not take place. This leads to the unintentional and unexpected triggering of the trauma memory when the individual is faced with a trauma cue.

Treatment for PTSD

Antidepressant medication of the SSRI class is the primary biological treatment for PTSD, and has been found to be effective in 59% of patients (Stein, Ipser, & Seedat, 2009). These medications work by increasing the availability of serotonin in the brain and this may diminish the activity of the amygdala (Gorman et al., 2000). The main psychological treatments for PTSD have been categorised into those where treatment is focused on the memory and meaning of the traumatic event (trauma-focused CBT–TFCBT), eye movement desensitisation and reprocessing), and those where the focus is more on coping with the symptoms of the disorder (Bisson et al., 2007).

TFCBT uses the techniques of stimulus confrontation where the individual is faced with the fearful material either in reality or in their imagination. They are then asked to describe the traumatic experience and relive it. This is similar to *implosion therapy* where after repeated fearful imaginings the individual will habituate to the traumatic experience and no longer feel fear. For example, Foa et al. (1999) asked female victims of sexual assault to imagine and describe the assault taking place on a daily basis. This technique has been found to be effective at reducing PTSD symptoms (Bisson et al., 2007).

Eye movement desensitisation and reprocessing involves the client focusing on the memory, emotions and thoughts associated with the traumatic event. Once the client is engaged with the traumatic event the therapist moves their fingers back and forth in front of the client's face as way of inducing eye movement to the left and right. Although remaining a controversial technique, there is evidence for its comparable efficacy with TFCBT (Bisson et al., 2007). It is proposed that this technique works by inducing a neurobiological state which facilitates the integration of traumatic memories into long-term memory and thereby reducing the negative emotions associated with the memory (Stickgold, 2002).

Other psychological techniques to treat PTSD include:

- cognitive restructuring – to identify and address dysfunctional thoughts about the traumatic event;
- psychoeducation – to educate the individual about PTSD;
- stress management – to help the individual to deal with stress;
- relaxation techniques – to reduce their physical tension.

A related type of anxiety disorder recognised by the DSM-5 is *acute stress disorder*. This shares many of the same symptoms as PTSD except that the duration of episodes is shorter, lasting up to one month from the time of the trauma as compared to those in PTSD which have a duration of *at least* one month. Another difference is that feelings of detachment from reality are more common in acute stress disorder than PTSD, although up to 80% of those with acute stress disorder go on to have PTSD (Murray, Ehlers, & Mayou, 2002).

> ✱ *Sample question* Essay

Describe the symptoms of PTSD and consider the key differences between this disorder and one other anxiety disorder.

Test your knowledge

4.14 What percentage of soldiers who served in Iraq or Afghanistan met the criteria for PTSD?

4.15 What happens during eye movement desensitisation and reprocessing?

4.16 What does TFCBT stand for?

Answers to the questions can be found on the companion website at: www.pearsoned.co.uk/psychologyexpress

---

Further reading Post-traumatic stress disorder

Key reading

Stickgold, R. (2002). EMDR: A putative neurobiological mechanism of action. *Journal of Clinical Psychology, 58*(1), 61–75.

Chapter summary – pulling it all together

→ Can you tick all the points from the revision checklist at the beginning of this chapter?

→ Attempt the sample question from the beginning of this chapter using the answer guidelines below.

→ Go to the companion website at www.pearsoned.co.uk/psychologyexpress to access more revision support online, including interactive quizzes, flashcards, You be the marker exercises as well as answer guidance for the Test your knowledge and Sample questions from this chapter.

Answer guidelines

> ✱ *Sample question* Essay

Critically consider psychological explanations for the acquisition of phobias.

Approaching the question

When asked to critically consider a particular approach it is necessary for you to be aware of the strengths and weaknesses of the approach, plus key research and theory in support of, and contradicting, the particular perspective. You should also give a reasoned opinion based on the evidence provided.

Important points to include

- Psychological explanations for phobias include classical conditioning, modelling and negative information. Be sure that you are familiar with each of these theories.
- The main contrasting approach to psychological explanations are biological explanations, so be sure you include these as a contrasting perspective.
- Remember to include research, where possible, which supports or contradicts the psychological or biological perspective on the acquisition of phobias. There is some evidence that different types of phobias stem from different causes, so include and discuss this evidence.

> **Make your answer standout**

A strong answer to this question would incorporate contemporary thinking and research on the causes of phobias. Therefore you should refer to the most recent theories and/or research in your answer. The subject of phobias is an extensive one. Try not to spend too much time describing each individual type, rather, briefly describe the different types and then focus on a specific type of phobia in order to answer the question.

Explore the accompanying website at www.pearsoned.co.uk/psychologyexpress

→ Prepare more effectively for exams and assignments using the answer guidelines for questions from this chapter.
→ Test your knowledge using multiple choice questions and flashcards.
→ Improve your essay skills by exploring the You be the marker exercises.

Notes

Notes

Notes

5

Schizophrenia and psychotic disorders

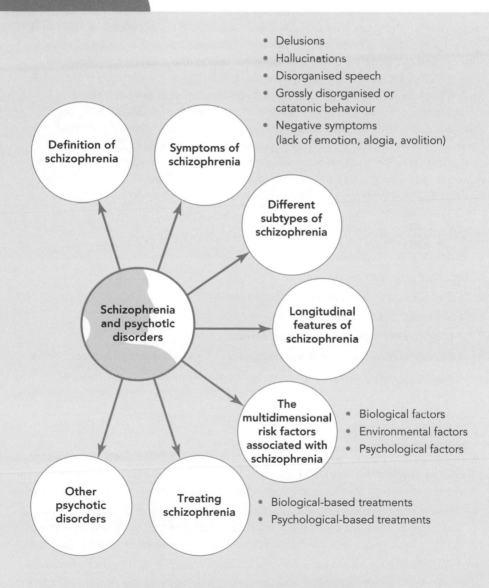

- Delusions
- Hallucinations
- Disorganised speech
- Grossly disorganised or catatonic behaviour
- Negative symptoms (lack of emotion, alogia, avolition)

Definition of schizophrenia

Symptoms of schizophrenia

Different subtypes of schizophrenia

Schizophrenia and psychotic disorders

Longitudinal features of schizophrenia

The multidimensional risk factors associated with schizophrenia

- Biological factors
- Environmental factors
- Psychological factors

Other psychotic disorders

Treating schizophrenia

- Biological-based treatments
- Psychological-based treatments

A printable version of this topic map is available from
www.pearsoned.co.uk/psychologyexpress

Introduction

The German psychiatrist Emile Kraepelin is credited with first defining the disorder we now know as schizophrenia in the late 19th century. He observed that three previously identified disorders seemed to have a similar pattern of onset, similar symptom fluctuation and comparable decline in mental functioning. These disorders were *catatonia*, which was typified by motor problems; *hebephrenia*, where emotional problems were prominent, and *dementia paranoids*, which featured hallucinations and delusions. Kraepelin suggested that these three disorders were actually manifestations of the same underlying pathology and coined the term 'dementia praecox' to emphasise the decline in mental faculties that patients seemed to experience. However, around 20 years later a Swiss psychiatrist, Eugen Bleuler, redefined the disorder as having four primary signs: autism, loss of associations, ambivalence and affect inappropriateness. A key feature of the disorder for Bleuler was the inappropriate affect shown by patients: he used the examples of someone smiling at their mother's death or crying with sadness at inheriting a fortune. To better describe the condition where there was a split between thought and emotion and also a split between threads of thought, Bleuler took inspiration from the Greek verb for splitting (*schizein*) and noun for mind (*phren*).

> **→ Revision checklist**
>
> *Essential points to revise are:*
> - Definition and symptoms of schizophrenia
> - Subtypes of schizophrenia
> - Longitudinal features of schizophrenia
> - Biological, environmental and psychological explanations of schizophrenia
> - Biological, psychological and family orientated treatment approaches

Assessment advice

- An important part of any essay on schizophrenia is a clear description of the core symptoms but it is also important to include an example of a particular symptom type to demonstrate your understanding.
- There is sometimes no clear distinction between one type of schizophrenia and another, and therefore the recognition that sometimes symptoms do not fit into neat categories as indicated by the DSM would strengthen your essay.
- If you are writing about explanations for schizophrenia, you need to focus on biological, environmental and psychological explanations and include key studies which support a particular standpoint.

- When considering treatment approaches to schizophrenia, you should clearly define the treatment before describing and evaluating its utility in schizophrenia. For example, in discussing Cognitive Behavioural Therapy (CBT) as a treatment approach the principles and methods in CBT should be outlined.

Sample question

Could you answer this question? Below is a typical essay question that could arise on this topic.

> ✱ *Sample question*   *Essay*
>
> Consider whether schizophrenia is primarily a *psychological* or *biological* disorder.

Definition of schizophrenia

Schizophrenia is defined as a group of disorders characterised by impairment in thought, emotion and behaviour. The term schizophrenia is often used incorrectly today as denoting a split personality. According to the DSM-5 (APA, 2013) the correct term for someone with two or more distinct personalities is 'dissociative identity disorder', a name which replaced the former 'multiple personality disorder'.

Symptoms of schizophrenia

The DSM-5 (APA, 2013) uses the following diagnostic criteria for schizophrenia:

- delusions;
- hallucinations;
- disorganised speech (incoherence or frequent derailment);
- grossly disorganised or catatonic behaviour;
- negative symptoms (lack of emotion, alogia, avolition).

Delusions

Delusions can be described as irrational beliefs which are held despite disconfirming evidence. For example, someone may believe that they are God, the devil, a secret agent or a pop star. Others may believe that they have special powers such as that they can communicate with trees. Different types

85

of delusions have been identified and the most common type of delusion experienced is that of persecution. Table 5.1 shows the different types of delusions that have been observed in schizophrenia.

Table 5.1 Delusions in schizophrenia

Type of delusion	Characteristic feature	Example
Persecution	The individual is being harmed, persecuted or harassed in some way.	Tony believes his mother is putting excrement in his food.
Grandeur	The individual has a special purpose in life, is famous or has a supernatural power.	Samantha believes that she is the devil.
Control	The individual believes that someone or something is controlling their thoughts and behaviour.	Emma believes her pet cat is controlling her thoughts.
Thought broadcasting	The individual believes that their thoughts are escaping their mind so that others can hear them.	Jim believes his psychiatrist can read all his thoughts.
Thought withdrawal	The individual believes their thoughts are being removed from their head.	Leigh believes that the Government has a machine to remove thoughts from his head.
Reference	The belief that things seen or heard during the course of the day have special relevance for the individual.	Trevor believes that the presenters on the TV news are discussing him.

Hallucinations

Hallucinations are sensory experiences which are not attributable to the environment so that, for example, someone might hear a voice when there is no one there or see a bug that no one else can see. In schizophrenia the most common type of hallucination is an auditory one, hearing voices. These voices can be of someone that the individual knows, e.g. mother, brother or friend, a personality from the television such as a Simpsons character, or an unknown individual. The voices can be solitary, or there could be two or more voices talking at the same time. Often the voices talk directly to the individual, but sometimes they provide a running commentary on the individual's actions ('He is making a cup of tea now'). They have even been reported to sing songs, and where there are two or more voices there have been reports of them having conversations between themselves. The voices can often be frightening and derogatory 'You may as well kill yourself as no one wants you' – and some command the individual to do certain things. Other reported voices can be helpful or reassuring.

In addition to auditory hallucinations, visual, olfactory and gustatory hallucinations are also experienced in some people. Visual hallucinations may involve seeing dead people, bugs or elves; olfactory hallucinations may involve a pervasive smell of garbage; and gustatory hallucinations might involve the individual tasting chemicals in all their food.

Disorganised speech

It is useful to consider that the symptom of disorganised speech is intrinsically related to disordered thinking rather than just being an expressive language impairment. Disorganised speech and thought is considered to be one of the hallmark features of schizophrenia and is characterised by the following:

- Jumbled or incoherent utterances/sentences: 'I am a Jurassic Park master and my mother was a chimney stack'.

- Loose associations; where someone shifts their thread of conversation in an irregular, unexpected way: 'When I am older I would like to retire but not like a bicycle, more like an aeroplane but my favourite type of chocolate is hot.'

- Neologisms; where the speaker makes up words: 'I am feeling clankered by shinters today.'

Grossly disorganised or catatonic behaviour

The case study of Jack in this chapter illustrates grossly disorganised behaviour in that he locked himself in his room until nightfall, took on a bizarre appearance and lost his ability to care for himself. Grossly disorganised behaviour can involve displaying highly agitated and unpredictable behaviour, such as running down the road screaming, or repeatedly making the sign of the cross. It can also include the display of inappropriate emotions such as crying at happy news or showing joy at a sad news story. Catatonic behaviour usually describes behaviour where there is extremely high or extremely low activity levels and low activity levels have the following behavioural features: social withdrawal, mutism, posturing (adopting a bizarre posture), **catalepsy** (staying in the same position) and muscle rigidity (Cornic, Consoli, & Cohen, 2007). Indeed, it is not uncommon for someone with withdrawn catatonia to stay in the same standing or sitting position in a strange posture and not talking for hours at a time. Extremely high activity levels in catatonia can involve constant movement and talking and sometimes include acts of violence (Sue, Sue, Sue, & Sue, 2010).

Key term

Catalepsy: muscular rigidity where limbs remain fixed in certain positions and there is a lack of response to external stimuli.

Negative symptoms (lack of emotion, alogia, avolition)

In general terms, negative symptoms are so called because they represent deficits in function, and the mathematical metaphor of 'negative' has been used to illustrate the removal or deduction of these normal behaviours or functions from the personality (Figure 5.1). An inability to display the usual range of emotions is one of the negative symptoms seen in schizophrenia, and someone may display little or no happy or sad emotion to any situation which would

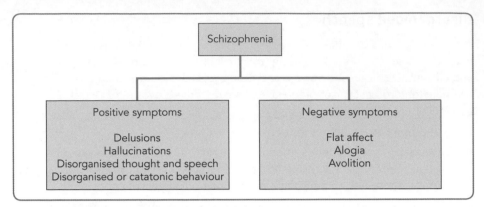

Figure 5.1 **Symptom classification in schizophrenia**

normally elicit an emotional response. Communicating in a very restricted way is also a negative symptom and this is termed alogia. Here, one-word utterances may be given in response to questions, and spontaneous speech, i.e. the patient initiating verbal contact, is not present. Similarly, avolition refers to the inability to take goal-directed action. Doing any task on a day-to-day basis, such as deciding to get out of bed, to make breakfast, to do the washing is goal-directed behaviour, i.e. behaviour that is initiated in order to achieve something. Patients with negative symptoms sometimes display an inability for any goal-directed tasks and so may be unable to care for themselves.

In addition to identifying negative symptoms as those which represent deficits in function, thought and feeling, other symptoms have been termed as *positive*. Here, delusions, hallucinations, disorganised thought and speech and disorganised behaviour are considered positive symptoms because they represent overt symptoms which are identifiable by their presence.

Although not included as part of the diagnostic criteria for schizophrenia, there is now widespread recognition that cognitive deficits are a core feature of the disorder. Studies have found that approximately 75% of patients have difficulty with aspects of memory, attention and executive function (planning and problem solving). These problems have been shown to be evident before the onset of the illness and also to affect the individual's ability to function (O'Carroll, 2000).

In addition to the positive and negative symptoms which are observed in schizophrenia, according to the DSM-5 (APA, 2013) there are other criteria which must be met before a diagnosis of schizophrenia can be made:

- Since the onset of symptoms, function in key areas of life must have been impaired, e.g. work or study, social relationships and self-care.
- There must have been signs of the disorder for six months or more.
- Other disorders with psychotic features (e.g. schizoaffective disorder) cannot explain the symptoms.
- Substance use (e.g. amphetamines) or organic factors (e.g. brain tumour) have been excluded as potential causes of the disturbance.

KEY STUDY

Jack had been a quiet child and did not take an interest in the outdoor activities that most other boys did. He would often prefer to stay inside by himself, watch TV and play video games. On trips to the beach with the family he would prefer to sit and read rather than swim in the sea or play. For these reasons Jack was considered a little different from other children. During adolescence his behaviour became very odd. He would lock himself in his room throughout the day and his mother would leave his meals outside the door for Jack to take when no one was around. At night he would sneak downstairs and hide behind the sofa, peering at the TV. His appearance became very unkempt and he refused to shower or brush his teeth. He wore the same clothes for weeks at a time and would always roll one trouser leg up to his knee, and whenever he was seen he was carrying a can of shaving cream in one hand and a teddy bear in another. When mental health services assessed Jack he said that he was a secret agent and that he had to be very careful with what he said as there were a network of spies observing who could access his thoughts using their 'mind machine'. He was in constant contact with his 'handlers', who communicated with him with messages sent directly into his head. Their voices told him of things he must do to avoid being caught by the British mafia.

Test your knowledge

5.1 What are the origins of the word 'schizophrenia'?

5.2 Give examples of a persecutory delusion and a delusion of grandeur.

5.3 What kind of voices might someone with schizophrenia hear?

5.4 What are loose associations?

Answers to the questions can be found on the companion website at:
www.pearsoned.co.uk/psychologyexpress

Further reading Cognitive deficits in schizophrenia

Key reading

O'Carroll, R. (2000). Cognitive impairment in schizophrenia. *Advances in Psychiatric Treatment*, 6, 161–168.

Assessing symptom type and severity in Schizophrenia

In the DSM-IV (APA, 2000), five different subtypes of schizophrenia were classified: Paranoid (fixation with paranoid delusions), Disorganised (speech and behavior are very disorganized), Catatonic (a lack of motor activity), Undifferentiated (mixed symptoms) and Residual (less prominent symptoms). However, in the DSM 5 (APA, 2013) these subtypes have been excluded because individuals often did not fit neatly into these categories, and they were not helpful in predicting response to treatment or the long term outcome for the individual. Instead, the DSM 5 focusses on symptom type and severity using a dimensional approach where the clinician rates the type and severity of symptoms on the scale: *Clinician-Rated Dimensions of Psychosis Symptom Severity* (APA, 2013). Table 5.2 illustrates this.

Table 5.2 Five subtypes of schizophrenia

Domain	0	1	2	3	4
I. Hallucinations	Not Present	Equivocal (severity or duration not sufficient to be considered psychosis)	Present but mild (little pressure to act upon voices, not bothered by voices)	Present and moderate (some pressure to respond to voices or is bothered by voices)	Present and severe (severe pressure to respond to voices, very bothered by them)
II. Delusions	Not Present	Equivocal (severity or duration not sufficient to be considered psychosis)	Present but mild (little pressure to act upon delusional beliefs, not bothered by beliefs)	Present but moderate (some pressure to act upon beliefs or is bothered by beliefs)	Present and severe (severe pressure to act upon beliefs, or is very bothered by beliefs)
III Disorganized Speech	Not Present	Equivocal (severity or duration not sufficient to be considered disorganization)	Present, but mild (some difficulty following speech)	Present and moderate (speech often difficult to follow)	Present and severe (speech almost impossible to follow)
IV Abnormal psychomotor behaviour	Not Present	Equivocal (severity or duration not sufficient to be considered abnormal psychomotor behavior)	Present, but mild (occasional abnormal or bizarre behavior or catatonia)	Present and moderate (frequent abnormal or bizarre behavior or catatonia)	Present and severe (almost constant abnormal or bizarre behavior or catatonia)
V Negative symptoms (restricted emotional expression or avolition)	Not Present	Equivocal decrease in facial expressions, prosody, gestures or self-initiated behavior	Present, but mild decrease in facial expressivity, prosody, gestures, or self- initiated behavior.	Present and moderate decrease in facial expressivity, prosody, gestures, or self- initiated behavior.	Present and severe decrease in facial expressivity, prosody, gestures, or self- initiated behavior

Domain	0	1	2	3	4
VI Impaired Cognition	Not Present	Equivocal (cognitive function not clearly outside range expected)	Present but mild (some reduction in cognitive function)	Present and moderate (clear reduction in cognitive function)	Present and severe (severe reduction in cognitive function)
VII Depression	Not Present	Equivocal (occasionally feels sad, depressed or hopeless)	Present but mild (frequent periods of feeling very sad, depressed or hopeless)	Present and moderate (frequent periods of deep depression, hopelessness, guilt)	Present and severe (deeply depressed or hopeless daily, delusional guilt)
VIII Mania	Not Present	Equivocal (occasional elevated, expansive or irritable mood)	Present but mild (frequent periods of elevated, expansive or irritable mood)	Present and moderate (frequent periods of extensively elevated, expansive or irritable mood)	Present and severe (daily and extensively elevated, expansive or irritable mood)

✳ Sample question   *Essay*

Individuals with schizophrenia used to be categorised into one of several subtypes (e.g., Paranoid or Catatonic). The DSM 5 no longer uses these categories and instead adopts a dimensional approach which has a focus on symptom type and severity. Consider the advantages and disadvantages of this dimensional approach in contrast to the previous categorical approach.

Longitudinal features of schizophrenia

Some studies have shown that those who go on to develop schizophrenia have certain premorbid personality characteristics which are observable in childhood. For example, they may have been an overly anxious child, had difficulty making friends or struggled academically at school (Cornblatt et al., 2003).

Prior to the onset of the full-blown disorder, a prodromal phase is often observed. This is where there is a gradual build-up of symptoms over a period which can last from days to years. Here, eccentric ideas and peculiar behaviours might start to appear and the individual may start to withdraw from family and friends. There may also be a lack of self-care evident or even an attempt to change appearance (Campo, Frederikx, Nijman, & Merckelback, 1998).

Key term

Prodromal phase: the gradual build-up of schizophrenic symptoms before the onset of the full disorder. For example, the individual may start to express odd ideas, have trouble concentrating and become withdrawn.

Following the *prodromal phase* is the *active phase* of the disorder where full-blown symptoms are observed. These are usually positive symptoms such as hallucinations and delusions and during this phase the individual's ability to function in key areas of life is impaired. This is the phase where mental health services usually become involved and treatment initiated to control the disorder. Following the active phase is the *residual phase* which is where symptoms are not predominant but may still be present in a limited capacity. However, studies of long-term outcome in schizophrenia have not shown a unitary pattern. Wiersma, Nienhuis and Slooff (1998) followed up 82 patients with schizophrenia over a 15-year period and observed different patterns of recovery, with:

- 12.2% of patients having one episode with no long-term symptoms or impairment;
- 14.6% of patients having repeated episodes with no symptoms or impairment between each episode;
- 17.1% of patients having one of more episodes with continuing symptoms and impairment after each episode;
- 33% of patients having repeated episodes with increasing severity of symptoms and impairment between each episode;
- 11% of patients show no recovery after the first episode and are substantially impaired over the long term.

The remaining 12.2% of patients were either untraceable or refused to cooperate with researchers.

Long-term studies of outcome in schizophrenia have also identified factors which are associated with better recovery (Irani & Siegel, 2006; Mihalopoulus, Harris, Henry, Harrigan, & McGorry, 2009; Shrivastava, Shah, Johnston, Stitt, & Thakar, 2010; Warner, 2009). These include:

- gender (women have better outcome);
- higher levels of education;
- being in a marriage;
- good occupational history;
- having independent living skills;
- lower levels of depression and anxiety;
- peer support;
- early intervention at onset of illness.

Further reading Long-term outcome in schizophrenia

Key reading

Jobe, T. H., & Harrow, M. (2005). Long-term outcome of patients with schizophrenia: A review. *Canadian Journal of Psychiatry, 50*(14), 892–900.

The multidimensional risk factors associated with schizophrenia

Schizophrenia is a multifaceted disorder incorporating a wide variety of emotional, behavioural and cognitive symptoms. As might be expected with such a complex condition, the aetiological features are also multidimensional. Evidence suggests that biological, environmental and psychological factors all play a role in the development of the disorder (Table 5.3).

Table 5.3 **Factors which have been found to be associated with schizophrenia**

Biological factors	Genetic predisposition Brain structure abnormalities Neurochemical abnormalities
Environmental factors	Birth complications and hazards Factors in upbringing Cannabis use
Psychological factors	Theory of mind Attentional overload Persecutory delusions as a defence mechanism Trauma

Biological factors

Genetic predisposition

There is insurmountable evidence that genes play a role in predisposing an individual to schizophrenia. The risk of developing the disorder is approximately 1% across the general population but if you have a relative who has the disorder then you have an increased likelihood of developing the condition. This likelihood increases the closer your genetic relationship is to the affected individual or individuals. For example, if you have one parent with the condition then you have approximately a 17% chance of developing the disorder, yet if you have two affected parents you have about a 46% chance of inheriting the condition. The highest probability of developing the condition is if you have an identical twin who is affected: you are at a 48% risk of schizophrenia. This is in contrast to a non-identical twin who has 17% chance of developing the condition if their twin is affected (Gottesman, 1991). It is important to note that even in adoption studies where the child who has a schizophrenic parent is brought up by unaffected adopted parents, they have still demonstrated a higher risk factor (e.g. Tienari et al., 2000). This negates the suggestion that the concordance rates are related to the home environment or learnt behaviour passed from parent to child. However, even with a 48% concordance rate between identical twins, there is still another 52% which is unaccounted for and is considered to relate to non-genetic factors.

Brain structure abnormalities

One of the first observable brain abnormalities to be detected in schizophrenia was that of enlarged ventricles. The ventricles are cavities within the brain containing cerebrospinal fluid, and a meta-analysis of magnetic resonance imaging (MRI) studies showed that on average the ventricles of patients with schizophrenia were 26% larger than those without schizophrenia (Wright, Rabe-Hesketh, Woodruss, David, & Murray, 2000). Enlarged ventricles may indicate that normal development of key brain regions has not taken place. Other brain areas have been found to be smaller in patients, including frontal and temporal areas (Lawrie, McIntosh, Hall, Owens, & Johnstone, 2008). These abnormalities may offer some explanation for the unusual experiences, behavioural problems and cognitive deficits that are seen in schizophrenia. For example, the temporal lobes are responsible for aspects of language and emotion and therefore difficulties with these abilities might be explained by structural abnormalities in these regions. Frontal areas are also associated with drive and motivation and therefore some of the negative symptoms observed in schizophrenia might be partially explained by these structural problems (Galderisi et al., 2008). Frontal lobe areas of the brain also play a role in the cognitive abilities of planning, decision making and memory and therefore structural abnormalities of these regions may be the basis for the reported deficits in these domains. Furthermore, one positron emission tomography (PET) study has even found that adolescents with schizophrenia show a loss of grey matter in parietal, temporal and frontal areas over a period of six years, indicating that the volume of these areas and total brain volume is decreasing (Thompson et al., 2001).

Neurochemical abnormalities

An excess of the neurotransmitter dopamine has been one of the predominant biological explanations for schizophrenia since the 1970s. The evidence for the role of dopamine in the disorder comes from a variety of sources:

- The class of medication which successfully reduces positive symptoms in schizophrenia, the antipsychotics, act by reducing the amount of dopamine within the brain (Stahl, 1996).

- The synthetic drug used to treat Parkinson's disease, L-DOPA, works by increasing the amount of dopamine. However, too much L-DOPA can lead to schizophrenic-like symptoms and, conversely, too much dopamine blocking by antipsychotic medication can cause Parkinson-like motor symptoms (Jaskiw & Popli, 2004).

- Amphetamines work by increasing the amount of dopamine and individuals who take amphetamines in high doses start to show schizophrenia-like symptoms (Harris & Bakti, 2000).

It has been suggested that one of the roles of dopamine is to tag certain thoughts, experiences and behaviours as important or special to us. However, if the dopamine system is overactive then many seemingly irrelevant events might be identified as having special importance, such as seeing a number 32 bus or hearing a conversation on television. This therefore may be a biological explanation for the delusions and hallucinations experienced in schizophrenia (Kapur, Mizrahi, & Li, 2005). In addition, there has also been the suggestion that positive symptoms are associated with increased dopamine and negative symptoms with a depletion of dopamine which usually occurs later on in the illness (Lieberman, Kinon, & Loebel, 1990).

The dopamine hypothesis, however, does not offer an all-encompassing explanation for schizophrenia. Studies have shown that up to 30% of patients with the disorder do not respond to treatment with antipsychotic medication and therefore they still exhibit symptoms despite reductions in their dopamine levels (Conley & Buchanan, 1997). In addition, recent research has implicated other neurotransmitter systems in the disorder, such as serotonin, noradrenaline and glutamate and it is likely that the disorder is the result of the complex interplay between these and other neurotransmitter systems. Indeed, second generation antipsychotic medication does exert its effects on multiple neurotransmitter systems and not just dopamine (Stahl, 1996).

Environmental factors

Birth complications and hazards

Studies have found that individuals who go on to develop schizophrenia have a higher likelihood of suffering from complications around birth than the general population. These complications include prematurity, low levels of oxygen to the brain, needing resuscitation or incubatory care and low birth weight (Cannon, Jones, & Murray, 2002; Geddes et al., 1999). These complications may lead to subtle brain damage which predisposes the individual to the disorder. There is also evidence that those at risk for schizophrenia have had a higher likelihood of being born in the winter months than summer months. One explanation for this is that viruses are more prevalent in the winter months and therefore individuals born during these months have a higher likelihood of being exposed to viruses, which predisposes them to developing schizophrenia later in life. Exposure to a virus either as a foetus or a young child does increase the risk of schizophrenia (Jones & Cannon, 1998; Takei, van Os, & Murray, 1995).

Factors in upbringing

Individuals from the lowest socio-economic group and those living in an urban environment appear to have an increased risk of developing schizophrenia (Eaton et al., 1989; Krabbendam & van Os, 2005). The most likely explanation for this is that there are increased stress levels associated with being within these environments and the interaction between genetic vulnerability and stress levels is a key precipitating factor for the onset of illness. Indeed, suffering stress as a result of adverse events during childhood appears to be related to schizophrenia as the following studies suggest:

- Suffering childhood trauma such as an accident, bullying and/or maltreatment increases the risk of psychotic symptoms at age 12 (Arseneault et al., 2011).
- Victims of bullying between the ages of 8 and 10 had double the risk of psychosis compared with non-bullied children and the more extreme the bullying the stronger the association with psychotic symptoms (Schreier et al., 2009).
- Psychosis is three times more prevalent in individuals who report maternal physical abuse before the age of 12 compared with controls (Fisher et al., 2010).

Experiencing such adverse events when the brain is not fully mature may hinder normal neural development and hence act as a predisposing factor in the development of schizophrenia. Indeed, stress has been shown to increase dopamine levels in animals, providing a potential biological mechanism of action for the link between childhood experiences and illness onset (Walker & Diforio, 1997). Furthermore, patterns of communication within the family have also been shown to be associated with the disorder. This research centres on the concept of *expressed emotion* which describes emotionally loaded communication patterns between family members which is of a critical or hostile nature. For example, a parent might be critical of an adolescent by saying 'you never lift a finger to help around the house' or 'you are an embarrassment to me with all your crazy ideas'. Research which has looked at communication patterns within families have found that expressed emotion is associated with relapse in individuals who already have the disorder (Breitborde, Lopez, & Nuechterlien, 2009). However, no studies have shown that expressed emotion acts as a precursor to the first onset of the illness. Interestingly, one study has shown that positive remarks in a family environment are associated with symptom improvement (O'Brien et al., 2006).

CRITICAL FOCUS

Cannabis use and schizophrenia

In addition to the use of amphetamine being associated with psychotic symptoms, a strong link has also been found between cannabis consumption and schizophrenia. Young users of cannabis have twice the risk of developing schizophrenia compared with non-users (Henquet, Murray, Linszen, & van Os, 2005). A dose–response relationship has also been reported where the more cannabis smoked, the greater the likelihood of developing the disorder (Andrèason, Allebeck, Engstrom, & Ryldberg, 1987). In individuals who already have schizophrenia, cannabis use predicts the rate of relapse and severity of symptoms (Linszen, Dingemans, & Lenoir, 1994). The link between cannabis use and schizophrenia is thought to be mediated by the primary active ingredient in the drug which is delta 9 tetrahydrocannabinol (Δ 9 THC). This metabolite has been found to increase cerebral dopamine activity and thereby potentially be one of the triggers for dopamine-led positive symptoms (Voruganti, Slomka, Zabel, Mattar, & Awad, 2001). However, not all cannabis users develop psychosis and therefore there may be a genetic component to the sensitivity

▶

of the dopamine system to cannabis (Henquet, Di Forti, Morrison, Kuepper, & Murray, 2008).

Key term

Delta 9 tetrahydrocannabinol (Δ 9 THC): the psychoactive part of the cannabis plant which causes mood and perceptual changes. It has been linked to the onset of schizophrenia.

Psychological factors

Theory of mind

The theory of mind is an influential psychological model of symptoms in schizophrenia which was originally proposed by Frith in 1992. A key element of normal cognitive processing involves us being able to understand the self-generated nature of our own thoughts, ideas and intentions, and also to have an idea about similar cognitive processes in others, i.e. we try to understand others based on our knowledge of our own minds. If this ability is impaired, then we do not know whether the thoughts we have are our own or have been 'planted' in our minds, and we may even think that we are being controlled externally because we do not recognise that our actions are generated by ourselves. We might also have auditory hallucinations because we think that our own thoughts (or inner speech) are external voices. Not being able to understand the minds of others might lead to difficulties interpreting the actions of others and might lead to ideas of reference or paranoid delusions. The theory of mind is a plausible explanation for many of the symptoms of schizophrenia and furthermore, has significant empirical support (Sprong, Schothorst, Vos, Hox, & Van Engeland, 2007). For example, one study found that patients with schizophrenia could not recognise geometric drawings they had made themselves (Stirling, Hellewell, & Ndlovu., 2001) and another study found they were poorer than controls in understanding cartoon jokes of which a key element was a seeing the situation from a particular character's perspective, i.e. they could not see the situation from another's point of view (Marjoram et al., 2005).

Attentional overload

One psychological explanation for auditory hallucinations in schizophrenia has proposed that there may be a problem in focusing attention appropriately (Hemsley, 1996). Here, the usual mechanisms which filter out irrelevant or unwanted material and only attend to salient information are not working properly. This results in individuals being bombarded with information and having a consequent difficulty in focusing on and interacting to the relevant environmental cues appropriately. There is also a failure of the system whereby stored memories are used to contextualise incoming sensory information in order to guide behaviour. For example, our behaviour whilst shopping is based on our stored memories (or script) of how to behave whilst shopping. According to these ideas, hallucinations stem from attention being paid to irrelevant sensory information (e.g. a voice heard in the street) whilst delusions are the result of the individual trying to derive meaning from a plethora of confusing information stemming from both internal and external sources. In addition to this hypothesis offering an explanation for some positive symptoms in schizophrenia, Hemsley (1996) also suggested that it explains negative symptoms (e.g. flat affect) in that these occur as a natural response to cope with the sensory overload.

Persecutory delusions as a defence mechanism

A psychological explanation of persecutory delusions suggests that they operate as a kind of defence mechanism when there is a discrepancy between who someone thinks they are (actual self) and who they would like to be (ideal self). So for example, if someone is unemployed, with few prospects and little money, then it would be a form of psychological defence to attribute this lack of success to a conspiracy between employers and the government rather than to the individual's own inadequacy (Bentall, Corcoran, Howard, Blackwood, & Kinderman, 2001).

Trauma

The trauma model of hallucinations proposes that voices occur as a result of traumatic experiences and their purpose is to draw attention to the trauma in order to promote recovery. The voices are in the third person as a defence mechanism against the emotional upset caused by the memories of the trauma (Romme & Escher, 1989).

From the preceding discussion it is clear that there is not a single overriding factor which causes the disorder, and it is likely that many of the above factors interrelate to cause an increased likelihood of developing the condition. For example, a genetic predisposition might result in brain abnormalities which interact with environmental factors to produce schizophrenia.

Test your knowledge

5.5 How do we know that schizophrenia has a genetic component?

5.6 What do the effects of L-DOPA tell us about the causes of schizophrenia?

5.7 Describe some of the childhood factors associated with the development of schizophrenia.

Answers to the questions can be found on the companion website at: **www.pearsoned.co.uk/psychologyexpress**

Further reading Cannabis and schizophrenia

Key reading

Henquet, C., Murray, R., Linzsen, D., & van Os, J. (2005). The environment and schizophrenia: The role of cannabis use. *Schizophrenia Bulletin, 31*, 608–612.

Treating schizophrenia

Biological-based treatments

Since the discovery of drugs that reduce the severity of psychotic symptoms in the 1950s, the 'antipsychotics' have become the primary front line treatment for individuals with schizophrenia (Stahl, 1996). There are two main classes of antipsychotic medication: the typical antipsychotics and the atypical antipsychotics. The typical antipsychotics (e.g. Chlorpormazine, Flupenthixol and Haloperidol) were the first class of medications to be developed and although they did reduce the intensity of psychotic symptoms, they had little effect on negative symptoms and also produced worrying side effects. Because of their neurochemical effect on a wide range of dopamine receptors, including those which play a role in voluntary movement, they produced side effects such as tardive dyskinesia, which is characterised by involuntary repetitive movements such as facial grimacing and lip smacking.

Although typical antipsychotics are still used today, they are gradually becoming less prominent in favour of atypical antipsychotics. These drugs (e.g. Clozapine, Olanzapine, Risperidone) have been developed to treat positive and negative symptoms and also reduce the incidence of side effects. They work on several neurotransmitter systems such as dopaminergic and serotinergic sites, but have much less of an effect on dopamine receptors which mediate movements. Therefore they have a much lower incidence of motor side effects, although they do have their own side effect profiles. For example, Clozapine has been found to decrease the number of white blood cells in some patients, whilst Olanzapine is associated with weight gain.

Psychological-based treatments

Cognitive Behavioural Therapy

The general aim of CBT in any setting is to change problematic thought and behaviour. In schizophrenia CBT used to be most commonly used to encourage behavioural change, such as in implementing strategies to assist someone with negative symptoms become more active or to help build independent living skills (Tai & Turkington, 2009). Although CBT is still used for these purposes, there is much more emphasis today on addressing the cognitive underpinnings of psychotic experiences and thereby reducing the stress associated with hallucinations and delusions (Turkington, Kingdon, & Weiden, 2006). Here, delusions might be challenged so that the client has an alternative interpretation of an event which is less stress inducing. For example, someone who believes that trees are talking to him might be encouraged to find evidence to suggest that trees have vocal apparatus and can speak English. Clients might also be taught to identify and thereby avoid *triggers* for psychotic experiences. Distraction techniques could also be implemented to reduce the impact of a psychotic experience and associated stress.

Family communication and education

The important role that families play in the care and well-being of individuals with schizophrenia should not be underestimated. As previously discussed, negative communication patterns within the family put individuals at greater risk of relapse if they already have the disorder (Breitborde et al., 2009). Therefore it is important that family members are educated about the disorder so that communication patterns can be blame free and empathic. It is also important that family members develop particular skills in order to help their relative, and these can include learning problem-solving strategies and stress management techniques. Indeed, a recent review of the literature has confirmed that family intervention strategies in schizophrenia reduce the incidence of relapse and hospital admission, and that they also improve social skills in those with schizophrenia (Pharoah, Mari, Rathbone, & Wong, 2010).

Other psychotic disorders

- **Schizophreniform disorder.** This is where an individual has an episode of schizophrenia-like symptoms which last for between one and six months. There is usually a return to premorbid functioning afterwards.
- **Brief psychotic disorder.** Here, schizophrenia-like symptoms are observed but these last between a day and a month with a full return to premorbid functioning afterwards.
- **Schizoaffective disorder.** This is where symptoms of schizophrenia such as hallucinations and delusions occur at the same time as symptoms of major depression or mania.
- **Delusional disorder.** The key symptom here is of a non-bizarre delusion which lasts for at least a month and there is no impairment in functioning. The delusion usually involves events that are within the realms of possibility rather than bizarre delusions seen in schizophrenia. For example, a delusion might involve the belief that someone is trying to poison you, that you omit a terrible smell, or that your partner is having an affair.
- **Shared psychotic disorder (*folie à deux*).** This is where two individuals, usually family members, share the same delusion such as that their neighbours are government agents and are monitoring their actions.
- **Substance-induced psychotic disorder.** Here the psychotic episode is related to substance intoxication or withdrawal.
- **Psychotic disorder not otherwise specified.** This category is used for disorders which do not fit into any of the preceding categories. Postpartum psychosis (or puerperal psychosis) where mothers who have just given birth become psychotic usually falls into this category.

Further reading Cognitive Behavioural Therapy for schizophrenia

Key reading

Turkington, D., Kingdon, D., & Weiden, P. J. (2006). Cognitive behavior therapy for schizophrenia. *American Journal of Psychiatry, 163*, 365–373.

Chapter summary – pulling it all together

→ Can you tick all the points from the revision checklist at the beginning of this chapter?

→ Attempt the sample question from the beginning of this chapter using the answer guidelines below.

→ Go to the companion website at www.pearsoned.co.uk/psychologyexpress to access more revision support online, including interactive quizzes, flashcards, You be the marker exercises as well as answer guidance for the Test your knowledge and sample questions from this chapter.

Answer guidelines

✱ *Sample question*   *Essay*

Consider whether schizophrenia is primarily a *psychological* or *biological* disorder.

Approaching the question

It is important that you recognise that the question requires you to adopt a critical perspective on psychological and biological explanations of schizophrenia. This means that an awareness of both the strengths and weaknesses of each approach is needed. These can be generic strengths and weaknesses (as outlined in Chapter 2), e.g. biological explanations have been criticised for their reductionist perspective.

Important points to include

● You will need to demonstrate an understanding of the main symptoms of schizophrenia so be sure you can briefly describe them. You should describe and evaluate the key biological explanations of schizophrenia (genetic, neuroanatomical and neurochemical) and include research which supports each explanation.

● You should describe and evaluate the key psychological explanations of schizophrenia (theory of mind, attentional overload, persecutory delusions and trauma) and include research which supports each explanation.

● Remember that although environmental explanations are not explicitly asked for in the question, demonstrating an awareness of them and how there is interplay between biological, environmental and psychological explanations would be useful.

Make your answer standout

A strong answer to this question would incorporate contemporary thinking and research on the proposed causes of schizophrenia. So, for example, when you consider the biological explanations you should refer to the most recent or most renowned research on genetic, neuroanatomical or neurochemical factors associated with the disorder. Remember that schizophrenia is likely to be caused by a complex interplay between biological, environmental and psychological factors and this should be emphasised in your conclusion.

Explore the accompanying website at www.pearsoned.co.uk/psychologyexpress

→ Prepare more effectively for exams and assignments using the answer guidelines for questions from this chapter.
→ Test your knowledge using multiple choice questions and flashcards.
→ Improve your essay skills by exploring the You be the marker exercises.

Notes

Personality disorders

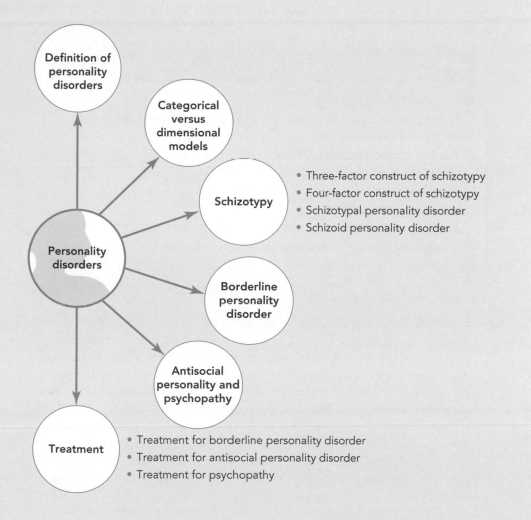

- Definition of personality disorders

- Categorical versus dimensional models

- Schizotypy
  - Three-factor construct of schizotypy
  - Four-factor construct of schizotypy
  - Schizotypal personality disorder
  - Schizoid personality disorder

- Personality disorders

- Borderline personality disorder

- Antisocial personality and psychopathy

- Treatment
  - Treatment for borderline personality disorder
  - Treatment for antisocial personality disorder
  - Treatment for psychopathy

A printable version of this topic map is available from
www.pearsoned.co.uk/psychologyexpress

Introduction

Personality disorders affect individuals across their lifespan: some personality disorders encompass the features of more disabling illnesses but do not impact upon the individual to the same degree and hence a formal diagnosis is not required.

This chapter will discuss the validity of the concept of personality disorders as distinct disorders, before considering a general theory explaining their development. Whilst there exists, according to DSM-IV-TR, an array of personality disorders, this chapter will focus on schizotype disorder, borderline personality disorder, antisocial personality disorder and psychopathy.

> **→ Revision checklist**
>
> *Essential points to revise are:*
> - ❑ The distinction between personality disorder and mental illness (e.g. psychotic-based disorder
> - ❑ The key components which a personality disorder impact upon: cognition; mood; interpersonal functioning; impulsive control
> - ❑ The categorical vs. dimensional approach to disorder and their implication on diagnosis
> - ❑ The distinction between psychopathy and antisocial personality disorder
> - ❑ Assessment and treatment approaches

Assessment advice

- Antisocial personality disorder, according to DSM-IV-TR (APA, 2000), includes aspects of psychopathic disorder, suggesting there to be some kind of overlap between these two concepts. When answering a question on psychopathy there is a potential for discussion around the assessment and diagnosis of antisocial personality disorder but make sure that you are clear about the differences in terminology. Make sure that you are able to discuss the issues related to personality disorders collectively.

- Assessments based on case studies are common in Clinical Psychology and require knowledge of both assessment and treatment. When reading a case study ensure you consider all of the information before providing an assessment of an individual and recommending treatment approaches. It is easy to make a decision after reading the first few sentences, although more important detail may be contained in the latter part of the case study.

Sample question

Could you answer this question? Below is a typical essay question that could arise on this topic.

> ✱ *Sample question*   *Essay*
>
> Critically discuss the contribution of the dimensional approach to understanding and diagnosing mental disorder.

Definition of personality disorders

Personality disorders, according to DSM IV-TR (APA, 2000), are axis 2 disorders, which means that they are thought to be stable long-term conditions and hence are experienced throughout much of an individual's life. Furthermore, personality disorders are characterised by individuals undergoing an enduring pattern of inner experience and behaviour that differs noticeably from the expectations of the individual's culture in at least two of the following:

- cognition;
- mood;
- interpersonal functioning;
- impulsive control.

The stable and prevalent patterns of traits, by definition, are evident across a range of personal and social situations and are noticeably ongoing for a long period of time. The onset of such features can usually be traced back to adolescence or early childhood. Often, personality disorders are accompanied by mood disorders, evidenced in between 24 and 74% of cases being accompanied by major depression and between 4 and 20% by bipolar depression. This comorbidity factor can make diagnosis challenging.

Personality disorders are therefore clusters of traits that are stable over time. However, the stability of these features has been brought into question particularly when examining dependent and schizotypal personalities (Loranger et al., 1994). Interestingly, 35–55% of people with substance misuse problems have symptoms of a personality disorder (Bennett, 2006). This is highlighted in American Psychological Association research (APA, 2000), which maintains that at least 50% of individuals who seek help with addiction or mental health treatment have co-occurring disorders.

Categorical versus dimensional models

The assessment and diagnosis of personality disorders can be extremely difficult. The DSM (APA, 2000) has evolved through several editions and major revisions which arguably reflects the advances in both research and clinical practice. In some cases, the revisions have entailed improved descriptive criteria, more behavioural references, theoretical definitions of symptoms and clearer boundaries for diagnosis.

According to this framework, and other similar frameworks such as the *International Classification of Disease* – 10 (World Health Organization, 1994), personality disorder exists in distinct categories that can be identified by an individual presenting a group of symptoms. Despite ongoing and long-standing efforts to improve the diagnostic tools, problems remain with categorical conceptualisation of personality disorders (Widiger & Samuel, 2005; Widiger & Sanderson, 1995; Wiggins & Pincus, 1994).

Partly in response to these issues, interests have been developed for research into a dimensional approach to personality assessment and diagnosis. Individuals' personalities can be assessed using various scales and psychometric tests and evaluated for psychopathology based on the test score (Huprich, 2003; Saulsman & Page, 2004; Strack, Lorr, & Campbell, 1990). This type of approach has the potential to create more comprehensive descriptions of patient functioning, improve the clinician's understanding of the individual being assessed, and provide a more accurate and natural representation of the organisation of personality and personality pathology (Livesley, 2006; Widiger & Simonsen, 2005; Widiger, Trull, Clarkin, Sanderson, & Costa, 2002). Often the characteristics and experiences of people with personality disorders are not distinctly differentiated from the normal population. Consequently, it helps to consider these individuals to be at the extreme of the distribution as opposed to categorically different from the normal population.

The dimensional model can be argued on theoretical and philosophical grounds, but in addition it provides a tool that is better at predicting outcome compared to the categorical approach used by the DSM. For example, scores on personality tests were able to produce better predictions of subsequent offending behaviour than categorical diagnosis of antisocial personality disorder (Ullrich, Borkenau, & Marneros, 2001). Dimensional scores have proved to be more reliable across clinicians than categorical diagnosis (Heumann & Morey, 1990).

✱ *Sample question*   *Essay*

Critically discuss the contribution of the dimensional approach to understanding and diagnosing mental disorder.

Further reading Assessment, diagnosis and categorical vs. dimensional models

Key reading

Huprich, S. K., & Bornstein, R. F. (2007). Overview of issues related to categorical and dimensional models of personality disorder assessment. *Journal of Personality Assessment* 89(1), 3–15.

Schizotypy

Schizotypy captures a group of personality traits which have been found to leave individuals susceptible to delusional-like beliefs and, consequently, individuals who score high for schizotypal traits can also produce similar findings associated with schizotypal personality disorder and other schizotype disorders (Sellen, Oaksford, & Gray, 2005; Galbraith, Manktelow, & Morris, 2008, 2010). Schizotypy as a construct provides further support for the idea that schizotypal psychopathological characteristics existing along a continuum (Claridge & Brooks, 1984; Eysenck & Eysenck, 1975), in which they present themselves to varying degrees. Van Os, Hanssen, Bijl and Ravelli (2000) suggest that this is due to a continuous phenotype which opposes the categorical approach of mental illness which maintains that symptoms are either present or not. Consequently, there exists a major subclinical category of psychopathological behaviour, referred to as schizotypes (Claridge, 1988).

Schizotypes share a number of common characteristics with not only personality-based disorders but also, psychotic-based disorders such as schizophrenia. For example, phenomenology (Kendler, 1985) and performance deficits are found on the Wisconsin card-sorting task (Lenzenweger & Korfine, 1994), which Tsakanikos (2004) notes are largely associated with the negative symptoms of schizophrenia. Executive functioning deficits have therefore been detected in non-clinical participants who score highly on psychometric measures of schizotypy (e.g Poreh, Ross, & Whitman, 1995; Suhr, 1997; Tsakanikos & Reed, 2003). Impaired performances on executive functioning tasks have been specifically associated with negative schizotypy (Poreh et al., 1995; Suhr, 1997; Tsakanikos & Reed,

2003), and Roitman et al. (1997) provide evidence for the common biological, phenomenological and cognitive similarities that exist between schizophrenia, schizotypal personality and schizotypy. Their research particularly highlights the abnormality in attention that is common in both schizophrenia and schizotypy.

In some cases it appears that individuals may progress through schizotypy, as a prodromal phase or state, prior to entering into and developing an active phase of schizotypal personality disorder (Yoon, Kang, & Kwon, 2008). Schizotypes are often characterised by an individual being quirky but awkward in social interaction, showing signs of 'odd' behaviour and language (Bentall, Claridge, & Slade, 1989).

A number of methods have been developed to assess schizotypy in non-clinical populations. In most cases, this has led to psychometrics tools, which aim to measure features of schizotypy according to a particular approach and theory. Many of these have used variations of factor analysis to explore the factors and constructs that relate to schizotypy, which confirms that schizotypy is a multifactor construct (Claridge et al., 1996). The number of constructs differs among models but contemporary studies have explored a five-factor model; however, this has largely been inconsistent and therefore not conclusive (Vollema & van den Bosch, 1995).

Three-factor construct of schizotypy

It is generally accepted by psychologists and increasingly by psychiatrists that schizophrenia and schizotypal personality disorder symptoms are clustered around three factors: positive symptoms; negative symptoms; and disorganisation (Figure 6.1; Peters, Joseph, Day, & Garety, 2004). Similarly, various studies

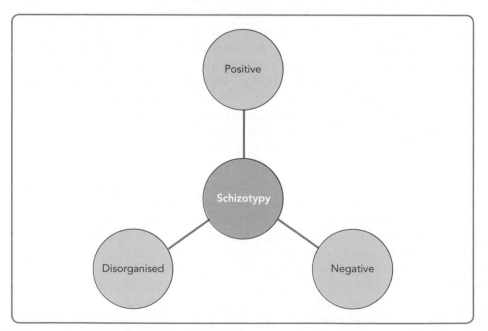

Figure 6.1 **Three-factor model of schizotypy**

suggest that schizotypal features are also clustered on three factors in the general population (Chen, Hsiao, & Lin, 1997; Gruzelier, 1996; Reynolds, Raine, Mellingen, Venables, & Mednick, 2000), in accordance with Raine, Reynolds, Lencz and Scerbo's (1994) three-factor model (cognitive-perceptual, interpersonal and disorganisation) and Bergmann et al.'s (1996, 1997) model of cognitive-perceptual, interpersonal and paranoid dimensions.

Four-factor construct of schizotypy

Other research has explored schizotypy as a four-factor construct (Figure 6.2; Bentall et al., 1989; Vollema & van den Bosch, 1995). The first three dimensions correspond with the three-factor model (Liddle, 1987): a positive ('unusual experiences'), a negative ('introvertive anhedonia') and a disorganised dimension ('cognitive disorganisation'), and the additional fourth dimension is 'impulsivity non-conformity'.

Schizotypal personality disorder

Schizotypal personality disorder has a number of similarities and associations with schizophrenia which you will have read about in Chapter 5. Seeber and Cadenhead

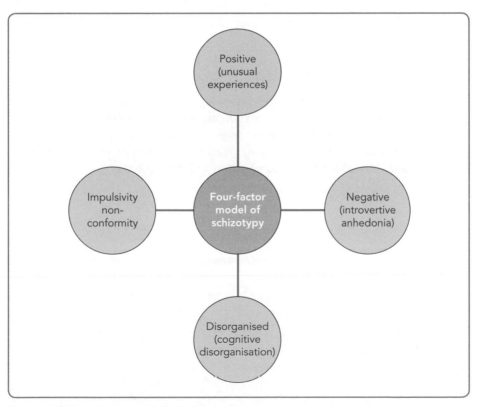

Figure 6.2 Four-factor model of schizotypy

(2005) report that 3–10% of first-degree relatives of individuals with schizophrenia, met the criteria for schizotypal personality disorder. However, these disorders differ quite significantly when considering their development and foundation. Schizophrenia is an episodic psychotic-based disorder, whilst schizotypal personality disorder is grounded in a long-term, and fairly stable, development of personality (Bennett, 2006). Therefore, SPD features as an axis 2 cluster A disorder within the DSM IV-TR (APA, 2000) criteria, forming a stable long-term condition whereby symptoms are continuously and consistently presented that are long-lasting if not permanent. In order for an individual to be diagnosed with schizotypal personality disorder five or more of the following symptoms must be present:

- ideas of reference (excluding delusions of reference);
- odd beliefs or magical thinking that influence behaviour and are inconsistent with subculture norms;
- unusual perceptual experiences, including bodily illusions;
- odd thinking and speech;
- suspiciousness or paranoid ideation;
- inappropriate or restricted affect;
- odd behaviour or appearance;
- lack of close friends or confidants other than first degree relatives;
- excessive social anxiety that does not diminish with familiarity and tends to be associated with paranoid fears.

Schizoid personality disorder

Schizoid personality disorder to some extent represents a less intense form of schizotypal personality disorder. It is characterised by a pattern of reduced attachment from social relationships accompanied by a restricted range of expression of emotions. Individuals diagnosed with schizoid personality disorder present at least four of the following symptoms (Bennett, 2006):

- neither desires nor enjoys close relationships;
- almost always chooses solitary activities;
- takes little interest in sexual experiences;
- takes pleasure in few activities;
- lacks close friends or confidants;
- emotional coldness/detachment;
- indifferent to praise or criticism of others.

It appears that schizoid personality disorder and schizotypal personality disorder have many similar, and possibly related, characteristics. However, the main difference between these two disorders lies in the reasons for withdrawal from social interactions. Schizotypal personality disorder is characterised by a fear of social interaction and therefore includes aspects of paranoia, suspicion and anxiety. In comparison, schizoid personality disorder is rooted in a 'lack of desire' for social interaction, particularly with close relationships. With both of these disorders there are notions of being 'split'. Schizophrenia is defined as being a 'split' from reality whereas schizotypal personality disorder and schizoid personality disorder inhabit features that show a 'split' from others (Bennett, 2006). Elements of both schizotypal personality disorder and Schizophrenia have been found in the subclinical category schizotypy (Bentall et al., 1989; Vollema & van den Bosch, 1995).

✳ Sample question   *Essay*

Critically discuss how the core feature, 'split', differs between schizotypal personality disorder and schizoid personality disorder.

Test your knowledge

6.4 How is schizotypal personality disorder defined?

6.5 How is schizoid personality disorder defined?

6.6 What is the prevalence rate of schizotypal personality disorder and schizoid personality disorder?

6.7 What is the relevance of schizotypy?

Answers to these questions can be found on the companion website at: **www.pearsoned.co.uk/psychologyexpress**

Further reading Schizotype and crime-based reasoning

Key reading

Wilkinson, D. J., Jones, T., & Caulfield, L. S. (2011). Time to reason about crime. *The Howard Journal of Criminal Justice, 50*, 393–405.

Borderline personality disorder

So far we have discussed disorders that are categorised as Cluster A diagnosis; we now turn to examine Cluster B disorders such as borderline personality disorder. Borderline personality disorder is characterised by the symptoms outlined below. A clinician may make the diagnosis of borderline personality disorder if the patient has five or more of the symptoms below and if the symptoms have a significant impact on their everyday life:

- emotions that are up and down (for example, feeling confident one day and feeling despair another), accompanied by feelings of emptiness and often anger;

- difficulty making and maintaining relationships;
- an unstable sense of identity, such as thinking differently about oneself depending upon other social influencers;
- risk taking or doing things without thinking about the potential consequences;
- self-harming or thinking about self-harming (for example, thinking about cutting oneself or taking an overdose);
- a fear of being abandoned or rejected or being alone;
- believing in things that are not real or true (i.e. delusional beliefs) or seeing or hearing things that are not really there (i.e. hallucinations).

Borderline personality disorder impacts around 2% of the US population with around 75% of these cases being women (APA, 2000). This figure drops to less than 1% in the UK, although women still make up 75% of the diagnosed population. This over-representation in females is particularly noticeable in forensic settings (Nee & Farman, 2005). Typically this disorder emerges during adolescence and continues through adulthood. An alarming 10% of diagnosed individuals eventually commit suicide (Zanarini, Frankenburg, Henne, Reich, & Silk, 2005), along with a good proportion of individuals who commit acts of self-harm. This is thought to be in response to the negative emotions often experienced in borderline personality disorder which contribute to patterns of negative thoughts.

It is quite common for a diagnosis of borderline personality disorder to be accompanied by other mental health-related problems, such as depression, anxiety, eating disorders or substance misuse (misusing drugs or alcohol). Naturally, the comorbidity creates further complexity around both diagnosis and treatment of the disorder.

Further reading Borderline personality disorder in female offenders

Key reading

Nee, C., & Farman, S. (2005). Female prisoners with borderline personality disorder: Some promising treatment developments. *Criminal Behaviour and Mental Health, 15*(1), 2–16.

Antisocial personality and psychopathy

KEY STUDY

Craig

Craig, a 25-year-old man, had attended an appointment with his local general practitioner (GP) where he had complained of recurrent backache. He had disclosed that he had tried many analgesics previously but overall they were either ineffective or caused intolerable side effects, with the exception of high doses of codeine. The GP

▶

conducted a physical examination of Craig and discovered significant disease of the lumbosacral spine secondary to a congenital defect in the alignment of the vertebrae.

The GP has been concerned about Craig's specific request for a potentially addictive narcotic that also had high resale value in the illicit drug market and consequently she inquired further into Craig's work and occupational history. Craig, typically, demonstrated an unstable pattern of impulsive and manipulative interpersonal relations, including an irregular work history and other features characteristic of antisocial personality disorder. A respectful but appropriately tough tone of inquiry into Craig's previous use of analgesics revealed a history of morphine addiction following lower back surgery. The GP's resistance to the request for codeine led to an angry outburst, with Craig declining alternative treatment. Several months later, however, Craig reappeared with legitimate complaints of upper respiratory tract infection. He told the physician, 'I came back to see you again because I figure you're nobody's fool, but you're not going to lecture me about how I should live my life either.'

Antisocial personality disorder is a term used by clinicians, to describe 'a pervasive pattern of disregard for, and violation of, the rights of others that begins in childhood or early adolescence and continues into adulthood' (APA, 2000, p. 645). The core characteristics include:

- repeatedly performing illegal acts;
- repeatedly lying or conning others for personal profit and/or pleasure;
- impulsivity or failure to plan ahead;
- reckless disregard for the safety of self and others;
- consistent irresponsibility;
- lack of remorse for others.

When an offender is diagnosed with antisocial personality disorder they are considered to be a 'mentally disordered offender'. This label is given for a number of underlying issues: mental illness; personality disorder; learning difficulties; drug dependency.

Lynam and Gudonis (2005) suggests a hypothetical profile for antisocial personality disorder based on the Costa and McCrae (1995) five-factor model of personality. They propose that an individual with antisocial personality disorder will score low on the following five dimensions of personality:

- low neuroticism;
- low extroversion;
- low openness;
- low agreeableness;
- low conscientiousness.

Scoring low for neuroticism would indicate that the individual lacks the appropriate concern for potential problems in health or social adjustment; emotional blandness. A low score for extroversion (introversion) would indicate that an individual may be socially isolated and therefore interpersonally detached with lack of support networks. They may experience a flattened affect and are unlikely to assert self or assume leadership roles even if qualified to do so. Low openness suggests that an individual has difficulty adapting to social or personal change, low tolerance and understanding of differing opinions or points of view, and excessive conformity to authority. Low agreeableness is characterised by cynical and paranoid thinking, an inability to trust even close friends and relatives, being quarrelsome, exploitive and manipulative, which limits social support, a lack of respect for social conventions, and arrogance. Low conscientiousness is evident in underachievement, poor performance, disregard of rules and responsibilities, lack of self-discipline, and aimlessness in both personal and occupational life.

CRITICAL FOCUS

Legal and clinical definitions

There is some overlap, as well as clear distinctions, between the clinical diagnosis of antisocial personality disorder, which is a clinical disorder featured in the DSM (APA, 2000), and the legal and sometimes more globally used term psychopathy, a concept developed by Hare (1993). Psychopathy is often associated with criminal or antisocial behaviours, and it is highly likely that individuals considered to be a psychopath could also be classified as having antisocial personality disorder. However, the majority of individuals with antisocial personality disorder are not psychopaths. The clinical classification of antisocial personality disorder is much more diverse, whereas the assessment of psychopathy is much more precise and indepth.

The term 'psychopath' describes an individual who demonstrates an apparent cluster of psychological, interpersonal, and neurological features. According to Hare (1993) psychopaths are social predators who charm, manipulate, and ruthlessly plough their way through life, leaving a broad trail of broken hearts, shattered expectations and empty wallets. Completely lacking in conscience and empathy, they selfishly take what they want and do as they please, violating social norms and expectations without the slightest sense of guilt or regret (p. xi).

Hare (1993) devised three categories of psychopathy which to some degree reflect the severity and focus of psychopathic personality:

- *Primary psychopath*. The primary (true) psychopath has certain psychological, emotional, cognitive and biological differences.

- *Secondary psychopaths*. Secondary psychopaths commit antisocial or violent acts because of severe emotional problems or inner conflict.

- *Dyssocial psychopaths*. Dyssocial psychopaths display aggressive, antisocial behaviour they have learnt from their subculture, like their gangs or families.

The primary psychopath, according to Hare, is the only 'real' psychopath; however, the media sometimes incorrectly portray secondary and dyssocial psychopaths as 'psychopathic' in headlines due to their rates of recidivism. Individuals with psychopathic disorder were found to be seven times more likely to commit a serious offence on discharge compared to individuals with a mental illness (Bartol & Bartol, 2011).

Given what we know about psychopathy, along with the extent of research conducted by Hare, there have emerged a number of psychometric assessment tools that assess psychopathy. The most widely used tool is the Psychopathy Check List – Revised (Hare, 1980, 1991; Hare & Vertommen, 2003). The PCL-R measures 20 items based on the typical characteristics that would be expected in a prototypical psychopath. These items are rated using data based on interviews and file information:

1 Glibness/superficial charm

2 Grandiose sense of self-worth

3 Need for stimulation/proneness to boredom

4 Pathological lying

5 Conning/manipulative

6 Lack of remorse or guilt

7 Shallow affect

8 Callous/lack of empathy

9 Parasitic lifestyle

10 Poor behavioural controls

11 Promiscuous sexual behaviour

12 Early behavioural problems

13 Lack of realistic, long-term goals

14 Impulsivity

15 Irresponsibility

16 Failure to accept responsibility for own actions

17 Many short-term marital relationships

18 Juvenile delinquency

19 Revocation of conditional release

20 Criminal versatility

The prevalence of psychopathy in the prison population is fairly high. For example, Hare, Clark, Grann and Thornton (2000) found 13% of a sample of 728 male offenders scored high on the PCL-R, indicating psychopathy. Some 22% were Category B prisoners, 15% Category C prisoners and 9% Category D prisoners. In the UK prison system, adult prisons are category A, B, C or D, with Category A the highest security, and Category D typically being low-secure open prisons. Other studies have found as many as 73% of males in special units scoring high for psychopathy (Coid, 1998), 26% at HMP Grendon (Shine & Hobson, 1997) and 8–12% in the general prison population in England and Wales (Coid, 1998).

✳ *Sample question*   *Essay*

Critically consider the impact and influence of psychopathy and/or antisocial personality disorder on an individual's behaviour.

Test your knowledge

6.8 How is psychopathy defined?

6.9 How does DSM-IV-TR (APA, 2000) define antisocial personality disorder?

6.10 What is the prevalence rate of psychopathy in the prison system?

Answers to these questions can be found on the companion website at: www.pearsoned.co.uk/psychologyexpress

---

Further reading Prevalence of psychopathy in the prison population

Key reading

Coid, J., Yang, M., Ullrich, S., Roberts, A., Moran, P., Bebbington, B., and Hare, R. (2009). Psychopathy among prisoners in England and Wales. *International Journal of Law and Psychiatry*, 32(3), 134–141.

Treatment

The treatment approaches that have been trialled, and in some cases are still used, to treat personality disorders include the broad categories of psychological and pharmacological interventions. There have, however, historically been some interesting approaches to addressing personality disorders. For example, it was once thought that antisocial personality disorder could be address through a 'boot camp' style intervention. The focus here, like many other interventions for antisocial personality, being on criminal behaviour and violence in adolescents. The consensus is that the classic 'boot camp' or incarceration does not work. This section will outline some of the interventions and treatments that have been used or are still being used to address the personality disorders featured in this chapter.

Treatment for borderline personality disorder

Borderline personality disorder is not easy to treat, and there are few controlled trials examining the effects of therapy. However, Roth and Fonagy (1998) made attempts to establish guidelines and overall goals for treatment:

● Psychotherapy is more effective for less severe cases.

● Patients under 30 years of age are at great risk of suicide and therefore prevention rather than cure is an important target of therapy.

- Individuals with good social support, chronic depression, who are psychologically minded and have low impulsivity benefit most from 'talking therapies'.
- The commitment and enthusiasm of the therapist are important, and finding the right therapist for the patient is key.

Cognitive therapy

Cognitive therapy involves the identification and modification of the cognitions and underlying schemata that drive inappropriate behaviours, using schema therapy or cognitive analytic approach (Ryle, 1975).

Emotional awareness training

There is evidence to suggest that individuals with borderline personality disorder lack the ability to understand and describe their emotional state (Farrell & Shaw, 1994). This training is a structured programme which encourages the skills to gain awareness. The individual works through a hierarchy of emotional awareness, starting with bodily sensation.

Pharmacological treatment

There has been a combination of limited trials and mixed results when considering pharmacological treatment for borderline personality disorder. Soloff et al. (1993) found major tranquillisers, such as Haloperidol, reduce a broad spectrum of symptoms, including anxiety, hostility and paranoid ideation. However, these findings were inconsistent in subsequent studies. In some cases, this has led to heightened suicide threats, suicide ideation and aggressive behaviour.

Treatment for antisocial personality disorder

Family and peer interventions

As mentioned previously, 'boot camp' style interventions were first trialled for individuals with antisocial personality disorder. However, the focus of intervention has since changed. For example, Borduin (1999) described a multi-systemic, family-based approach to equip individuals with the skills to cope with family life. Family interventions were intended to improve parenting skills, encouraging support for the offender and reducing levels of stress in the family environment. There have also been peer-orientated interventions to encourage pro-social interaction. However, despite the relatively high success rates (Henggeler, Melton, & Smith, 1992) there are issues around engagement with the intervention from all parties.

Treatment for psychopathy

Therapeutic communities

Therapeutic communities emerged in the UK in the 1940s. They provide an intensive 24:7 intervention to change psychopathic behaviour. Each individual is responsible for the physical and emotional care of others within the community. Rice, Harris and

Cormier (1992) evaluated the successfulness of therapeutic communities' situation in a maximum secure prison. Individuals responded well when they were involved in leading a therapeutic group and administering the programme.

This model is used in the forensic setting where there are a high percentage of offenders with personality disorders, for example HMP Grendon.

Further reading Therapeutic communities

Key reading

Shine, J. (2001). Characteristics of inmates admitted to Grendon Therapeutic Prison and their relationship to length of stay. *International Journal of Offender Therapy and Comparative Criminology, 45*(2), 252–265.

Chapter summary – pulling it all together

→ Can you tick all the points from the revision checklist at the beginning of this chapter?

→ Attempt the sample question from the beginning of this chapter using the answer guidelines below.

→ Go to the companion website at www.pearsoned.co.uk/psychologyexpress to access more revision support online, including interactive quizzes, flashcards, You be the marker exercises as well as answer guidance for the Test your knowledge and Sample questions from this chapter.

Answer guidelines

✳ *Sample question*   *Essay*

Critically discuss the contribution of the dimensional approach to understanding and diagnosing mental disorder.

Approaching the question

This question requires you to carefully consider how a dimensional approach to mental health has contributed towards *both* our understanding and the diagnosis of mental disorder. Therefore, you will need to consider the categorisation of mental disorder by DSM-IV-TR (APA, 2000) alongside other models of mental disorder.

A good response to this question will explore the debate between the continuity and categorical models of mental disorder, whilst arguing a position based on the evidence from relevant research papers.

The question specifically states 'critically discuss' and therefore it is essential that you demonstrate this element. This will require that you explore both historical and contemporary (within the last ten years) research evidence to both support the points you raise and to construct a balanced argument throughout, before reaching a conclusion.

Important points to include

● It is important that you define what is understood by mental illness, personality disorder and sub-clinical categories as this will allow you to both demonstrate your knowledge of categorical vs. continuity models as well as allowing you to construct a balanced debate and discussion around the topic area.

● You should present the various historical theoretical models alongside more contemporary models.

Make your answer stand out

Strong answers will adhere to a clear and organised structure and, therefore, demonstrate a competent understanding of the complexities of diagnosing personality disorders. In doing so, a good response will consider the limitations and advantages of exploring mental disorder from either approach. When answering questions in this topic area you should be careful to base your claims on presented research evidence and avoid personal opinion or emotive language.

Explore the accompanying website at www.pearsoned.co.uk/psychologyexpress

→ Prepare more effectively for exams and assignments using the answer guidelines for questions from this chapter.

→ Test your knowledge using multiple choice questions and flashcards.

→ Improve your essay skills by exploring the You be the marker exercises.

Notes

Notes

7

Sexual disorders

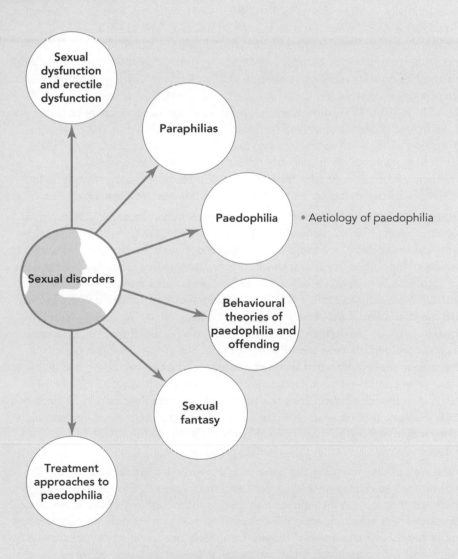

A printable version of this topic map is available from
www.pearsoned.co.uk/psychologyexpress

Introduction

Sexual disorders fall into two distinct, albeit broad, categories: sexual dysfunction, characterised by problems of sexual arousal and response, and paraphilias, characterised by repeated sexual urges, fantasies and behaviour deemed socially inappropriate. The socially constructed nature of paraphilias is arguably best reflected in homosexuality since changes to its categorisation as a 'sexual disorder' and the ensuing treatment approaches, broadly tracks changes in Western societal attitudes towards same-sex relationships. Homosexuality was partially dropped from DSM-II (APA, 1974) when the American Psychiatric Association (APA) declared that some homosexuals still experienced 'sexual orientation disorder' requiring treatment (Silverstein, 2009). The partial removal from previous iterations of DSM can largely be attributed to the work of the pro-homosexuality and political activist Barbara Gittings who actively campaigned and lobbied the APA during the mid-1970s. It was not until DSM-III-R (APA, 1987), however, that references to homosexuality were dropped fully from the classification and replaced by 'Sexual disorders not otherwise specified'. The relationship between homosexuality and societal attitudes is both historical and temporally bound with same-sex relationships documented globally and cross-culturally (Rothblum, 2000). Homosexuality, therefore, is reflective of the changing attitudes and societal views attributed to paraphilias.

The categorisation of paraphilias is further problematic since many of the more common paraphilias categorised by DSM-IV-TR (APA, 2000), including fetishism and sadomasochism, are frequently practised between like-minded and consenting adults of legal age. The extent to which these behaviours can therefore be viewed as 'problem behaviours' is difficult to define, and unless the individual spends considerable time and effort either fantasising about or partaking in the activity (to the detriment of activities associated with daily living, e.g. employment) it is questionable as to whether the behaviour is problematic. If the individual does spend considerable time and effort thinking about and engaging in paraphilic behaviour it is arguable that such behaviour would be better addressed in line with assessment and treatment approaches for addictive behaviour (Chapter 8). The issue is further compounded by the very nature of paraphilic behaviour since many individuals neither experience distress nor wish to change their sexual behaviour. They may therefore be more appropriately positioned at the edge of a sexual interest distribution rather than disordered per se.

One way of disentangling the issue of whether an individual should be considered as displaying a 'disorder', and therefore eligible for treatment, is perhaps through the investigation of relative harm either to the individual or to others. For many, paedophilia epitomises the most harmful and dangerous of all paraphilias since sexual activity frequently occurs without consent and is entwined with persuasion, guilt and secrecy. Even this highly contentious and deeply emotive paraphilia should not be considered in the absence of a wider debate. Does an individual who frequently fantasises and self-masturbates to sexual gratification about children (but in the absence of any contact behaviour) demonstrate problematic behaviour? Consider in particular that 'thinking' does not necessarily lead to 'doing' (Jones & Wilson, 2008). Further, global attitudes towards paedophilia have changed considerably since the accepting Renaissance period (14th to 17th centuries) towards almost universal condemnation of adult–child relationships. Even the issue of harm is not without contention since male adult members of a Manchester-based sadomasochistic club were arrested in September 1989 for violation of The Offences Against the Person Act 1861, even though the genital manipulation acts were fully consensual (Green, 2001; Thomas, 2000). Even so, 16 men were eventually prosecuted and found guilty of a number of offences, including assault occasioning actual bodily harm, resulting in the incarceration of some group members.

This chapter will consider the two branches of sexual disorders (sexual dysfunction and paraphilias) although paraphilias are of considerably more interest to clinicians. The social and cultural context in which sexual behaviours are considered is of critical importance and the preceding introduction has outlined the blurred and non-liner distinction between problem and non-problem behaviour.

> **→ Revision checklist**
>
> *Essential points to revise are:*
> ❑ Distinction between sexual dysfunction and paraphilia
> ❑ Paraphilias including fetishism, exhibitionism, voyeurism, sadomasochism and frotteurism
> ❑ Sexual fantasies
> ❑ Paedophilia
> ❑ Models of paedophilia
> ❑ Assessment and treatment approaches

Assessment advice

- Paraphilias classified by DSM-IV-TR (APA, 2000) include both legal and illegal behaviours and the extent to which a behaviour is perceived as socially acceptable is largely socially constructed. When answering a question on paraphilias the difficulty in assessing whether a behaviour is problematic or not should be discussed and debated. Clearly, paedophilic behaviour is problematic, and as such the classification, aetiology and treatment approaches of this disorder can be focused on.

- Assessments based on case studies are common in Clinical Psychology and require knowledge of both assessment and treatment. When reading a case study ensure you consider all of the information before providing an assessment of an individual and recommending treatment approaches. It is easy to make a decision after reading the first few sentences, although more important detail may be contained in the latter part of the case study.

- Although some of the paraphilias can be emotive to discuss, try to remain neutral in your approach and consider the weight of empirical evidence when presenting your arguments. Endeavour to present information in a non-biased and non-derogatory way to help you reach a reasoned conclusion.

- Due to the legality of some paraphilias, e.g. paedophilia and necrophilia, many of the theoretical models and treatment approaches are based in both forensic and clinical fields. Conducting literature searches in the forensic literature will help you to strengthen your essay and further aid your understanding of both different disorders and how psychology professionals approach treatment.

Sample question

Could you answer this question? Below is a typical essay question that could arise on this topic.

✳ Sample question   *Essay*

Critically discuss the extent to which paedophilia can be considered alongside other paraphilias.

Sexual dysfunction and erectile dysfunction

Sexual problems are both distressing to individuals and may be an integral symptom of other psychiatric disorders (e.g. depression), medical conditions (e.g. cardiovascular disorders) or a side effect of pharmacological treatments (Adegunloye & Ezeoke, 2011). Despite the relative severity and high prevalence of sexual disorders including premature ejaculation, erectile dysfunction (persistent inability to gain or maintain an adequate erection until completion of sexual activity marked by distress or interpersonal difficulties) and lack of pleasure in sex associated resulting from vaginismus (persistent involuntary spasm of the musculature of the outer third of the vagina), relatively few individuals discuss their sexual problem(s) with a doctor and few doctors seek information about such problems during routine examinations (Nazareth, Boynton, & King, 2003). In a more recent UK-based study (Moreira, Glasser, Nicolosi, Duarte, & Gigell, 2008), the most common male sexual problems included early ejaculation (20%) and erectile dysfunction (18%), and the most common female problems included lack of pleasure in sex (25%); however, despite these figures only 26% of men and 17% of women reported these issues to their doctor. Similar prevalence and reporting rates are reflected in non-Western countries with 23% of Nigerian males reporting premature ejaculation or erectile dysfunction in one study (Adegunloye & Ezeoke, 2011) and 32% of Korean males experiencing erectile dysfunction in another (Moreira et al., 2008). Erectile dysfunction is often incorrectly associated with older men with Laumann, Palik and Rosen (1999) reporting a 7% prevalence rate among men aged 18–29 and 9% among men aged 30–39. Although these figures do increase to 11% for men aged 40–49 and 18% for men aged 50–59 this may partly be accounted for by the relationship between the disorder and other psychiatric or medical conditions. When males do report sexual dysfunction problems to their doctor, erectile dysfunction is the most common complaint of males seeking help (Simons & Carey, 2001). Although sexual dysfunction may have a physical basis, this is relatively rare (particularly in relation to erectile dysfunction), and psychological explanations of sexual dysfunction include the following:

- The attitudes an individual holds towards sexual activities may be in direct contrast to the attitudes held by their partner, which in turn may result in conflict. If an individual holds a conservative attitude towards sex and their partner a more conservative view, this can be a source of conflict (Masters & Johnson, 1970).

- Anxiety is reported as a major factor associated with sexual dysfunction (McConaghy, Armstrong, Blaszczynski, & Allcock, 1983). The effect of conditioned anxiety following early traumatic experiences (e.g. abuse, non-satisfying sexual relationships) on later sexual experiences is well documented; however, anxiety can also arise from adulthood experiences. Performance anxiety is a relatively common factor associated with erectile dysfunction, particularly if a situation is not conducive to sexual intercourse, e.g. shared house, sharing a bedroom with a sibling or sexual intercourse in the family home.

- Spectatoring, associated with anxiety (Masters & Johnson, 1970), refers to when an individual will watch themselves during sexual activity and negatively self-appraise their performance. Spectatoring per se is not problematic and many men and women report watching themselves during sexual activity

Key term

Sexual dysfunction: problems with sexual response including both aversion to sexual activity and problems with orgasm, marked by premature ejaculation in men or a failure to reach orgasm in both men and women. Problems are frequently treated using a combination of behavioural and pharmacological approaches although are most successful when the biopsychosocial influences of the client, partner and couple are addressed.

as enjoyable and stimulating, but the problem arises when spectatoring behaviour features in the sexual activities of someone who is already nervous, since this only serves to perpetuate the level of anxiety.

- Various psychological causes are associated with erectile dysfunction including performance anxiety, childhood sexual trauma, sexual identity or orientation issues, partner intimacy problems and lack of sexual stimulation. Zilbergeld (1992) reported that many men perceive their sexual performance as the 'cornerstone' of every sexual experience and that their masculinity is undermined if they do not perform with a firm erection on every sexual encounter. The self-pressure levied by men during sexual activities can help to perpetuate underling anxieties or attitudes about sexual performance and in turn reduce sexual performance.

- Psychological treatment approaches for erectile dysfunction focus on reducing the level of stress associated with sexual activity (Masters & Johnson, 1970). The couple are encouraged to mutually touch each other in pleasurable ways but without touching each other's genitals since the goal is intimacy rather than sexual satisfaction. The next stage focuses on genital touching but again in the absence of sexual satisfaction (orgasm) and without a focus on erection maintenance although the latter frequently occurs. Finally the couple are encouraged to engage in sexual intercourse but only when both parties feel comfortable with the preceding levels of intimacy. Although the effectiveness of psychological approaches is reported to be relatively high, a dearth of research evidence exists, due in part to the dominance of pharmaceutical research (Melnik, Soares, & Nasello, 2008).

- Pharmacological approaches to treating erectile dysfunction have dominated both the research and treatment approaches due to their effectiveness and limited cost. Sildenal (more commonly referred to as Viagra) has been reported as highly successful in the treatment of erectile dysfunction with Goldstein et al. (1998) finding that 70% of men treated with the drug reported improvements in the quality and frequency of erections and 70% of intercourse attempts were successful versus 22% for men treated with a placebo. In common with other pharmacological approaches, some users have reported side effects including headaches and facial flushing. Owing to the widespread availability of Sildenal other approaches including vacuum pumps and direct injection of drugs into the penis are now far less common (Ralph & McNicholas, 2000).

KEY STUDY

Sexual dysfunction

Joe, a 17-year-old male from Hounslow, London, has recently reported to a GP following his failure to achieve and then maintain an erection during sexual intercourse with his 22-year-old girlfriend. Joe is exceptionally embarrassed about the situation and has started to self-label himself as 'abnormal', having had reoccurring thoughts that he

▶

will never be able to maintain an erection during intercourse. Joe has been dating his girlfriend for the last six months and whilst he has some previous sexual experience with both females and males, he has never had full intercourse. Joe's girlfriend was with her previous boyfriend for five years before meeting Joe and has told him that she enjoyed an active sex life with her ex-partner. Joe lives at home with his two older brothers, Martin and Tyrone, and Joe's girlfriend also lives at home with her sister (Tulsia) and her two step-brothers, Reggie and Max. Although they frequently spend nights at each other's houses, Joe shares a room with his brother Tyrone, and Joe's girlfriend's mother, a practising Christian, frequently disrupts them when he stays at her house. Joe's GP has referred Joe to visit a clinician since she believes the underlying cause of his erectile dysfunction is psychological rather than physical.

What are the most prevalent psychological explanations for Joe's condition?

How might the environment negatively affect Joe?

What anxiety reduction and cognitive techniques could be employed to help Joe manage his condition?

Test your knowledge

7.1 How is sexual dysfunction defined?

7.2 How does DSM-IV-TR (APA, 2000) define paraphilias and how is this likely to change in DSM-5?

7.3 What is the prevalence rate of sexual dysfunctions cross-culturally?

7.4 To what extent are the causes of erectile dysfunction predominately psychological?

Further reading Sexual dysfunction

Key reading

Moreira, E. D., Brock, G., Glaber, B. D., Nicolosi, A., Laumann, E. O., Paik, A., Wang, T., & Gingell, C. (2005). Help-seeking behaviour for sexual problems: The Global Study of Sexual Attitudes and Behaviours. *International Journal of Clinical Practice, 59*(6), 6–16.

Paraphilias

Despite relatively few individuals receiving a formal diagnosis of paraphilia, the number of individuals engaged in paraphilic activities is reported as high (Bennett, 2011). Males account for 90% of cases of paraphilia, with the exception of sexual masochism, which is significantly higher in women (Thibaut et al., 2010). Individuals frequently develop an interest in a paraphilia before the age of 18 years, with the paraphilia lasting for many years and often across an entire lifespan. Frequently, individuals experiment with, and hold, an interest for more than one paraphilia (Thibaut et al., 2010), making it exceptionally difficult to determine an accurate number of individuals with a paraphilic interest. The most common paraphilias categorised by DSM-IV-TR (APA, 2000) are outlined in Table 7.1.

Table 7.1 **Paraphilias as categorised by DSM-IV-TR (APA, 2000)**

Fetishism	Intense and recurring sexual urges, fantasies or behaviours involving non-living objects such as female shoes or underwear.
Exhibitionism	Recurrent urges and fantasies of exposing genitalia to an unsuspecting stranger.
Voyeurism	Recurrent and intense urges to observe an unsuspecting person who is naked, disrobing or engaged in sexual activity.
Sadomasochism	The act (real not simulated) of being humiliated, beaten or bound, or otherwise made to suffer (e.g. hot wax).
Frotteurism	Touching or rubbing against a non-consenting person.
Sadism	Physical suffering of a person (including humiliation) is sexually exciting to the perpetrator/sadist.

Key term

Paraphilia: DSM-IV-TR (APA, 2000: 566) defines the essential features of a paraphilia as 'recurrent, intense sexually arousing fantasies, sexual urges or behaviours generally involving 1) nonhuman objects, 2) the suffering or humiliation of oneself or one's partner or 3) children or other nonconsenting persons that occur over a period of at least 6 months'. It should be noted that the proposed definition of paraphilia is subject to change in DSM-5 where the term is mooted to refer to 'any intense and persistent sexual interest other than sexual interest in genital stimulation or preparatory fondling with pheonotypically normal ('normal' physical and psychological characteristics), consenting adult partners' (Blanchard, 2009). Similar to sexual dysfunction, paraphilias are treated using both pharmacological and psychological approaches where the aims are to reduce or abolish the prevalence of (paraphilic) sexual fantasies, control sexual urges, where distress exists, to decrease this level of distress in the paraphilic individual and to encourage a 'normal' sex life.

In addition to the most common paraphilias outlined in Table 7.1, other paraphilias include necrophilia (corpses), coprophilia (faeces), zoophilia (animals) and telephone scatologia (obscene telephone calls of a sexual nature). With a few notable exceptions (frotteurism, necrophilia and zoophilia), many paraphilias can be practised legally and among consenting adults, making their classification as 'problem' behaviour difficult to determine. The final paraphilia, paedophilia (intense and recurrent sexual urges and sexually arousing fantasies involving children), has received considerable interest from both clinicians and forensic psychologists alike who have sought to understand the prevalence, aetiology and treatment approaches for the disorder. As a result many of the aetiological explanations for paedophilia are presented as a common pathway for other paraphilias.

Key term

Aetiology: the cause or the origin of a clinical disorder. The aetiology of paedophilia has been attributed to disruptive child–parent relationships (Hanson & Slater, 1988), experiencing sexual advances as a child (Cohen et al., 2002) and sexual arousal following exposure to images of children (Barbaree, 1990).

Further reading Paraphilias

Key reading

Bhugra, D., Popelyuk, D., & McMullen, I. (2010). Paraphilias across cultures: Contexts and controversies. *Journal of Sex Research, 47*(2–3), 242–256.

Paedophilia

Paedophilia is marked by intense and recurrent sexual urges and sexually arousing fantasies involving sexual activity (although not necessarily penetration) with a prepubescent child or children (APA, 2000). Since paedophilia in the UK and other Western countries is illegal and therefore constitutes an offence, terms such as perpetrator and offending are used to reflect paedophilic behaviour. In addition to the diagnostic definition of paedophilia further criteria are also acknowledged:

- The perpetrator has to be 16 years or older, and at least five years older than the victim.

- Sexual activities vary, although frequently involve genital touching, oral sex and undressing.

- Paedophiles attracted to females usually prefer children aged 8–10 years of age and those attracted to males prefer slightly older children (APA, 1994). However, whilst the ages are not mutually exclusive, and paedophiles can be attracted to children and infants of any age, almost all paedophiles are either exclusively attracted to males or females.

- Many victims of paedophilia are either relatives, neighbours or family friends of the children's parents since access, along with opportunity and motivation, are preconditions of offending (Wilson, 1997). Access refers to the physical access afforded to perpetrators and many perpetrators will know their victim since gaining access to strangers is much more difficult to achieve. In acknowledging the issue of access, Murray (2000) suggests that paedophilic 'relationships' are dependent on persuasion, guilt and friendship. As most paedophilic relationships involve coercion and not force, opportunity exists when paedophiles are 'trusted' with a child or children, therefore providing the opportunity for contact offending to occur. Finally, motivation plays a significant part in whether an individual will act out their sexual urges and whilst the other components (access and opportunity) may be available, if motivation is lacking, offending is unlikely to occur.

Aetiology of paedophilia

It is important to distinguish between factors that may contribute towards individuals developing a paedophilic paraphilia and those that contribute towards the likelihood of an actual contact offence taking place. Aetiological factors that have attempted to account for the development of a paedophilic paraphilia include both the paedophile as a childhood abuse victim (Lee, Jackson, Pattison, & Ward, 2002) and as experiencing disruptive early childhood experiences (Marshall & Marshall, 2000):

- Hanson and Slater (1988) have found that 67% of paedophiles report disruptive early parent–childhood relationships or they experienced childhood sexual abuse. In a matched study (paedophilic offender vs. non-offender), 60% of offenders reported childhood sexual advances. Although surprisingly high, this figure does not account for why individuals may in turn offend against a child, and may be seen as a way of rationalising their behaviour (Wilson & Jones, 2008), or as developing a new identity from being the 'abused' to the 'abuser' (Cohen et al., 2002).

- Other explanations include a maladaptive attractiveness of youthfulness (Quinsey & Lalumière, 1995), whereby hairlessness, large eyes and slender physical form is preferred to a more mature body, deviant sexual fantasies involving children (Dandescu & Wolfe, 2003) and an inability to inhibit sexual behaviour due to poor frontal lobe function (Stone & Thompson, 2001).

- Factors contributing towards contact offending occurring include comorbidity with other disorders including major depression and anxiety, low self-esteem, low ability to emphasise, cognitive distortions (e.g. 'The child enjoys their time with me'), inappropriate masturbatory behaviour (masturbating whilst viewing child-based material), poor sex education and inappropriate infant attachment.

Further reading Aetiology of paedophilia

Key reading

Seto, M. C. (2008). Etiology of paedophilia. In M. C. Seto (Ed.), *Paedophilia and sexual offending against children: Theory, assessment and intervention* (pp. 101–122). Washington: American Psychological Association.

Behavioural theories of paedophilia and offending

Theories aid the understanding and evaluation of the causal mechanisms involved in paedophilic sex offending and hold important clinical implications in the management and treatment of individuals.

- Finkelhor (1984) suggests via the 'preconditions theory' of paedophilic offending that many paedophiles fail to develop satisfying psychological and sexual relationships with adults and in addition may report high levels of adult loneliness, making them more likely to seek the intimacy of children who they find it easier to engage with both psychologically and intimately. The preconditions theory suggests that paedophilic activity is the result of four factors: sex with children is emotionally satisfying; sex with children is sexually satisfying; an inability to meet the sexual needs in a more appropriate manner; and disinhibited behaviour at times of stress. Indeed the level of disinhibition is an important factor since disinhibition may result in the motivation to commit an offence (Wilson, 1997) and may be related to suppressed frontal lobe function (Stone & Thompson, 2001).

- The quadripartite model (Hall & Hirschman, 1992), suggests four conditions are required ahead of a contact offence taking place: deviant arousal or sexual preference to children; distorted beliefs of children as competent sexual partners able to make decisions about sexual activity; emotional disturbance; and problematic personality traits.

- The pathways model of paedophilic behaviour and offending (Ward & Siegert, 2002) proposes the following five pathways to child sex offending:

  1 *Intimacy and social skills deficits.* Sexual abuse arises from dysfunctionality with intimacy and social skills. Insecure attachment styles with parents or caregivers and abuse and neglect in childhood result in poor relationships characterised by a lack of self-esteem, emotional loneliness and isolation.

  2 *Deviant sexual scripts.* Distorted sexual scripts and dysfunctional attachment styles may result in sexual abuse as interpersonal contact is only achieved via sexual contact. Individuals are likely to demonstrate deviant patterns of sexual arousal, intimacy deficits, inappropriate emotional experience and inappropriate cognitive distortions.

  3 *Emotional dysregulation.* Individuals may have 'normal' sexual scripts and do not face the same issues as individuals with deviant sexual scripts; however, they have difficulties in the self-regulation of their emotions. Individuals are likely to experience becoming overwhelmed and sexually inhibited by their emotional state or adopt sexual behaviour to help soothe their emotional dysregulation.

  4 *Antisocial cognitions.* Individuals with antisocial cognitions do not experience deviance in sexual scripts but have a general tendency towards deviance and criminality. Individuals are more likely to experience difficulties with impulsivity and engage in behaviours consistent with conduct disorder from an early age.

  5 *Multiple dysfunctional mechanisms.* Individuals hold both deviant sexual scripts which coincide with dysfunctions on all of the other psychological mechanisms.

- Ward and Hudson (1998, 2000) argue that desire to engage in deviant sexual activity results in the establishment of an offence-related goal and it is at this point a paedophile will make a decision about the acceptability of her/his desire and what (if anything) (s)he will do about it (Bickley & Beech, 2002). Ward and Hudson (1998, 2000) propose a four-pathways model that paedophiles may adopt once an offence-related goal has been selected. Although at the point of selection self-regulation could prevent an offence from occurring, a paedophile will frequently engage in their first contact offence or seek to re-offend (Table 7.2).

Table 7.2 **Paedophilic offender pathways**

Pathway	Self-regulatory style	Description
Avoidant – passive	Under-regulation	Desire to avoid sexual offending but lacking the appropriate coping skills to prevent offending from occurring.
Avoidant – active	Misregulation	Direct attempt to control deviant thoughts and fantasies but use of ineffective or counter-productive strategies (e.g. alcohol consumption or visiting a park playground).
Approach – automatic	Under-regulation	Overlearned sexual scripts (schemas) for offending, combined with impulsive and poorly planned behaviour.
Approach – explicit	Effective regulation	Desire to sexually offend and the use of careful planning to execute offence goal. Harmful goals concerning sexual offending.

Source: Ward & Hudson (1998, 2000).

Each of the theoretical perspectives embellishes many of the proposed aetiological factors for offending including inappropriate parent–child attachment, inappropriate cognitions, lack of self-esteem, loneliness and disinhibited behaviour regulation.

Test your knowledge

7.5 How is paedophilia defined?

7.6 To what extent does sexual fantasy play a role in paedophilic paraphilias?

7.7 What are the proposed causes of paedophilia?

7.8 How does Finkelhor's (1984) account of paedophilic offending differ from Ward and Hudson (1998)?

Answers to these questions can be found on the companion website at: www.pearsoned.co.uk/psychologyexpress

Further reading Theoretical models of paedophilia

Key reading

Bickley, J. A., & Beech, A. R. (2002). An investigation of the Ward and Hudson pathways model of the sexual offence process with child abusers. *Journal of Interpersonal Violence, 17*(4), 371–393.

Sexual fantasy

One aspect common to all paraphilic behaviour is the role of sexual fantasies, and despite their prevalence in paedophilic offending in particular (Dandescu & Wolfe, 2003), they remain largely underexplored (Wilson & Jones, 2008). Sexual fantasies enable individuals to create, rehearse and indulge in paraphilias without ever needing to 'act them out' in the physical world, and to some extent may provide a more socially acceptable place for such extreme sexual behaviours to reside. The dominance of sexual fantasies is evident in both research studies and the very definitions of paraphilic behaviour. Sexual fantasies frequently remain non-verbalised and, when they are, are likely to be shared between consenting adults and only ever acted out in part. Jones and Wilson (2008: 235), suggest that 'Sexual fantasies are not temporarily constrained. Their fluidity enables them to be recalled, rehearsed, manipulated and abandoned as the individual chooses. Neither are they constrained by ethnicity, age, gender, duration or frequency'.

- Sexual fantasies may form either a fleeting thought or may represent a significantly longer period of reflection. Doskoch (1995) suggests that on average men fantasise about sex 7.2 times per day and women 4.5 times per day. The three 'primary' types of sexual fantasies are forbidden imagery referring to thoughts focusing upon images of unusual partners (e.g. celebrities) and positions, sexual irresistibility in relation to seductiveness, multiple partners and dominance, and submission-based fantasies.

- The role of sexual fantasies is important since it enables individuals to be 'relatively free to indulge their primitive lusts and brutish impulses in ways that might be unacceptable in reality' (Wilson, 1997: 14).

- Hicks and Leitenberg (2001) suggest that erotic fantasies serve to sexually arouse and are mental 'images' occurring over long periods or as simple fleeting thoughts.

- Although sexual fantasies are relatively private and for the large part remain as such, in contemporary society it is more acceptable than ever before to both share and act out fantasies, including those deemed as paraphilic (Jones & Wilson, 2008). Fantasies can be physically acted out in socially acceptable environments and between consenting adults. Retail outlets such as Ann Summers provide a high-street shopping experience for paraphilic materials, e.g. sadomasochistic clothing, whilst online spaces, such as Second Life, provide opportunities to 'virtually act-out' being a sadist. Further, the consumption of pornography provides a pseudo-reality where images of fantasy are coupled with reality. Despite pornography being widely available since the mid-1800s it is since the advent of the Internet into mainstream society that pornography has become more widely and freely available.

- The consumption of pornography may prevent individuals from acting out their sexual fantasies in the physical world, and satisfy their particular paraphilia. For others it may seek to exacerbate a paraphilia and in turn provide them with the opportunity to meet others, discuss their paraphilic interest and in turn provide opportunities to physically act out their fantasy. This itself is not problematic, providing the behaviour is consensual, legal and between like-minded individuals. It is problematic, however, when the paraphilia is illegal, without consent and poses significant harm, e.g. paedophilia. Quayle and Taylor (2003) argue that there appears to be little support for a 'direct causal link between viewing pornography and subsequent offending behaviour'. However, Wyre (1992) reports that paedophiles view inappropriate images of children to generate and reinforce sexual fantasies, and in turn reinforce the fantasies though subsequent masturbation. This is particularly problematic since masturbatory reconditioning (a behavioural therapy) aims to promote masturbation following exposure to appropriate stimuli and fantasies. More contemporary research (Jones & Wilson, 2008; Wilson & Jones, 2008) acknowledges the importance of sexual fantasy in paedophilia and argues for a direct causal link between pornography consumption, inappropriate fantasy rehearsal and acting out the fantasy, including sexual gratification via masturbation.

As sexual fantasies are core to paraphilic behaviour these should not be overlooked in assessment and treatment approaches. Where behavioural techniques such as masturbatory reconditioning occur, this should include targeting and reconditioning held fantasies.

CRITICAL FOCUS

Offending behaviour and fantasy

Although many of the existing theories (e.g. Ward & Hudson, 1998, 2000) take into consideration the role of fantasy in offending behaviour, Wilson and Jones (2008) argue that it is central to offending behaviour. Many existing theories pre-date the mainstream advent of the Internet, and more importantly fail to take into consideration the portability and ubiquity of mobile devices, e.g. smartphones and tablet computers. Despite the important role that sexual fantasies may play in offending behaviour, few studies have empirically studied them in relation to offending, and those that do, often utilise small case-study samples, e.g. Wilson and Jones (2008).

Further reading Sexual fantasy and paedophilia

Key reading

Wilson, D., & Jones, T. (2008). In my own world: A case study of a paedophile's thinking and doing and his use of the Internet. *Howard Journal of Criminal Justice, 47*, 1–14.

Treatment approaches to paedophilia

Treatment for paedophilia often occurs in either a prison or a secure forensic unit due to the legal status of sex with children. Many paedophiles are convicted under the Sexual Offences Act (2003), which incorporates a number of sex offences including rape, sexual assault, causing sexual activity without consent, rape and other offences against children under 13 and child sex offences. Upon conviction, offenders receiving a caution or non-custodial sentence are placed onto the register for a period of five years and those with a sentence of 30 months or over are placed onto the register indefinitely. Despite the diagnostic classification for paedophilia being relatively clear, determining whether an individual *is* a paedophile is less easy to determine. Katheryn Roach, a 24-year-old religious education teacher from Bolton, received a two-year sentence in 2011 for 'inciting a child to engage in sexual behaviour' following a series of text messages sent to one of her pupils. Roach was placed onto the Violent and Sex Offender Register for seven years but was not classed as a paedophile since her behaviour did not constitute recurrent and intense urges and fantasies about children in general, but instead focused on one child.

Both physical and behavioural treatment approaches are adopted in the treatment of sex offenders:

- Androgen deprivation therapy (ADT), colloquially referred to as 'chemical castration', suppresses the production or action of androgens and in turn reduces the level of the male libido. Despite studies (Losel & Schmucker, 2005) reporting successful treatment and reductions in recidivism (re-offending) following treatment, Rice and Harris (2011) argue that the quality of studies investigating the effectiveness of ADT are insufficient, particularly as a result of the self-selecting samples, patient self-reports about libido and circulating testosterone levels. Rice and Harris (2011: 315) conclude that more research is necessary before 'ADT has a scientific basis to be relied upon as a principal component of sex offender treatment'.

- The point at which recidivism is considered should also be questioned as Berlin and Meinecke (1981) suggest relapse rates in one study were relatively low during treatment (3 out of 20 offenders); however, this was substantially increased once treatment ceased. Further, many offenders fail to take the treatment (between 30 and 100% according to Barbaree & Seto, 1997), making it difficult to determine the true effectiveness of ADT.

- Behavioural therapies (Table 7.3), including aversion therapy and masturbatory reconditioning therapies, have been adopted in the treatment of paedophilia.

Craig and Campbell-Fuller (2009: 180), state 'arguably, given that deviant sexual arousal has been shown to be one of the strongest predictors of sexual recidivism (Craig, Beech, & Browne, 2006), the focus of redirecting sexual arousal is of critical importance … achieved most probably through the use of behavioural strategies'.

Table 7.3 Overview of behavioural therapies

Therapy	Characteristics
Aversion therapy	Exposure to 'deviant' stimulus followed by an aversive stimulus, e.g. mild electric shock or strong aversive odour.
Covert sensitisation	Imagine (fantasise) about a deviant sexual experience until point of arousal and then imagine a powerful negative experience, e.g. divorce by spouse, family conflict or arrest.
Olfactory conditioning	Powerful (aversive) smell paired with a high-risk sexual situation, e.g. walking past a school playground.
Masturbatory reconditioning	Initial arousal to inappropriate stimulus (child-based imagery), followed by a switch to appropriate material (adult-based imagery) at point of arousal and continue concentration on appropriate imagery to point of orgasm.

- Although masturbatory reconditioning is relatively easy to implement, can be practised between therapy sessions and is less ethically problematic than aversion therapy, Fagan, Wise, Schmidt and Berline (2002) argue there is little empirical evidence of its effectiveness, whilst Laws and Marshall (1991) suggest there is a dearth of appropriate evidence to support the initially encouraging results presented in the literature.

- Combined behavioural therapy (Craig & Campbell-Fuller, 2009) marries aversion therapy with masturbatory reconditioning. During the olfactory aversion phase, offenders carry a bottle of smelling salts (ammonium carbonate) and are instructed to sniff the salts when they enter a high-risk situation, e.g. beginning to fantasise about children or upon release from prison if they enter a shopping centre. The salts enable the offender to appraise the situation since the olfactory stimulus disrupts the current thought patterns. Whilst the offender is in the olfactory aversion phase they also begin directed masturbation, a form of masturbatory reconditioning, where the offender is instructed to reinforce non-deviant fantasies (sexually appropriate fantasies of legal-aged adults) through directed masturbation and to record a 'fantasy' diary to monitor which fantasy techniques were implemented. Craig and Campbell-Fuller report a significant decrease in the frequency of deviant fantasies and time spent masturbating to deviant fantasies. The reduction corresponded to an increase in the frequency and time spent masturbating to non-deviant fantasies. VanDeventer and Laws (1978), however, argue extinction of olfactory aversion occurs very rapidly as the individual both habituates to the smell and may choose not to sniff the salts when entering a high-risk situation, therefore, therapy using such techniques should be time-limited to under 26 weeks.

- Cognitive Behavioural Therapy (CBT; Beck, 1977, 1997; Ellis, 1977) has also been used with some success. CBT challenges the cognitive distortions held by offenders, e.g. 'I will never be able to maintain a satisfying sexual relationship with an adult' or 'I'm helping children to explore sex', raises awareness of the effects of sexual offending (on the victim), enhances victim empathy and develops release prevention strategies (Craig, Browne, & Stringer, 2003). CBT is frequently implemented in group settings due to its effectiveness (Beech, Fisher, & Beckett, 1999), and forms the basis of sex offender treatment in England, Canada, New Zealand and the USA.

- Relapse prevention techniques (Marques, Nelson, Alaarcon, & Day, 2000) help to re-educate offenders to identify situations in which they are at a high risk of offending behaviour, get out of the risky situation, consider lapses as something to be learned from and identify the factors that led to relapse and plan how these may be avoided in the future. A pioneering programme initiated in Canada and now implemented in the UK entitled 'Circles of Support & Accountability' (COSA) aims to promote the successful integration of offenders back into the community by providing support to help prevent relapse through advocacy and accountability in the community. Various professionals and volunteers support individuals through the provision of a network to help identify high-risk situations with the aim of relapse prevention (Wilson, 2007).

Test your knowledge

7.9 How are sexual fantasies defined?

7.10 To what extent do sexual fantasies play a role in paraphilic behaviour?

7.11 What are the four behavioural techniques employed in treating paedophilia?

7.12 How successful is androgen deprivation therapy (ADT) in treating paedophilia?

Answers to the questions can be found on the companion website at: www.pearsoned.co.uk/psychologyexpress

Further reading

Topic	Key reading
Androgen deprivation therapy	Rice, M. E., & Harris, G. T. (2011). Is androgen deprivation therapy effective in the treatment of sex offenders? *Psychology, Public Policy & Law, 17*(2), 315–332.
Circles of support and accountability	Wilson, R. J., McWhinnie, A., Picheca, J. E., Prinzo, M., & Cotroni, F. (2007). Circles of support and accountability: Engaging community volunteers in the management of high-risk sexual offenders. *The Howard Journal of Criminal Justice, 46*(1), 1–15.

> ✳ **Sample question**   *Essay*
>
> With reference to empirical examples critically discuss the role of sexual fantasies in offending behaviour.

Chapter summary – pulling it all together

→ Can you tick all the points from the revision checklist at the beginning of this chapter?

→ Attempt the sample question from the beginning of this chapter using the answer guidelines below.

→ Go to the companion website at www.pearsoned.co.uk/psychologyexpress to access more revision support online, including interactive quizzes, flashcards, You be the marker exercises as well as answer guidance for the Test your knowledge and Sample questions from this chapter.

Answer guidelines

> ✳ **Sample question**   *Essay*
>
> Critically discuss the extent to which paedophilia can be considered alongside other paraphilias.

Approaching the question

This question requires you to carefully consider whether paedophilia should be categorised by DSM-IV-TR (APA, 2000) alongside other paraphilias, or whether it would be more appropriate to classify it as its own sexual disorder.

Upon reading the question you should consider whether *you* will argue that paedophilia belongs with other paraphilias or whether it should be classed as its own discrete disorder. You should also consider the role that sexual fantasy plays in paraphillic behaviour since fantasy underpins many of the paraphilias including paedophilia.

As the question contains a critical element you should ensure that you provide both historical and contemporary research evidence (within the last ten years) to both support the points you raise and to construct a balanced argument throughout, before reaching a conclusion.

Important points to include

● Defining paraphillic behaviour and distinguishing this from sexual dysfunction is important to ensure that you demonstrate your understanding of the two different branches of sexual disorders. In doing so, you should ensure that you base your definition on DSM criteria and acknowledge that criteria change over time. With the advent of DSM-5 (2013), hypersexual disorder (marked by extreme amounts of time spent in sexual activity, using sexual activity to alleviate low mood states and failed attempts at reducing the behaviour) is likely to be added to the classification of sexual disorders. Therefore, you should demonstrate an appreciation of how such additions change and refine previous definitions.

- You should outline the various paraphilias, indicate any commonalities (e.g. role of fantasy) and differences between them. You should also briefly outline the diagnostic criteria and treatment approaches for paraphilias other than paedophilia.

- In discussing paedophilia you should demonstrate the complexity of behaviours prevalent in the disorder, and in particular, make a reasoned decision based on research evidence as to whether paedophilia is best placed alongside other paraphilias or whether it should be presented as a single sexual disorder in its own right.

- You should consider presenting information both on the aetiology and prevalence of paedophilia and the extent to which this is different from other paraphilias.

- Presenting the various historical theoretical models (e.g. Hall & Hirschman, 1992; Ward & Hudson, 1998, 2000), alongside more contemporary models (e.g. Wilson & Jones, 2008) will help you to run a sexual fantasy strand through your essay which in turn will help you to link paedophilia to other paraphilias, whilst at the same time allowing you to make a case for paedophilia as its own sexual disorder.

- You should also discuss the treatment approaches to paedophilia and whether these are more complex than those for other paraphilias. You should outline where approaches share a common base (e.g. CBT) and where they are significantly different (e.g. androgen deprivation therapy and circles of support and accountability).

- It is important that you clearly answer the question and make a reasoned decision as to whether paedophilia should be considered (i.e. classified, diagnosed, treated and researched) alongside the other paraphilias. The strength of evidence you present throughout your essay will enable you to make this decision and write a well-defined concluding paragraph.

Make your answer stand out

Strong answers will present a clear demonstration of the complexities of diagnosing and treating sexual disorders, and the fluidity of sexual behaviour. In doing so, strong answers will reflect upon the relative levels of distress caused to both the individual and others, and question whether a paraphilia such as fetishism is as problematic and dangerous to the individual and others, as paedophilic behaviours. When answering questions in this topic area you should be careful to base your claims on presented research evidence and avoid personal opinion or emotive language. You should also base your wider discussion around theoretical models and avoid media representations of sexual disorders.

Explore the accompanying website at www.pearsoned.co.uk/psychologyexpress

→ Prepare more effectively for exams and assignments using the answer guidelines for questions from this chapter.

→ Test your knowledge using multiple choice questions and flashcards.

→ Improve your essay skills by exploring the You be the marker exercises.

Notes

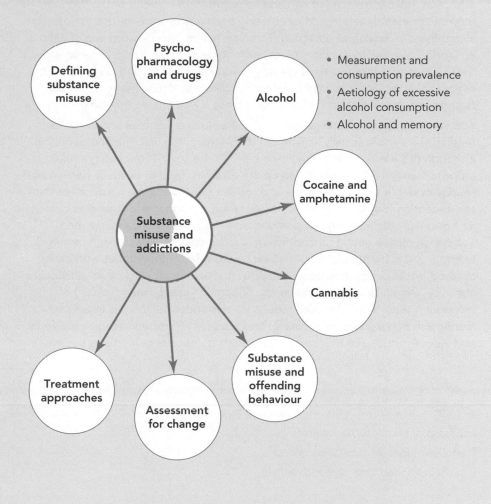

8

Substance misuse and addictions

- Measurement and consumption prevalence
- Aetiology of excessive alcohol consumption
- Alcohol and memory

Defining substance misuse

Psycho-pharmacology and drugs

Alcohol

Substance misuse and addictions

Cocaine and amphetamine

Cannabis

Treatment approaches

Assessment for change

Substance misuse and offending behaviour

A printable version of this topic map is available from
www.pearsoned.co.uk/psychologyexpress

Introduction

Defining addictive behaviour is not necessarily a straightforward task. Consider how you would respond if you were asked to define an 'addict'. The majority of people will provide a highly stereotypical response of someone addicted to 'hard' and illegal drugs such as cocaine or amphetamine; they are unlikely to consider someone addicted to caffeine, nicotine, gambling or exercise, despite each of these addictions resulting in a similar neurochemical reaction. As definitions of addictive behaviour are influenced by social, moral and political factors this in turn makes defining an addict even more complicated. Consider John, 34, who drinks a bottle of vodka every day and is now homeless as a result of his alcohol addiction. His partner has left him and he is suffering sclerosis of the liver. We may clearly identify this individual as being both a substance misuser (misuser of alcohol) and as having an addiction. To some extent, this classification of John as an 'addict' also reinforces the societal stereotype of an alcoholic. If we consider Sarah, 26, who drinks two large glasses of wine every night and drinks in excess every Friday and Saturday night, we are less likely to define her as an addict despite her overall alcohol consumption across a week being the same as John's.

Furthermore, some substances (alcohol, caffeine and nicotine) and behaviours (exercise) are more socially acceptable than others, e.g. cocaine and gambling, although this has not always been the case. In the early 19th century, opium (approximately 16% morphine and opiate alkaloid, used to produce heroin) was readily available from pharmacists and 'opium dens' were the norm rather than the exception (Berridge, 1978). It was not until 1916 that addiction was perceived as a social problem in England and one that required significant attention. Substance misuse and in turn addiction is cross-cultural, affects both men and women, and is frequently characterised by complex comorbidities with other medical, social or psychological problems. It is also reinforced by an individual's social system and psychological needs. Substance use, however, does not necessarily equate to substance misuse (or dependence) and it is important to distinguish between use and misuse. This chapter will focus on substance (legal and illegal) misuse and how such substances influence cognition and behaviour.

→ Revision checklist

Essential points to revise are:

❑ Definitions of substance misuse
❑ Psychopharmacology and drugs
❑ Alcohol
❑ Cocaine and cannabis
❑ Assessment and treatment approaches

Assessment advice

- It is important when answering a question on substance misuse that you define the terminology you will be using. Substance use, misuse and dependence all mean different things and although an individual may use a substance, e.g. alcohol, their use may not be problematic. Likewise, an individual may abuse or misuse a particular drug, e.g. cocaine, although they may not be dependent on that drug. Understanding the differences between use, misuse and dependence is key to answering assessment on substance misuse and addictive behaviour.

- Individuals who misuse substances may have other psychological disorders, e.g. depression or anxiety disorders, therefore understanding comorbidity and the role comorbid disorders play in substance misuse is important when discussing the wider issues of assessment and treatment approaches.

- Clinical psychologists strive to work with individuals to help them alleviate symptoms of distress, and in relation to substance misuse, terminate their substance use. When answering questions on substance misuse and addiction it is important to recognise the complexity of different drugs including their cognitive and behaviour affects, the polydrug nature of substance use, and how clinicians both assess and treat individuals with substance misuse disorders.

- As substance use and misuse are issues cross-culturally, you can strengthen your answer by including contemporary research from different cultures. Psychology is frequently criticised for its ethnocentric and masculinity biases; however, research in many areas of psychology is not available cross-culturally. Research on substance use and misuse is one area where cross-cultural research is available and you are encouraged to compare and contrast prevalence, aetiology and treatment approaches in different cultures.

Sample question

Could you answer this question? Below is a typical essay question that could arise on this topic.

✳ *Sample question*   *Essay*

To what extent are substance use disorders effectively treated using Cognitive Behavioural Therapy?

Defining substance misuse

Definitions of substance use and misuse are problematic due to the range of social, moral and political factors. The Diagnostic and Statistical Manual of the American Psychiatric Association (DSM-IV-TR; APA, 2000) acknowledges the rich complexity of substance and particularly drug-associated problems and provides a relatively loose definition of the harmful use of substances.

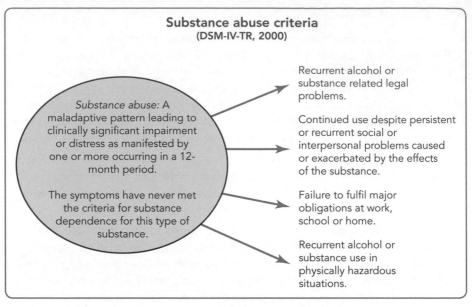

Figure 8.1 Substance abuse criteria (DSM-IV-TR; APA 2000)

- DSM-IV-TR (APA, 2000) defines substance addiction as a 'maladaptive pattern of substance use leading to clinically significant impairment or distress and one or more of the following'; failure to fulfil major role obligations at work, school or home, use in physically hazardous situations, legal problems and social or interpersonal problems.

- DSM-IV-TR (APA, 2000) also provides a distinction between substance abuse (Figure 8.1) and substance dependence (Figure 8.2) since it is possible that an individual can demonstrate substance abuse without suffering any of the classic symptoms of substance dependence (e.g. increasing levels of substance intake to achieve intoxication or presentation of withdrawal symptoms).

- An individual can only qualify for substance abuse if the symptoms for that particular substance (e.g. alcohol) have never met the criteria for substance dependence.

- Substance dependence is more common than substance abuse without dependence since individuals frequently require an increased level of a substance to achieve intoxication as the body becomes tolerant (psychologically or physically) to a particular substance.

- In addition to tolerance and intoxication in dependence, the individual spends substantial time and effort sourcing the substance and demonstrates a history of repeated and unsuccessful attempts to stop using the substance.

- Alternative approaches to defining substance misuse include the medical model (Kraepelin, 1883/1981), the contemporary medical model (McLellan, Lewis, O'Brien, & Kleber, 2000) and the substance problems perspective model.

- The medical model lists 'species' of alcoholics with a 'gamma' alcoholic defined as an individual who is unable to abstain and demonstrates a total loss of control. The

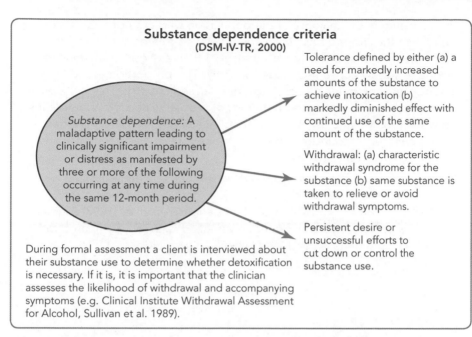

Substance dependence criteria
(DSM-IV-TR, 2000)

Substance dependence: A maladaptive pattern leading to clinically significant impairment or distress as manifested by three or more of the following occurring at any time during the same 12-month period.

Tolerance defined by either (a) a need for markedly increased amounts of the substance to achieve intoxication (b) markedly diminished effect with continued use of the same amount of the substance.

Withdrawal: (a) characteristic withdrawal syndrome for the substance (b) same substance is taken to relieve or avoid withdrawal symptoms.

Persistent desire or unsuccessful efforts to cut down or control the substance use.

During formal assessment a client is interviewed about their substance use to determine whether detoxification is necessary. If it is, it is important that the clinician assesses the likelihood of withdrawal and accompanying symptoms (e.g. Clinical Institute Withdrawal Assessment for Alcohol, Sullivan et al. 1989).

Figure 8.2 Substance dependence criteria (DSM-IV-TR; APA 2000)

contemporary medical model defines substance use disorders as medical disorders with a specific aetiology, predictable course and specific treatment basis.

- The substance problems perspective (Figure 8.3) is a continuum perspective and does not make any assumption about aetiology or course and is not specific to any particular substance. Instead at one end of

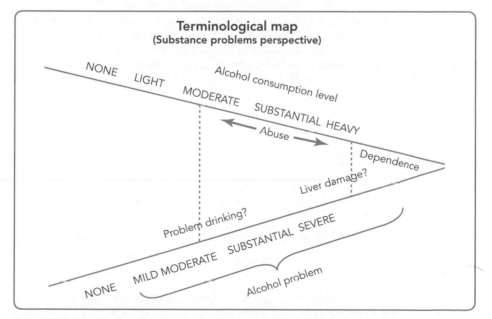

Terminological map
(Substance problems perspective)

NONE LIGHT Alcohol consumption level MODERATE SUBSTANTIAL HEAVY

← Abuse →

Dependence

Liver damage?

Problem drinking?

NONE MILD MODERATE SUBSTANTIAL SEVERE

Alcohol problem

Figure 8.3 Terminological map (substance problems perspective)

the spectrum is the majority of the population who are not substance users, and therefore do not have any substance-related problems. It is acknowledged that this is lower for alcohol than any other substance as alcohol is widely consumed cross-culturally. The proportion in the 'none' category further varies by age, race, gender and country. This perspective demonstrates that there are gradations of problems and that boundaries between problematic use and non-problematic use are blurred rather than the more pronounced distinction made by the medical model and contemporary medical model.

- Substance use and misuse vary by country, sex, age and ethnicity. Grant et al. (2004), for example, report higher rates of alcohol dependence in men (12.4%) than women (4.9%) across cultures and Hibell et al. (1997) suggest 41% of UK 16-year-olds admit to having smoked cannabis, compared with 34% of US, 10% of Italian and 2% of Greek 16-year-olds.

CRITICAL FOCUS

Substance abuse

Historical models of substance abuse fail to take into consideration the fluidity of behaviour demonstrated by substance users. Further, there are key differences between substance abuse and substance dependence, which should be acknowledged since some abusers may not be dependent. Finally, the complexity of the definition becomes more clouded when sociocultural factors are taken into consideration; the sociability, desirability and acceptability of alcohol consumption in Western countries is markedly different from countries where cultural and religious practices forbid its consumption. In Middle Eastern countries, however, the consumption of tobacco and caffeine is widely practised. Therefore, it is important to fully appreciate that an individual may move through a spectrum of consumption and question the universality of substance consumption.

Test your knowledge

8.1 In clinical terms what does comorbidity refer to?

8.2 What are the differences between substance abuse and substance dependence?

8.3 How does DSM-IV-TR (APA, 2000) define substance addiction?

8.4 What alternative definitions to the DSM-IV-TR (APA, 2000) of substance misuse exist?

Answers to the questions can be found on the companion website at: www.pearsoned.co.uk/psychologyexpress

Psychopharmacology and drugs

Although clinicians are predominately interested in the resulting psychological and physical changes associated with substance use, the neurotransmitter changes accompanying substance use are also of interest. Psychopharmacology (derived from the Greek word for drug *pharmakon*) is the study of drug-induced changes in mood, thinking and behaviour resulting from natural (plants and animals) and artificial (laboratory processed chemicals) psychoactive drug use (Table 8.1).

Table 8.1 **Psychoactive drug groups and associated neurotransmitters**

Drug group	Drug	Neurotransmitter	Main properties
Mimic natural transmitters	Alcohol	GABA	Drowsiness and relax mood state
	Opiates (heroin, morphine and codeine)	Endorphins	Reduce pain and increase pleasure
	Cannabis	Anandamide	Relaxation and various effects
	Nicotine	Acetylcholine	Various effects
Release transmitters	Cocaine	Dopamine	Increase alertness and intensify mood state
	Amphetamine	Dopamine	Increase alertness and intensify mood state
	Nicotine	Dopamine	Various effects
	Ecstasy	Dopamine	Increase alertness and intensify mood state
Block transmitters	Barbiturates	Glutamate	Sedation

- Drugs are any biologically active chemical not occurring naturally in the human body. Drugs can be used to prevent and/or treat disease (medical use), alter mood and cognition or otherwise change behaviour (Parrot, Morinan, Moss, & Scholey, 2005).
- Drugs are ordinarily classified by their 'family' – chemical structure or pharmacological affect (mimic natural neurotransmitters, release neurotransmitters or block transmitters).

Key terms

Neurotransmitters: chemicals that allow the transmission of signals from one neuron to the next via synapses.

Psychoactive: a drug that alters mood, cognition and/or other aspects of behaviour.

Further reading Pharmacological properties of drugs

Key reading

Nutt, D. J., & Law, F. D. (2000). Pharmacological and psychological aspects of drugs of abuse. In M. G. Gelder, J. J. Lobez-Ibor & N. C. Andreasen (Eds.), *New Oxford Textbook of Psychiatry*. Oxford: Oxford University Press.

Alcohol

Alcohol is consumed in many cultures globally and it is the most widely consumed, and socially acceptable, psychoactive drug in the Western world. Consumed in small quantities, some alcohol such as red wine has been linked with increased health benefits including lowering the risk of coronary heart disease (Zakhari & Gordis, 1998), and for the antioxidant properties contained within the drink (Cao & Prior, 2000). Excessive alcohol consumption, however, has been linked to increased emergency in-patient hospital admissions (O'Farrell, Allwright, Downey, Bedford, & Howell, 2004), increased violent crime rates (Martin, Maxwell, White, & Zhang, 2004) and both fatal and non-fatal driving accidents (Allan, Roberts, Allan, Pienaar, & Stein, 2001). Furthermore, the age at which alcohol consumption begins has been shown to be reliable predictor of crime and sexual risk taking (Mason et al., 2010).

Measurement and consumption prevalence

Alcohol consumption in the UK is measured in relation to the number of units of alcohol contained within a drink. A standard (175ml) glass of wine contains 2 units of alcohol, whilst a strong lager contains approximately 3 units of alcohol. Current UK Government guidelines suggest men should consume no more than 21 units of alcohol per week (approximately 7 pints of strong lager or 10 standard glasses of wine) and women should consume no more than 14 units per week (approximately 4½ pints of strong lager or 7 standard glasses of wine).

The Office for National Statistics (ONS, 2009) reports that 41% of men drank over 4 units of alcohol (equating to 28 units per week) and 34% of women drank over 3 units of alcohol (equating to 21 units per week) in the week prior to interview in 2007. Of equal concern is the consumption pattern of children and young adults. In 2007, 20% of 11–15-year-olds reported drinking alcohol in the week prior to interview consuming an average of 12.7 units.

Measuring actual alcohol consumption is problematic since measurements are predominately based on self-report measures, which fail to reflect the full extent of variability of drinking over limited time periods and do not take into consideration variability across calendar events (e.g. birthdays, seasonal periods and family gatherings) where consumption is increased (Neal & Fromme, 2007). Despite the variability in self-report measures, such measures have demonstrated acceptable reliability and validity (Del Boca & Darkes, 2003).

In addition to self-report measures, blood alcohol content (BAC) provides an accurate measure of the level of alcohol circulating in the blood at a particular point in time, although it does not provide information regarding consumption behaviour. One standard 175ml of wine will increase the BAC by approximately 15%, although the actual figure is in part determined by weight and sex since females have slightly higher BAC due to a higher content of body fat.

Whilst the health benefits of moderate alcohol consumption are well documented, alcohol misuse and dependence have been inextricably linked to alcohol-related illness and death. The ONS (2009) reports that 9% of males and 4% of women (aged 16–74) demonstrated alcohol dependence in 2007 and in the same year there were 6541 alcohol-related deaths, an increase of 19% from 2001.

Further reading Alcohol consumption

Key reading

Goldman, M. S., Greenbaum, P. E., Darkes, J., Brandon, K. O., & Del Boca, F. K. (2011). How many versus how much: 52 weeks of alcohol consumption in emerging adults. *Psychology of Addictive Behaviour, 25*(1), 16–27.

Aetiology of excessive alcohol consumption

Excessive alcohol consumption has been linked to genetic, sociocultural and psychology determinants:

● Alcohol releases dopamine within the reward and pleasure area of the brain (including the thalamus and amygdala).

● Genes for enzymes involved in alcohol metabolism have been linked to alcohol misuse and dependence. The dopamine D2 receptor gene DRDA1(+) allele (the dopamine D2 receptor gene can take a number of forms, therefore DRDA1(+) is just one of the various forms) is more prevalent in alcohol-dependent individuals than individuals without such dependence (Lawford et al., 1997).

● Individuals more genetically predisposed are more likely to be encouraged to initiate and maintain alcohol use as they experience an easy 'high' following consumption. Continued alcohol use reduces the response of the reward system, resulting in increased consumption to maintain the original effects, in turn leading to dependence.

- Sociocultural factors are also influential in excessive alcohol consumption and dependence. UK teenagers and young adults favour a drinking 'culture' and whilst for many consumption reduces with age (Bartholow, Sher, & Krull, 2003), for some the early exposure increases consumption throughout later adulthood. Individuals have a tendency to use alcohol in line with their familial or social group and teenagers are typically part of peer groups where interests are similar. Although previously it was perceived that peers could have either a 'positive' or 'negative' influence on an individual, more recent research suggests that teens actively 'seek' out like-using peers as friends, demonstrating a desire to belong to a particular social group (Donohew et al., 1999). Sociocultural factors are important when considering treatment approaches to alcohol misuse since changing an individual's social network forms an important part of this process (McCrady, 2004), but may place the individual under considerable stress and anxiety, which could exacerbate the level of consumption.

Across cultures, excessive alcohol consumption is associated more with men than women, and particularly those who are less educated and on lower incomes (Hemmingsson, Lundberg, Romelsjö, & Alfredsson, 1997). Family history of alcoholism, however, has been associated with early onset alcohol misuse in females (Capone & Wood, 2008). Alcohol consumption has also been linked to stress reduction, both in terms of reducing short-term anxiety (Ham, Casner, Bacon, & Shaver, 2011) and post-traumatic stress disorder (McCarthy & Petrakis, 2010).

The media frequently represent drinking 'cultures', for example, 86% of British television soaps (e.g. *Emmerdale*, *Coronation Street*, *EastEnders* and *Hollyoaks*) contain verbal or visual references to alcohol at a rate of one reference every 3.5 minutes (Furnham, Ingle, Gunter, & McClelland, 1997).

Key terms

Thalamus: part of the forebrain. It plays an important role in relaying sensory information from the sense organs to the cortex.

Amygdala: an almond-shaped bunch of neurons located within the medial temporal lobe. It is associated with emotional processing and is a key part of the limbic system, a set of structures located either side of the thalamus involved in both emotional processing and the formation of new memories.

✳ Sample question   Essay

'Alcohol use is solely related to sociocultural factors.' Critically examine the accuracy of this statement.

Alcohol and memory

Although working memory is negatively affected by alcohol misuse (Park et al., 2011), low alcohol consumption has been associated with improved memory recall when the encoding state matched the recall state. The real impact on memory, however, arises in prolonged alcohol consumption and alcoholism. Korsakoff's syndrome is an organic amnesia associated with chronic alcoholism, resulting in both anterograde (inability to lay down new memory traces) and retrograde (inability to recall past events prior to amnesia onset) amnesia. Korsakoff's syndrome is a result of poor diet and particularly deficiency of thiamine (vitamin B$_1$), associated with chronic alcoholic misuse. It is prevalent in approximately 5% of individuals. Although individuals can be treated with thiamine, improvement is seen in only roughly one-third of all cases and many aspects of the disease are seen as irreversible. Individuals often fill out retrograde gaps with elaborate and far-fetched stories known as confabulation. In addition to a deficit of memory, deficits are also noted in abstract reasoning, skill learning and visuospatial ability.

Test your knowledge

8.5 What is the relationship between dopamine and the limbic system?

8.6 What is the role of sociocultural factors in alcohol misuse?

8.7 What is the difference between alcohol units and blood alcohol concentration?

Answers to these questions can be found on the companion website at: www.pearsoned.co.uk/psychologyexpress

Further reading

Topic	Key reading
Alcohol and social stress	Ham, L. S., Casner, H. G., Bacon, A. K., & Shaver, J. A. (2011). Speeches, strangers and alcohol use: The role of context in social stress response dampening. *Journal of Behaviour Therapy and Experimental Psychiatry, 42,* 462–472.
Predictors of alcohol misuse	Harrell, Z. A. T., Slane, J. D., & Klump, K. L. (2009). Predictors of alcohol problems in college women: The role of depressive symptoms, disordered eating, and family history. *Addictive Behaviors, 34,* 252–257.
Korsakoff's syndrome	Spiegel, D. R., & Lim, K. J. (2011). A case of probable Korsakoff's syndrome: A syndrome of frontal lobe and diencephalic structural pathogenesis and a comparison with medial temporal lobe dementias. *Innovations in Clinical Neuroscience, 8*(6), 15–19.

Cocaine and amphetamine

Cocaine and amphetamine are both associated with dopamine release and are stimulant drugs. They increase alertness through increased dopamine and noradrenaline activation and whilst moods are initially intensified, on withdrawal positive moods are frequently replaced by more negative mood states. The initially positive mood states (alertness, increased energy, power and confidence) are due to the stimulation of the median forebrain bundle with underlies pleasure and reward (Pinel, 2008). Both cocaine and amphetamine boost activity in the ascending reticular activating system (ARAS), the brainstem underlying alertness and arousal.

- Cocaine use is not unequivocally associated with positive moods states, since negative moods can be induced if negative feelings are present at the onset of use. Further, cocaine use can increase feelings of irritability, suspiciousness, power and invincibility, which in turn can lead to violence (Licata, Taylor, Berman, & Cranston, 1993).

- Frequent cocaine use increases the risk of cardiac arrest and stroke due to increased heart rate and elevated blood pressure. Further, nasal cocaine ingestion can weaken the septum and cartilage on the bridge of the nose resulting in the bridge collapsing.

Cannabis

Cannabis is the most widely consumed illicit substance cross-culturally and the number of young people using the drug has risen sharply in the last 30 years (Hall & Acula, 2003) combined with a fall in age of first-time use (Monshouwer, Smit, de Graaf, van Os, & Vollebergh, 2005). The European Monitoring Centre for Drugs and Drug Addiction (EMCDDA, 2003), suggests that a minority of school-aged young people (15–16-year-olds) have tried cannabis and that despite its relative popularity with young users, more recent research suggests that levels of cannabis use may have peaked in the early 21st century, and are now beginning to decline (Murphy & Rose, 2007).

Individuals cite a number of reasons for cannabis use, with pleasure and relaxation noted as the primary reasons, alongside heightened sensations and experience of getting 'high'. Younger adults also perceive cannabis as a relatively low-risk drug that does not lead to dependence (Highet, 2004), despite cannabis being frequently used alongside nicotine and alcohol.

- Young people hold relatively pro-cannabis attitudes in comparison to other illicit drugs, e.g. cocaine, and perceive other drugs as resulting in more serious consequences (particularly addiction), and that cannabis is no more harmful than alcohol or tobacco (McIntosh, MacDonald, & McKeganey, 2003).

- Early adoption of cannabis use, however, has been linked to future problem use and dependence (Chen, O'Brien, & Anthony, 2005), and to antisocial behaviour, particularly aggression, theft and destruction of property (Miller & Plant, 2002).

- Cannabis use results in acute cognitive effects and in particular impairment of short-term memory both evident in small doses and in frequent users. This may be a result of the demands placed upon attentional systems and a failure to encode relevant information.

- Driving performance is significantly affected by cannabis use, with tasks such as reversing, risk judgement and braking tasks substantially impaired by 33–42% in low cannabis doses and 55–63% in high cannabis doses (Klonoff, 1974). Importantly, impairments in cognitive and motor tasks remain present at approximately the same level eight hours after inhalation (Robb & O'Hanlon, 1993).

- Educational achievement and school satisfaction are also affected by frequent use, with regular cannabis users more likely to be excluded from mainstream education (McCrystal, Higgins, Percy, & Thornton, 2005).

Substance misuse and offending behaviour

There is an inextricable link between substance use and offending behaviour, with serious offenders reporting higher use of alcohol and other drugs than non-offenders. The polydrug nature of alcohol and cannabis makes disentangling cause and effect problematic, although cannabis users are less likely to be involved in serious crime than cocaine users (Childs, Dembo, Belenko, Wareham, & Schmeidler, 2011). Further, research (Dembo, Wareham, & Schmeidler, 2007) also suggests that young male offenders report higher cannabis use than females, although young female offenders are more likely to use cocaine and amphetamines (Neff & Waite, 2007), providing some evidence for gender differences in use behaviour. Interestingly, US research (Belenko, Sprott, & Peterson, 2004) suggests that Caucasian young offenders report higher rates of lifetime use of all drugs than Black, Hispanic and Asian offenders.

Key term

Polydrug: when individuals use more than one drug at the same time (e.g. alcohol and cannabis), this is known as polydrug use. Olszewski, Matias, Monshouwer and Kokkevi (2010) report that teenage polydrug (15- to 16-year-olds) use across Europe is fairly consistent with alcohol and nicotine being the most widely consumed polydrugs, followed by alcohol and cannabis.

153

Test your knowledge

8.8 What are the key reasons for cannabis use?

8.9 What are the psychopharmacological effects of cocaine use?

8.10 What evidence exists for gender and race differences in drug use?

Answers to the questions can be found on the companion website at:
www.pearsoned.co.uk/psychologyexpress

Further reading

Topic	Key reading
Gender differences and drug use	Wagner, F. A., & Anthony, J. C. (2007). Male–female differences in the risk of progression from first use to dependence upon cannabis, cocaine and alcohol. *Drug & Alcohol Dependence, 86*, 191–198.
Polydrug use	Epstein, J. A., Botvin, G. J., Griffin, K. W. & Diaz, T. (1999). Role of ethnicity and gender in polydrug use among a longitudinal sample of inner-city adolescents. *Journal of Alcohol & Drug Education, 45*(1), 1–12.

Assessment for change

The role of a clinical psychologist (as part of a wider multidisciplinary team) is to help change or eradicate the pattern of substance use. In the case of alcoholism, there is considerable debate as to whether total abstinence or moderation of use is more appropriate (Vaillant, 1995). The first stage of working with an individual is known as 'engagement' which can be either self-directed or coerced (e.g. court order, employer or external agent). During the engagement stage, clients may not view their use as misuse or problematic, and the role of the clinician at this stage is to motivate the client to change. In recognising the importance of motivation, Prochaska, DiClemente and Norcross (1992) suggest individuals move through three stages of motivation before a substance is no longer use:

- *Stage 1*: Precontemplation – At this stage the individual views their substance use as non-problematic and may need to be coerced into viewing their use as problematic.

- *Stage 2*: Contemplation – At this stage the individual questions whether their use may be problematic and begins their journey of substance use termination.

- *Stage 3*: Preparation – At this stage the individual is motivated to change and begins working towards termination.

The model proposed by Prochaska et al. (1992) enables the individual to regress to earlier stages, e.g. move from preparation to precontemplation since motivation is recognised as a state rather than a trait, and acknowledges the difficulty in substance use termination. The end goal, however, is always to maintain motivation in the individual so that preparation for change leads to termination.

During engagement the individual is assessed for their drinking and drug-use history and the individual's perceptions of her/his substance use pattern. Although this is initially completed as part of the initial stages of assessment it is revisited throughout a treatment programme. If the individual is being treated for alcoholism, their BAC is assessed at the start of each session (using a hand-held breathalyser), and a urine test is required to screen for major drugs (in part recognising the importance of polydrug use in substance users). Further, a timeline follow-back interview (TLFB, Sobell et al., 2001) may be completed to assesses substance use behaviour in a set time-window to provide information about quantity, frequency and pattern of substance use.

Based on the information provided as part of the TLFB and initial interview with the individual, the clinician determines whether the individual is likely to suffer from withdrawal symptoms following reduction or cessation of substances. Sudden cessation of substance use can result in both psychological (reduction in consciousness, memory impairments, insomnia and hallucinations) and physical (nausea, sweating and shaking) symptoms, which need to be managed throughout the treatment process.

Daily self-reporting cards including the inventory of drinking situations (Annis, Graham, & Davis, 1987) enable clinicians to assess substance use throughout the treatment process. These self-report measures assess the situations in which an individual may use a particular substance, e.g. alcohol, and in turn allow the clinician to focus on the trigger of use.

Further reading **The alcohol timeline follow-back interview and inventory of drinking situations**

Key reading

Sobell, L. C., Agrawal, S., Annis, H., Ayala-Velazquez, H., Echeverria, L., Leo, G. I., Rybakowski, J. K., Sandahl, C., Saunders, B., Thomas, S., & Ziólkowski, M. (2001). Cross-cultural evaluation of two drinking assessment instruments: Alcohol timeline followback and inventory of drinking situations. *Substance Use & Misuse, 36*(3), 313–331.

Treatment approaches

Following assessment, the initial treatment phase focuses upon establishing a therapeutic alliance (creating an atmosphere for reflection and change), agreeing treatment goals, agreeing a treatment plan and attending to motivational issues. The initial stage of treatment is aligned to Stage 2 (Contemplation) of Prochaska et al.'s (1992) model of motivation since the individual is receptive to change, but the clinician must work with them to ensure that progress to Stage 3

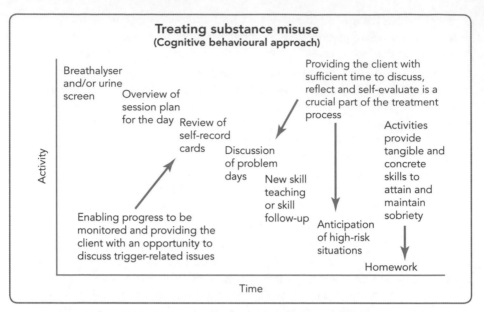

Figure 8.4 Treating substance misuse (cognitive-behavioural approach)

(Preparation) is met. One of the key treatment approaches adopted by clinicians is Cognitive Behavioural Therapy (CBT, see Chapter 2).

Figure 8.4 provides an overview of the role of CBT in treating substance misuse and addictions. During each treatment session the client is initially tested for substances ahead of the session beginning. Self-recording cards are one of the first skills provided to the individual by the clinician and the cards allow both parties to record and graph substance-free days, high-substance days and money/time spent on sourcing substances. At the start of each session, the cards are reviewed and provide a focus for the session through the identification of triggers and reflection.

After identifying major triggers the clinician can develop a high-risk hierarchy of use-related situations that are rated by the individual and incorporated into a change plan. Clients are taught to deal with high-risk stimuli in three ways:

● Avoid high-risk stimuli or situations in which stimuli will be present.

● Rearrange route or pattern of behaviour so that contact with high-risk stimuli is avoided.

● Respond differently when confronted with high-risk stimuli or situations.

In addition to behavioural changes, clinicians work with individuals to challenge their irrationally skewed (positive beliefs) about substance use. Successful self-changers focus on the negative consequences of use rather than the positive uses, e.g. 'I have lost my job as a result of my cocaine use' rather than 'I am invited to lots of parties where cocaine is freely available and I always have a good time'.

Cognitive restructuring techniques enable the client to challenge their thoughts by firstly recognising their thoughts as irrational and then through the development of more rational and accurate beliefs. Clinicians may also choose to work with clients on their lifestyle skills to help them avoid high-risk situations and to provide support during treatment:

● *Social support.* Encourage movement away from original social network to networks where substances are not the focus e.g. sports clubs.

● *Self-help groups.* Interaction with people dealing with similar substance use problems, role models and learning additional skills and new attitudes, e.g. Alcoholics Anonymous.

● *Communication skills.* New communication skills are taught through role-play, discussion and problem solving to help the client express and discuss their previous substance use and understand criticism surrounding such use.

● *Substance alternatives.* Focus on long-term behaviour change.

Although individuals may terminate their substance use, relapse is relatively common. Miller and Wilbourne (2002) report 35% of individuals maintain continuous abstinence or moderate/non-problematic use a year after treatment, suggesting a relapse rate of 65%. Relapse prevention focuses on educating individuals to the possibility of relapse, devising sessions to avoid relapse and preparing the individual with techniques to help manage relapse should it occur. Relapse warning workshops, for example, help to identify and target warning signs of where relapse may occur and provide alternatives to substance use, e.g. feeling lonely may be a warning sign and rather than using a substance to alleviate the feeling of loneliness, the individual is encouraged to take part in a social activity.

Test your knowledge

8.11 What are the three stages of motivation ahead of change?

8.12 How do clinical psychologists assess individuals wishing to terminate their substance use?

8.13 What treatment approaches do clinical psychologists adopt when treating substance misuse?

Answers to these questions can be found on the companion website at: www.pearsoned.co.uk/psychologyexpress

---

Further reading

Topic	Key reading
Skills training and substance use	Grawe, R. W., Hagen, R., Espeland, B., & Mueser, K.T. (2007). The better life program: Effects of group skills training for persons with severe mental illness and substance use disorders. *Journal of Mental Health, 16*(5), 625–634.
CBT and alcohol misuse	Kavanagh, D. J, Sitharthan, G., Young, R. M., Sitharthan, T., Saunders, J. B., Shockley, N., & Giannopoulos, V. (2006). Addition of cue exposure to cognitive-behaviour therapy for alcohol misuse: A randomized trial with dysphoric drinkers. *Addiction, 101*, 1106–1116.

Chapter summary – pulling it all together

→ Can you tick all the points from the revision checklist at the beginning of this chapter?

→ Attempt the sample question from the beginning of this chapter using the answer guidelines below.

→ Go to the companion website at www.pearsoned.co.uk/psychologyexpress to access more revision support online, including interactive quizzes, flashcards, You be the marker exercises as well as answer guidance for the Test your knowledge and Sample questions from this chapter.

Answer guidelines

✳ *Sample question*   *Essay*

To what extent are substance use disorders effectively treated using Cognitive Behavioural Therapy?

Approaching the question

This question requires you to firstly define what is meant by the terms substance use disorders and cognitive behavioural therapy (see Chapter 2). It is important to demonstrate a full appreciation of how substance use, abuse and dependence differ both across time and within different cultures. The historical background to substance use disorders will prove invaluable in helping to provide the wider context necessary to fully answer the question.

In answering 'to what extent' you should consider whether substance abuse and dependence are effectively treated or managed using Cognitive Behavioural Therapy, and to what extent alternative treatment approaches are more applicable.

You should ensure that your answer contains research-based evidence and theoretical approaches to support the claims that you make and to help you construct an argument before reaching a reasoned conclusion.

Important points to include

● You should start your answer with an overview of the different terminology since substance use, abuse and dependence mean quite different things and whilst an individual may use a substance their behaviour may not be problematic and as such would not be classed as either abuse or dependence. Further, you should acknowledge the comorbidity issue of substance abuse and prevalence with other disorders, e.g. anxiety and mood disorders. Strong answers will also demonstrate a critical appreciation of polydrug use, particularly in adolescence, since this highlights the fluidity between substance use.

- You should discuss at least two substances and preferably two substances that differ in terms of aetiology, prevalence and treatment approaches since you can compare and contrast the substances, and highlight a particular substance that is effectively treated with Cognitive Behavioural Therapy.
- It is important to include the theoretical approaches and respective models (e.g. medical model and substance perspective continuum) since these will also provide the basis for discussion of treatment approaches. In adopting the medical model, the treatment approach for Korsakoff's syndrome is thiamine treatment to increase vitamin B1 levels; however, this is very different from a CBT approach that would seek to address the underlying behaviours leading to alcohol consumption.
- The role of CBT should be considered in relation to theoretical models, particularly those focusing on motivation and pre-contemplation (e.g. Prochaska et al., 1992). Answers should provide an understanding of what CBT is, the historical origins of the treatment approach and its relative effectiveness in treating disorders. You should also consider the effectiveness of using CBT as a treatment approach both when comorbidity exists and as a multi-faceted approach with other approaches (e.g. medical model).
- In questioning the universality of substance abuse and the cross-cultural differences associated with substance use, you should also question the applicability, prevalence and effectiveness of CBT as a treatment approach in different cultures.

Make your answer stand out

Including an example of how CBT may work in practice when working with a client will help you to provide an overview of the techniques employed in the therapeutic approach and allow you to critique the effectiveness of CBT for substance use disorders. You could provide an example of how a client would be taught cognitive restricting techniques, how to access substance alternatives, e.g. leisure activities, and revised communication skills as part of their treatment approach. As part of the discussion you could question the role of social influence, particularly in polydrug use in adolescence, and the role of both complementary and alternative treatment approaches.

Explore the accompanying website at www.pearsoned.co.uk/psychologyexpress
- → Prepare more effectively for exams and assignments using the answer guidelines for questions from this chapter.
- → Test your knowledge using multiple choice questions and flashcards.
- → Improve your essay skills by exploring the You be the marker exercises.

159

Notes

9

Eating disorders

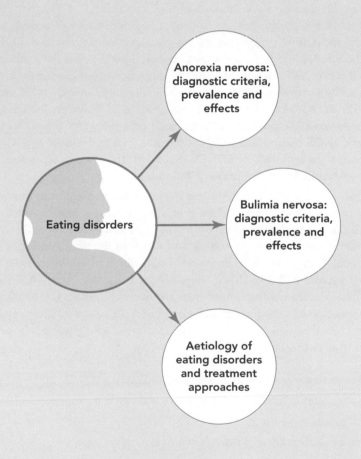

- Anorexia nervosa: diagnostic criteria, prevalence and effects
- Eating disorders
- Bulimia nervosa: diagnostic criteria, prevalence and effects
- Aetiology of eating disorders and treatment approaches

A printable version of this topic map is available from
www.pearsoned.co.uk/psychologyexpress

Introduction

According to Stice, Marti and Rohde (2012), approximately 10% of young women meet the DSM-IV-TR (APA, 2000) criteria for anorexia nervosa (AN), bulimia nervosa (BN) or an eating disorder not otherwise specified (EDNOS), including binge eating disorder (BED). Whilst each disorder has its own prevalence, incidence and behavioural pattern, they are interrelated by the individual's desire to control weight and may involve movement from one disorder to another, e.g. some individuals with AN will shift to bulimic eating patterns. Additionally, there are specific differences between the two primary eating disorders, AN and BN, since individuals with the latter are rarely underweight and value sexual attraction, and as such are in direct contrast to individuals with AN. Eating disorders are marked by their comorbidity with other disorders including substance abuse, anxiety disorders and depressive disorders, and by their chronic nature, propensity for relapse, level of distress and morbidity rates. Although AN and BN are the two specified eating disorders according to DSM-IV-TR (APA, 2000), the most common eating disorder diagnosis in clinical and community samples is within the EDNOS category (Smink, van Hoeken, & Hoek, 2012). Because of the heterogeneous nature of disorders including partial aspects of AN and BN, over half of individuals presenting for an eating disorder receive an EDNOS diagnosis (Eddy, Celio Doyle, Hoste, Herzog, & le Grange, 2008). Despite the high rate of EDNOS diagnosis, the literature predominately focuses on AN and BN as the primary eating disorders.

This chapter will consider both AN and BN in terms of diagnosis, prevalence, aetiology and treatment approaches. It is worth noting at the outset that eating disorders per se are more commonly reported in women, with men only accounting for between 5 and 12% of all cases (Button, Aldridge, & Palmer, 2008). Clinical studies report AN figures in men between 5–10% and BN figures between 10 and 15% (Striegel-Moore, Garvin, Dohm, & Rosenheck, 1999). Whilst prevalence figures for men and women remain relatively static, an increasing rate of eating disorders have been observed in Spain and other European countries, which may partly be accounted for by sociocultural factors discussed later in this chapter.

→ *Revision checklist*

Essential points to revise are:
- ❑ Definition, aetiology and prevalence of eating disorders
- ❑ Anorexia nervosa (AN)
- ❑ Bulimia nervosa (BN)
- ❑ Sex differences and prevalence of eating disorders
- ❑ Assessment and treatment approaches

Assessment advice

- Whilst AN and BN are the primary eating disorders classified by DSM-IV-TR (APA, 2000) and DSM-5 (APA, 2013), it is important to acknowledge the prevalence and extent of EDNOS, particularly as many individuals will be diagnosed with the latter due to the partial presence of other eating disorders. You should carefully consider the role of diagnostic criteria and whether such criteria account for the full spectrum of eating disorders.

- Individuals with eating disorders may have other psychological disorders, e.g. depression or anxiety disorders, therefore understanding comorbidity and the role comorbid disorders play is important when discussing the wider issues of assessment and treatment approaches.

- The role of sociocultural factors is important in the emergence and maintenance of eating disorders; however, ensure that your answer is rooted in psychological literature and does not draw more widely on media reports and representations. Further, consider the extent to which Western views of 'thinness' and 'attractiveness' are permeating other cultures and whether this is resulting in increased reports of eating disorders in these populations.

- Although men represent only a relatively small proportion of individuals reporting with eating disorders, consider whether assessment and treatment approaches adequately account for this group. Weltzin et al. (2012), for example, report that men should be treated in all-male groups to reduce stigma. Comorbidity issues for men include: excessive exercise, body image, sexuality and spirituality. When answering a question on eating disorders attempt to consider the prevalence of men with eating disorders and reflect the comorbidity issues outlined above in your answer.

Sample question

Could you answer this question? Below is a typical essay question that could arise on this topic.

> ✳ *Sample question*   *Essay*
>
> Critically examine the evidence that anorexia nervosa and bulimia nervosa are primarily a result of sociocultural influence.

Anorexia nervosa: diagnostic criteria, prevalence and effects

Anorexia nervosa (AN) refers to behaviour that is adopted to keep the body as thin as possible. It goes beyond 'dieting behaviour' since the individual has a desire to be significantly underweight combined with an intense fear of weight gain, leading to maintenance of body weight below 85% of expected weight for age and height (DSM-IV-TR; APA, 2000). Weight maintenance occurs through either Type 1 behaviour characterised by self-imposed starvation or Type 2 behaviour characterised by binging, purging and laxative behaviour.

Individuals with AN may also demonstrate marked increases in physical activity alongside either Type 1 or Type 2 behaviour (Bulik, Reba, Siega-Riz, & Reichborn-Kjennerud, 2005). Despite significant weight loss, individuals continually obsess about weight gain, remain dissatisfied with the perceived size of their body and engage in behaviours to further perpetuate weight loss. Individuals with AN score high on scales of perfectionism (Halmi et al., 2000) and low on scales of self-esteem (Karpowicz, Skarsater, & Nevonen, 2009).

Neuropsychological research suggests that individuals with AN may have executive function deficit, associated with the prefrontal cortex, resulting in excessive self-control (Fassino et al., 2006), cognitive rigidity and excessive attention to detail (Friederich & Herzog, 2011) and increased thinking (Fairburn & Harrison, 2003). Excessive self-control has been associated with increased activation in the prefrontal and visual cortex when thinking about images of food (Brooks et al., 2012), suggesting a cognitive bias towards food stimuli and its subsequent control.

DSM-IV-TR (APA, 2000) and ICD-10 adopt slightly different diagnostic criteria for the diagnosis of AN (Table 9.1). The key difference between DSM-IV-TR and DSM-V (APA, 2013) is the requirement for (female) individuals to present with amenorrhea (Keel, Brown, Holm-Denoma, & Bodell, 2011). It has been argued that amenorrhea, the absence of a menstrual cycle in women, is not a good predictor of AN since there are no reported differences in women with AN who do and do not menstruate (Watson & Anderson, 2003).

The age of AN onset is typically associated with puberty and as such spans between 14 and 18 years of age (Kimura, Tonoike, Muroya, Yoshida, & Ozaki, 2007; Pike, 1998). Feighner et al. (1972) suggested age of onset before 25 years should be adopted as part of diagnostic criterion. Although incidence rates have remained relatively stable a notable exception to this is the increase in the number of 15–19-year-old females being diagnosed with the disorder during the last ten years (Smink et al., 2012), and it is unknown whether the increase in this 'high-risk' group reflects early detection or earlier age of onset. Both early and late ages of onset are reported in the literature (e.g. Bayes & Madden, 2011; Kimura et al., 2007) despite the clustering of onset coinciding with puberty. Late onset AN is commonly associated with separation experiences and anxiety following the death of a spouse or children leaving home (Joughin, Crisp, Gowers, & Bhat, 1991).

Prevalence figures for AN in females range from between 0.5% (Hudson et. al., 2007) to 2% (Rooney, McClelland, Crisp, & Sedgwick, 1995) with average prevalence reported as 0.3%. Taking the previously reported figure of between 5 and 10% of males accounting for all AN diagnosis (Striegel-Moore et al., 1999)

Table 9.1 Diagnostic criteria for anorexia nervosa

	DSM-IV-TR (2000) diagnosis criteria	ICD-10 diagnosis criteria
Weight	Refusal to maintain body weight at or above minimally normal weight for age and height (<85% expected weight) or failure to make expected weight gain during growth period leading to <85% expected weight.	Body weight maintained at least 15% below expected weight or prepubertal individuals fail to make expected weight gain during growth period or weight loss self-induced by avoidance of fattening foods.
Phobic behaviour	Intense fear of weight gain despite being underweight due to either restrictive behaviours (not engaging in binge eating or purging behaviour – Type 1) or purging behaviour (engaging in purging behaviour – Type 2).	Self-induced weight loss through the avoidance of fatty foods and one or more of the following: self-induced vomiting, purging, excessive exercise, appetite suppressants and/or diuretics.
Body perception	Disturbed view of body weight and shape or denial of seriousness of current low body weight.	Body-image distortion characterised by a dread of 'fatness' and self-imposed low weight threshold.
Amenorrhea/hormonal fluctuations	Absence of three consecutive menstrual cycles, and whereby menstrual cycle is started via hormone induction.	Amenorrhea in females and lack of sexual interest in males.
Pubertal development		Delayed or arrested pubertal events, e.g. juvenile male genitals in males and delayed breast development in females. Females may also demonstrate primary amenorrhea.

Source: adapted from Bulik et al. (2005).

against the average of 0.3%, this suggests male AN prevalence is between 0.015 and 0.03%.

Male eating disorders are frequently associated with other predictive factors including excessive exercise, body image and sexuality (Weltzin et al., 2012). Men may demonstrate lack of control, increased tolerance and reduce alternative activities when exercising (Hausenblas & Symons Downs, 2002), and homosexual men have both increased rates of eating disorder diagnosis than heterosexual men and score higher on ratings of body image concerns (Russel & Keel, 2002).

AN results in a range of health complications including amenorrhea, anaemia, high or low blood pressure, increased tooth cavities and gum disease, cracked skin, brittle bones, cardiotoxicity (damage to the heart muscles) and immune infections due to a weakened immune system.

Eating disorders, alongside substance misuse disorders, constitute the major contribution to mortality in clinical disorders (Harris & Barraclough, 1998) with mortality rates estimated at approximately 5% per decade (Smink et al., 2012) and between 0 and 21% of individuals with AN dying as a result of the disorder (Birmingham, Su, Hlynsky, Goldner, & Gao, 2005).

Test your knowledge

9.1 What are the key differences in diagnostic criteria for anorexia nervosa?

9.2 What is the prevalence rate of anorexia nervosa?

9.3 To what extent does amenorrhea play a role in diagnostic criteria and why might this be controversial?

9.4 What behaviours do individuals with anorexia nervosa demonstrate?

9.5 What is the difference between Type 1 and Type 2 anorexia nervosa?

Answers to the questions can be found on the companion website at: www.pearsoned.co.uk/psychologyexpress

Further reading

Topic	Key reading
Self-esteem and anorexia nervosa	Karpowicz, E., Skarsater, I., & Nevonen, L. (2009). Self-esteem in patients treated for anorexia nervosa. *International Journal of Mental Health Nursing, 18,* 318–325.
Anxiety disorder and anorexia nervosa comorbidity	Swinbourne, J., Hunt, C., Abbott, M., Russell, J., St Clare, T., & Touyz. (2012). The comorbidity between eating disorders and anxiety disorders: Prevalence in an eating disorder sample and anxiety disorder sample. *Australian & New Zealand Journal of Psychiatry, 46*(2), 118–131.

Bulimia nervosa: diagnostic criteria, prevalence and effects

According to DSM-IV-TR (APA, 2000) bulimia nervosa (BN) is characterised by recurrent binge eating, recurrent and inappropriate use of compensatory behaviours, including vomiting after eating, to control weight gain, high frequency of eating binges and compensatory behaviour and self-evaluation unduly influenced by body weight and shape (Bowman, 1998). Compensatory behaviours should occur, on average, for a period of at least twice a week for three months. Proposed diagnostic changes in DSM-5 (APA, 2013) result in a change of frequency for inappropriate compensatory behaviours to once a week for three months (Keel et al., 2011).

Individuals with BN demonstrate a fear of weight gain (similar to individuals with AN) and consider themselves to be heavier than they actually are (McKenzie, Williamson, & Cubic, 1993). Food is consistently eaten in secret, often rapidly consumed and without pleasure. Periods of binge eating can result in excess of 5000 calories being consumed (twice the recommended daily male calorie intake), with approximately 80–90% individuals following binge periods with excessive vomiting. A further third of individuals adopt laxative use and excessive exercising to help counteract binge periods (Anderson & Maloney, 2001). A number of key differences exist between AN and BN (Table 9.2).

Table 9.2 Differences between anorexia nervosa and bulimia nervosa

Anorexia nervosa	Bulimia nervosa
High and excessive self-control	Impulsivity and emotional instability
Weight loss not driven by desire to appear feminine	Social concept of femininity drives behaviour
Body weight significantly (<85%) below expected for age/height	Fluctuations in weight although weight remains relatively close to norms for age/height
Less likely to have been overweight in the past	More likely to have been overweight in the past
Less likely to have substance misuse disorder	More likely to have substance misuse disorder

BN is estimated to affect between 1 and 3% of adolescent and young women (Keel, Heathertom, Dorer, Joiner, & Zalta, 2002) with a lifetime prevalence rate of 1.5% and a median onset age of 18 (Hudson, Hiripi, Pope, & Kessler, 2007). If symptom frequency reflects proposed DSM-5 (2013) changes to once a week, lifetime prevalence for women rises to 2.3% (Keski-Rahkonen et al., 2009). Conversely, the lifetime prevalence rate for men is estimated between 0.1% and 0.5% (Hudson et al., 2007).

Due, in part, to the purging behaviour associated with BN, visits to health services are higher in the 12 months before and 12 months after a diagnosis, reflecting the health complications associated with the disorder (Striegel-Moore et al., 2008). Individuals may experience a number of oral and gastrointestinal complications as a result of self-induced vomiting, including dental erosion, periodontal disease and chronic inflammation of the lips (Studen-Pavlovich & Elliott, 2001).

Despite the relative ineffectiveness of laxatives in reducing calorie absorption, with between 10 and 12% of ingested calories being lost from laxative use (Turner, Batik, Palmer, Forbes, & McDermott, 2000), individuals with BN continue to use laxatives during purging. Laxatives are ineffective since the majority of calorie absorption takes place before the bowel (Steffen, Mitchell, Roerig, &

Lancaster, 2007). Sustained laxative use can result in cathartic colon syndrome (nerve damage to the colon associated with sustained laxative use; Xing & Soffer, 2001).

Further reading Health complications and bulimia nervosa

Key reading

Brown, C. A., & Mehler, P. S. (2012). Successful 'detoxing' from commonly utilised modes of purging in bulimia nervosa. *Eating Disorders, 20*(4), 312–320.

KEY STUDY

Eating disorder: Gemma

Following a recent dental examination, Gemma, a 14-year-old-girl from Edinburgh, has been referred to her GP. Gemma's dentist has become concerned about rapid erosion on her teeth and poor condition of her lips and inside of her mouth. Upon examining Gemma, her GP noticed that her weight was within the normal range, although Gemma became quite upset when asked about her eating behaviour. Gemma commented that she used to regularly skip meals and had infrequent periods but now eats regularly, adding that sometimes she eats too much. Upon further questioning, Gemma commented that she doesn't really enjoy eating although doesn't believe that she has a particular 'problem' with food. Although Gemma's GP attempted to ask more questions about her eating habits, Gemma became more frustrated and declined to answer the questions in detail.

Would Gemma's GP diagnose her with AN or BN based on the above description and why?

To what extent could Gemma have previously had AN and since moved to BN?

Which elements of the diagnosis criteria are missing from the above description to enable a full diagnosis to be made?

Notes

Although early diagnosis is associated with favourable prognosis, the average time between symptom onset and treatment contact is approximately four years (Cachelin, Striegel-Moore & Regan, 2006). This in part is due to the individual's recognising the need for help and disclosing their eating behaviour (Becker, Grinspoon, Kilbanski, & Herzog, 1999).

Further reading Disclosure and eating disorders

Key reading

Gilbert, N., Arcelus, J., Cashmore, R., Thompson, B., Langham, C., & Meyer, C. (2012). Should I ask about eating? Patients' disclosure of eating disorder symptoms and help-seeking behaviour. *European Eating Orders Review, 20*, 80–85.

Aetiology of eating disorders and treatment approaches

Biological mechanisms associated with eating disorders (AN and BN) include dysfunction of dopaminergic neurotransmission (Frieling et al., 2010). The dopaminergic system is involved in the regulation of body weight, eating behaviour and the reward system (Volkow, Fowler, Wang, & Swanson, 2004), domains compromised in individuals with eating disorders. Individuals prone to binge eating may demonstrate low levels of dopamine release (Jimerson, Lesem, Kaye, & Brewerton, 1992).

Sociocultural factors play an important role in the development and maintenance of eating disorders, with over half the families in which an individual develops an eating disorder placing a strong emphasis on weight and shape (Haworth-Hoeppner, 2000). Since values and attitudes towards 'thinness' are perceived as favourable in Western countries, this has resulted in being overweight drawing prejudice. Whilst eating disorders continue to be most prevalent in Western countries and among middle- and upper-class Caucasian women, the number of different ethnic and socioeconomic groups affected by these disorders is increasing (Steiner & Lock, 1998).

Social factors can be translated into behavioural outcomes via cognitive processes. Thinness and weight loss become prioritised due to the high status associated with looking thin and attractive, and this prioritisation prevents individuals from weight gain. Additionally, individuals judge their self-worth on the basis of achieving a low body weight as part of a weight-related self-schema. In turn, the schema drives all behaviour in relation to whether others are perceived as thinner or fatter than the individual, and any weight change has a significant effect on the individuals thoughts and feelings.

As part of a distorted body image perspective, individuals with AN considerably overestimate their body proportions, maintain a low opinion of their body shape and consider themselves unattractive even when their weight is clinically subnormal (Gupta & Johnson, 2000). Slade and Brodie (1994), however, argue that many anorexics are uncertain about their body size and err on the side of caution when making a judgement, resulting in overestimation errors.

Further reading Distorted body image and anorexia nervosa

Key reading

Espeset, E. M. S., Nordbo, R. H. S., Gulliksen, K. S., Skarderud, F., Geller, J., & Holte, A. (2011). The concept of body image disturbance in anorexia nervosa: An empirical inquiry utilizing patients subjective experiences. *Eating Disorders, 19*, 175–193.

Initial treatment approaches for AN involve promoting weight gain through operant conditioning and rewarding weight gain. Where an individual is hospitalised because their body weight is less than 75% of normal weight for height/age, an individual may be rewarded for weight gain by early hospital release, since few rewards focus intrinsically on food.

Treasure (2001), whilst acknowledging the inhumane nature of force-feeding individuals with AN, argues that such feeding can be used in extreme cases of AN where individuals are not mentally competent to make decisions that may result in their death. Treasure suggests that individuals must be able to do the following in order to demonstrate competency in refusing food:

- Absorb and retain information relevant to their decision and understand the likely consequences of having or not having the treatment.
- Believe the information.
- Weigh the information in balance as part of the process of arriving at a decision.
- Recognise they have a health problem and take action to remedy their condition.

Accordingly, Treasure (2001) proposes that individuals with anorexia do not conform to the above principles and as such are not competent to make a decision about whether to receive food or not. Dyer (2012), however, reports the case of 'L', a 29-year-old woman, who the judge described as 'intelligent' and ruled against her being forcefully fed as part of her treatment, questioning the legality of competency testing.

Despite there being little evidence regarding the optimum treatment approach for AN (Bulik et al., 2005), Cognitive Behavioural Therapy (CBT) has been proposed as a highly effective treatment approach (Fairburn et al., 2009), although the evidence for whether it is any more effective than other therapies is questionable (Bulik et al, 2005).

Cognitive behavioural approaches adopt a phased approach where gaining trust and not challenging individual thoughts occur at the outset. This leads to the evaluation of emotional and physical cost associated with extreme dieting, homework activities focusing on how thoughts are influenced, and mechanisms for reinterpreting weight and eating-related events in more positive ways. Both weight gain and the initial evaluative work underpins subsequent CBT treatment.

The focus of CBT in treating AN is:

- To challenge inappropriate cognitions and develop autonomy.
- To challenge perceptual/attitudinal distortions (resulting in the individual understanding that their distorted thoughts are leading to over-exaggerations of their weight).
- To promote and encourage individuals to trust their own feelings helping to reaffirm self-belief and control.
- To focus on problem-solving skills to help individuals become more resourceful with crises that may occur in the future, and to deal with such crises more effectively.

Many individuals respond poorly to treatment approaches and a high proportion drop out of therapy or fail to benefit from treatment (Dalle

Grave, Bohn, Hawker, & Fairburn, 2008); however, there is little indication of individuals who are likely to do well and those who are not (Bulik et al., 2005). Treatment research in BN suggests that early behavioural change, however, is a strong predictor of benefiting from CBT (Agras, Walsh, Fairburn, Wilson, & Kraemer, 2000).

In addition to CBT, family therapy approaches are also used, with the Maudsley Method (Le Grange & Lock, 2005), being one of the most widely implemented. The method is based on the work of Minuchin, Rosman and Baker (1978), who suggested that eating disorders were not the result of individual pathology but of dysfunctional family patterns. The model is an intensive outpatient treatment approach focusing on three core treatment goals (Treasure et al., 2008), within 15–20 treatment sessions and a 12-month duration:

● restoration of an individual's weight to normal levels;

● individual control over eating;

● return to normal adolescent development.

The Maudsley Method involves three phases, as described in Table 9.3.

Table 9.3 Maudsley Method of family therapy for eating disorders

Phase	Key developments
Phase 1: Re-feeding and weight restoration Approximately 10-week duration	Restoration of individual's weight through re-feeding and limitations on physical activity. Parental support of the individual is encouraged and parental guilt is minimised. Individual undergoes psychoeducation to inform of dangers of malnutrition alongside assessment and alignment of family interaction patterns and eating habits. Family meal conducted in presence of therapist to observe eating patterns and assist in weight-restoration process.
Phase 2: New patterns of eating as control returned to individual Approximately 7-week duration	Individual accepts family structure and support of increased food intake without conflict combined with weight gain. Parents encouraged to allow individual more autonomy in food choice and physical activities, and therapy sessions focus on healthy weight and reduction of symptoms. Familial issues, patterns and daily family functioning affecting the individual are addressed during therapy and a balance between weight gain and daily struggles are managed.
Phase 3: Establishing healthy identity and termination	Phase begins when individual's weight is >95% of their ideal weight for height/age and refrains from restrictions in a variety of social situations (both within and outside of family settings). Focus of treatment is on the negative role AN has on the individuals development and the establishment of a healthy identity through addressing issues of adolescence, personal autonomy, parental boundaries and preparation of leaving home.

Source: adapted from Smith and Cook-Cottone (2011).

CBT for bulimia contains three clear stages (Anderson & Maloney, 2001):

- Stage 1: Rationalisation of treatment and replace binge eating behaviour with stable eating behaviours. Eating is restricted to three meals a day and without compensatory behaviour. If the individual experiences compensatory behavioural thoughts, these are replaced with other (positive) activities, e.g. visiting friends, in an attempt to reduce compensation.

- Stage 2: Concerns focusing on shape and weight are countered and eating patterns for previously avoided foods are introduced. To some extent, Stage 2 reflects aspects of systematic desensitisation.

- Stage 3: Maintenance of progress at stages 1 and 2, and identification of factors and strategies to prevent relapse once therapy is terminated.

Pharmacological interventions for anorexia frequently involve the drug Fluoxetine, an antidepressant of the selective serotonin reuptake inhibitor (SSRI). Although some studies demonstrate positive results in relation to weight gain in individuals taking fluoxetine compared with a placebo (Kaye, Klump, Frank, & Strober, 2001), others have reported limited effectiveness (Attia & Schroeder, 2005). Although Fluoxetine may be beneficial in individuals with depressive symptoms and anorexia for the treatment of major depression, there is no evidence to suggest that it benefits anorexia per se. Similar results are reported in the literature for binge eating behaviour associated with bulimia. Grilo, Crosby, Wilson and Masheb (2012) report a 12-month follow-up study of individuals treated with CBT and Fluoxetine, and suggest treatment was most effective when individuals were treated with CBT and a placebo rather than Fluoxetine only or CBT and Fluoxetine.

✳ Sample question   *Essay*

With reference to one eating disorder, critically discuss the aetiology, prevalence and treatment approaches of the disorder.

CRITICAL FOCUS

Developments in eating disorder research

The relationship between eating disorders, treatment approaches and attachment theory is a relatively new development in eating disorder research. Early research studies suggest individuals with attachment-associated insecurities are the least likely to benefit from current symptom-focused therapies, and instead focus should be placed on attachment functioning. Cognitive behavioural therapies focusing on treating restrained eating, disinhibited eating and weight and size concerns are commonplace (Fairburn, Cooper, & Shafran, 2003); however, factors including intolerance, interpersonal problems, low self-esteem and clinical perfectionism, commonly associated with attachment theory, may hinder an individual's treatment.

Further reading Attachment theory and eating disorder treatment

Key reading

Tasca, G. A., Ritchie, K., & Balfour, L. (2011). Implications of attachment theory and research for the assessment and treatment of eating disorders. *Psychotherapy, 48*(3), 249–259.

Chapter summary – pulling it all together

→ Can you tick all the points from the revision checklist at the beginning of this chapter?

→ Attempt the sample question from the beginning of this chapter using the answer guidelines below.

→ Go to the companion website at www.pearsoned.co.uk/psychologyexpress to access more revision support online, including interactive quizzes, flashcards, You be the marker exercises as well as answer guidance for the Test your knowledge and Sample questions from this chapter.

Answer guidelines

✳ Sample question	Essay

Critically examine the evidence that anorexia nervosa and bulimia nervosa are primarily a result of sociocultural influence.

Approaching the question

This question requires you to firstly define what is meant by the terms anorexia nervosa (AN) and bulimia nervosa (BN). You should also discuss the prevalence and extent of EDNOS, particularly as many individuals will be diagnosed with EDNOS due to part-presence of other eating disorders. You should carefully consider the role of diagnostic criteria and whether such criteria account for the full spectrum of eating disorders.

In critically examining the evidence you should present research-based evidence to construct an argument as to whether AN and BN are primarily the result of sociocultural influence. In doing so, you should consider the role of social and cultural influences in eating disorders whilst maintaining a psychological answer and not one dominated by media references. You should also consider Western views of 'attractiveness' and 'thinness' and the extent to which these may be influencing other cultures, in addition to the role such values are having within their own culture.

You should ensure that your answer contains research-based evidence and theoretical approaches to support the claims that you make and to help you construct an argument before reaching a reasoned conclusion. The question is asking you to make a judgement, based on the presented evidence, as to whether AN and BN are predominately the result of sociocultural factors or whether there are other contributing factors.

Important points to include

- In answering the question you should outline the diagnostic criteria, definition, prevalence and aetiology for both AN and BN. You should state where there are similarities in prevalence patterns for example and any comorbidity issues. When discussing AN, it is important to distinguish between Type 1 and Type 2 behaviours. Your answer should also outline differences in diagnostic criteria. To further strengthen your answer and to provide the necessary critical strand required you should consider controversial aspects of diagnostic criteria and whether this is reflective of sociocultural influence, e.g. amenorrhea.

- The key element of the question is to carefully and critically consider the role of sociocultural factors, and as such, you should such an appreciation of how family systems may influence eating behaviour (e.g. Haworth-Hoeppner, 2000), and in turn any differences culturally, e.g. ethnicity differences as outlined by Steiner and Lock (1998). Whilst the question does not have an explicit focus on treatment approaches per se, through discussing how social factors are translated into behavioural outcomes via cognitive processes, you can consider the role of CBT as an effective treatment approach and whether such an approach is malleable to sociocultural influence, e.g. social groups.

- You should also consider the role of weight-related self-schema, and how the internalised self-schema governs behaviour in regards to whether other individuals are perceived as fatter or thinner than the individual and the resulting influence on the individual's cognitive thought process.

- Contemporary research, e.g. Tasca, Ritchie and Balfour (2011), suggests a link between infant attachment and eating disorders. You should critically consider the role of attachment theory both in relation to the onset of AN and BN, and treatment approaches. Attachment theory is highly relevant to the question since it is reflective of the sociocultural familiar environment.

● You should also consider whether other factors, beyond sociocultural ones, play a role in the onset of AN and BN, e.g. neuropsychological evidence suggesting deficits in frontal cortex function so resulting in poor executive functioning.

Make your answer stand out

In discussing the role of sociocultural factors you should not only concentrate on women but should also consider men with AN and BN. Whilst this group remains relatively small, male eating disorders can be associated with other predictive factors including excessive exercise regimes, distorted body image and sexuality (Weltzin et al., 2012) which are both reflective and non-reflective of sociocultural influence. Broadening the discussion of eating disorders to include both men and women will demonstrate a fuller appreciation of the issues associated with such disorders.

Explore the accompanying website at www.pearsoned.co.uk/psychologyexpress

→ Prepare more effectively for exams and assignments using the answer guidelines for questions from this chapter.

→ Test your knowledge using multiple choice questions and flashcards.

→ Improve your essay skills by exploring the You be the marker exercises.

Notes

Notes

10

Developmental disorders

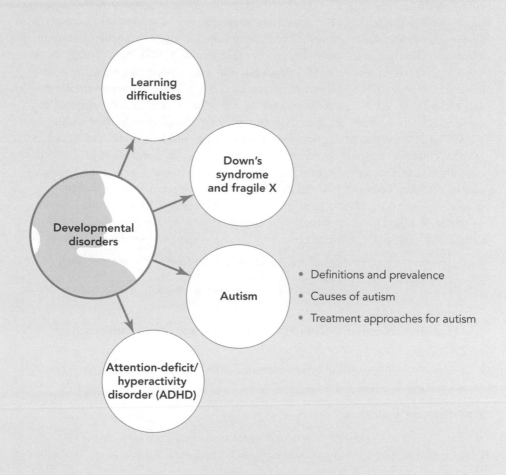

Learning difficulties

Down's syndrome and fragile X

Developmental disorders

Autism
- Definitions and prevalence
- Causes of autism
- Treatment approaches for autism

Attention-deficit/ hyperactivity disorder (ADHD)

A printable version of this topic map is available from
www.pearsoned.co.uk/psychologyexpress

Introduction

Developmental disorders can be broadly categorised into three groups: learning difficulties, autism and attention deficit/hyperactivity disorder (ADHD). The term 'learning difficulty' is the frequently, although not universally, adopted (Inglis & Swain, 2012; Kavale, Spaulding, & Beam, 2009) term, referring to conditions where the defining characteristic is one of significant impairment of intellectual functioning. Previously, individuals with learning difficulties may have been referred to as 'handicapped', 'retarded' or 'disabled' regardless of how profound their intellectual deficit may have been. The shift in terminology reflects a move away from prejudice-laden labels to understanding deficits in intellectual functioning.

Learning difficulties typically refer to developmental disorders where the onset occurs before the age of 18 and exclude onset caused by trauma or neurological illness later in life. An important distinction should be made, however, between learning difficulties more generally and specific learning difficulties (SpLD), since learning difficulties also refer to individuals who experience general difficulties in acquiring new skills and knowledge associated with an intelligence quotient (IQ) of less than 70. IQ is therefore seen as a marker of not just an individual's general cognitive ability but also their potential to learn. An individual with a low IQ will be assessed as having low learning potential and learning difficulty, which may be classified as 'low', 'medium' or 'severe'. This is in contrast to an individual with a SpLD as they will demonstrate variable ability to learn with good to high scores on many skills but marked deficits in specific areas. Dyslexia (deficits in reading, writing and automatic information processing), for example, is one example of a SpLD. Whilst educational psychologists will focus on both learning difficulties and SpLDs, clinicians primarily focus on general learning difficulties.

> ### → Revision checklist
>
> *Essential points to revise are:*
> ❏ Learning difficulties: definition, aetiology and social interventions
> ❏ Autism
> ❏ Attention-deficit/hyperactivity disorder (ADHD)

Assessment advice

● It is important to consider developmental disorders generally, and in particular autism spectrum disorders (ASDs) and ADHD, on a spectrum rather an absolute. Many children may demonstrate behaviours that could see them classified as lacking in attention or being hyperactive, however, it should be questioned whether such children have ADHD. Further, you should consider the usefulness of diagnostic criteria and the extent to which criteria may lead to both the over- and under-diagnosis of developmental disorders.

- The role of the environment and wider environmental factors is key in many developmental disorders and you should consider whether disorders have a primarily genetic or environmental component and the extent to which the two interact.

- Although psychopharmacological treatments may be applicable in some cases, for other developmental disorders, e.g. learning difficulties, such approaches are without merit. You should carefully consider how individuals with developmental disorders should be 'treated' and the approaches that should be adopted. Further, you should critically question whether behavioural techniques such as operant conditioning are effective, particularly in relation to their susceptibility for extinction, and whether they are ethical.

- The role of transactional relationships (Sameroff & Fiese, 2000) is key to many developmental disorders since this is the interrelation between parent, child and environment. You should consider the dyadic relationship between parents and children and in turn how the environment affects both.

Sample question

Could you answer this question? Below is a typical essay question that could arise on this topic.

✳ *Sample question*   *Essay*

With reference to empirical evidence and at least *two* developmental disorders, critically discuss the role of IQ in those disorders.

Learning difficulties

Approximately 1–3% of the population fall into the learning difficulty category (Hodapp & Dykens, 1996), that is falling two standard deviations below the population mean of 100. Within this category, four subcategories, reflective of both DSM-IV-TR (APA, 2000) and ICD-10 classification of 'mental retardation' exist (Table 10.1).

Key term

Learning difficulty: definitions have varied across time, groups and nations. However, many definitions retain two essential features at their core: deficit in intellectual function and deficit in adaptive function (MacKay, 2009). Adaptive function refers to an individual's ability to exercise personal independence and social responsibility (Doll, 1953). The role of intellectual function is most markedly assessed via the use of IQ scores with individuals categorised into one of four sub-groups reflecting the extent of their socio-intellectual functioning.

Table 10.1 Learning difficulty sub-categories in relation to IQ scores

IQ score range	Severity of learning difficulty	Percentage of all individuals classified with a learning difficulty	Characteristics
<20	Profound	2–3%	Profound physical, sensory and mental difficulties, unable to communicate using language and demonstrate mobility problems. Individuals require lifelong (care home or hospitalisation) care.
20–35	Severe	2–3%	Ability to communicate at a simple level although lack motivation and require institutionalised care regime.
35–50	Moderate	10%	Learning difficulties combined with other neurological difficulties, e.g. motor skills, and individual may demonstrate reduced mobility. Individuals live independently within family or group homes.
50–70	Mild	85%	Demonstrable learning difficulties at schools, e.g. behavioural problems and low achievement. More likely to have unskilled job as an adult and require ongoing financial and social assistance.

Whilst IQ is unequivocally associated with learning difficulties, recent research (e.g. Alloway, 2009) has argued that working memory plays a more important role in predicting learning ability in children with learning difficulties. The role of working memory is perceived as important since it is not influenced by prior experience or socioeconomic background and, as such, is linked to a direct capacity to learn (Alloway, Gathercole, Willis, & Adams, 2005), rather than assessing what has previously been learnt.

Although prevalence figures between 1 and 3% (Hodapp & Dykens, 1996) are widely acknowledged, prevalence varies both within and among countries. A study by King, State, Shah, Davanzo and Dykens (1997) suggests that although the overall percentage of children with learning difficulties (6–17 years of age) within the USA (based on the US Department for Education Database) fell within the 1% range, variability across the country ranged between 0.3 and 3%. Within the UK, prevalence figures are approximately 2.5% (derived from the number of individuals in the population who score at or less two standard deviations below the mean). Similar to US data, variability also exists within countries with Whitaker and Porter (2002), for example, suggesting prevalence rates in West Yorkshire of only 0.29%.

MacKay (2009) suggests that differences in prevalence rates can partly be attributed to the accuracy of administrative data of individuals receiving particular services and as such figures may underrepresent the true prevalence picture. Whilst epidemiological studies could provide a more accurate reflection of prevalence, such studies require significant control, are expensive and raise various ethical issues. Whitaker (2004) argues that epidemiological studies would identify 95% of the study population as non-cases and questions whether the 5% identified as having a learning difficulty would readily identify with either the label or service provision associated with it.

Although for many individuals there is no known biological cause, approximately 25% of learning difficulties have an identifiable cause, as given in Table 10.2.

Table 10.2 **Aetiology of learning difficulties**

Aetiology	Percentage of cases	Example conditions
Unknown	25	
Postnatal	10	Trauma, e.g. **encephalitis** (inflammation of the brain tissue caused by either a virus or autoimmune conditions)
Pre- and perinatal	10	Parental infection, e.g. rubella or herpes simplex meningitis
Genetic	55	Down's syndrome (trisomy-21) and fragile X syndrome

Source: adapted from Vahabzadeh, Delaffon, Abbas, & Biswass (2011).

Key terms

Epidemiology: the branch of medicine interested in mapping the pattern, causes, distribution and control of disease. An epidemiological study would therefore focus on monitoring aspects of occurrence, distribution and factors associated with spread in order to build a picture for effective control (MacMahon & Trichopoulos, 1996). Epidemiological research can adopt several study designs including experimental studies and observational studies such as cohort and case-control studies.

Encephalitis: a condition whereby the brain becomes inflamed, resulting in changes in mental state such as confusion, drowsiness or disorientation, seizures and personality changes. Encephalitis can be caused by infections such as rubella or post-infection when the auto-immune system reacts to a previous infection at a later date. Finally, the autoimmune system can also cause encephalitis in response to a non-infectious cause such as tumour or an autoimmune disorder, e.g. human immunodeficiency virus (HIV).

Further reading

Topic	Key reading
Classification and prevalence of learning difficulties	MacKay, T. (2009). Severe and complex learning difficulties: Issues of definition, classification and prevalence. *Educational and Child Psychology, 26*(4), 9–18.
Aetiology of learning difficulties	Vahabzadeh, A. B. N., Delaffon, V., Abbas, M., & Biswas, A. B. (2011). Severe learning disability. *InnovAiT, 4*(2), 91–97.

Down's syndrome and fragile X

Down's syndrome is the most common chromosomal anomaly in live born infants and the most frequent form of learning difficulty in industrialised countries (Frid, Drott, Lundell, Rasmussen, & Annerne, 1999). Down's syndrome, also referred to as trisomy-21, is characterised by the full or part presence of a third 21st chromosome (Lejeune, Gautier, & Turpin, 1959).

The prevalence of Down's syndrome has been studied extensively (de Graff et al., 2011) and is estimated at between 1 and 3% of all live births where differences are dependent on maternal age (higher maternal age carries an increased risk of Down's syndrome), distribution in general population and selective abortion rates (Dolk et al., 2005).

Down's syndrome infants are characterised by a single crease across the palm, upwards slanting eyes and sparse straight hair. Down's syndrome is typically associated with IQ scores in the range of 20–50 although higher IQ scores are typically observed during early infancy (Carr, 2012).

Fragile X is the most common cause worldwide of inherited intellectual disability with 1 in 1000 male and 1 in 2500 female births affected by the syndrome. Fragile X results as a deficit within the FMR-1 (fragile X mental retardation) gene located on the X chromosome. Fragile X is more common in men due to XX vs. XY chromosome in women. Women, however, remain a carrier as fragile X is only masked by the normal chromosome.

Fragile X is caused when the FMR-1 gene repeatedly duplicates amino acids, unnecessarily resulting in a longer gene. When repeats are small (fewer than 200) there is no sign of the disorder but when repeats are large, learning deficits associated with fragile X are observed. Fragile X is associated with anatomical abnormalities in the striatum, which in turn results in a deficit in procedural learning (Bussy, Charrin, Brun, Curie, & des Portes, 2011). Procedural learning refers to rule-based motor skill learning and storage.

The characteristics of fragile X can be classified into physical, developmental and behavioural:

- *Physical*. Smooth and soft skin with prominent ears and high forehead, resulting in an elongated face. Following the onset of puberty the individual may develop an enlarged jaw.
- *Developmental*. Intellectual disability (including reduced IQ) is the most marked characteristic of fragile X. Individuals demonstrate poor fine motor skills and females tend to have a higher propensity towards anxiety disorders.
- *Behavioural*. Problems with self-regulation, e.g. inability to control emotions, toilet-training problems during infancy and hyperactivity.

The normalisation movement (Wolfensberger, 1972) proved to be a pivotal movement for individuals with learning difficulties and sparked a move away from institutionalised settings towards more 'normal' living conditions. The movement focused on individuals being able to live a life as close to normal as possible, maintain behaviour close to their cultural norms and live with normal rhythms to their lives.

Psychological interventions for individuals with learning difficulties utilise principles of operant conditioning to either reduce inappropriate behaviour or teach skills to maximise ability. Behaviourists (e.g. Skinner) believe that all behaviour is learned and maintained by consequence, which can either be positive via reinforcement or negative via punishment. When behaviour is reinforced either though a positive stimulus or the removal of an aversive stimulus, behaviour increases. When behaviour is punished either through the presentation of an aversive stimulus or isolation from a reinforcer, behaviour decreases (Table 10.3).

Table 10.3 Reinforcement and punishment in operant conditioning

Reinforcement		
Positive reinforcement	Presentation of positive stimulus	Behaviour increases
Negative reinforcement	Removal of aversive stimulus	Behaviour increases
Punishment		
Positive punishment	Presentation of aversive stimulus	Behaviour decreases
Time-out	Isolation from reinforcer	Behaviour decreases
Response cost	Positive stimulus removed, e.g. pocket money	Behaviour decreases

Test your knowledge

10.1 How are learning difficulties defined?

10.2 What role does IQ play in the definition of learning difficulties?

10.3 What is the prevalence and aetiology of learning difficulties?

10.4 What problems exist in determining the prevalence of learning difficulties?

Answers to the questions can be found on the companion website at: www.pearsoned.co.uk/psychologyexpress

Further reading Operant conditioning and learning difficulties

Key reading

Wishart, J. G. (1991). Learning difficulties in infants with Down's syndrome. *International Journal of Rehabilitation Research, 14*(3), 252–255.

Autism

Definitions and prevalence

Autism is characterised as a pervasive developmental disorder with impairments most notably in social interaction and communication skills. For a child to be classified as autistic or as having an 'autistic disorder', the child should demonstrate the following prior to reaching three years of age: a qualitative impairment in social interaction, qualitative impairments in communication, and restricted, repetitive and stereotyped patterns of behaviour and interests. Further, the child should demonstrate a total of six symptoms with at least two from the first section and one from each of the second and third sections in Table 10.4.

Table 10.4 DSM-IV-TR (APA, 2000) autism classification

Section	Characteristics
Section A: Qualitative impairment in social interaction	Impairment in using non-verbal behaviours such as eye contact, body language and facial expressions.
	Inability to develop and maintain peer relationships.
	Lack of social or emotional reciprocity.
	Inability to seek spontaneously enjoyment, achievements or interests with other people.
Section B: Qualitative impairments in communication	Developmental delay in the onset of language development or total absence of spoken language development.
	Inability to initiate or sustain spoken conversation.
	Use of idiosyncratic language or repetitive use of language.
	Lack of spontaneity in play.
Section C: Restricted, repetitive and stereotyped patterns of behaviour and interests	Stereotyped and repetitive behaviour.
	Preoccupation with parts of objects.
	Inflexible and persistent use of non-functional routines.

Autism is more commonly characterised on a spectrum ranging from full autism (reflective of the classification above) to pervasive developmental disorder not otherwise specified (PDD-NOS), to the milder version of Asperger's syndrome (Solomon & Chung, 2012). Therefore, it is more common to refer to autism spectrum disorders (ASDs) rather than 'autistic disorder' and other associated diagnostic labels. This will be reflected by the changes to both diagnostic criteria and the labels used for ASDs in DSM-5 (Swedo, 2009).

In proposed revisions for DSM-5, ASD diagnosis will focus on two domains: persistent deficits in social communication and social interaction across contexts, and restricted, repetitive patterns of behaviour, interests or activities (Solomon & Chung, 2012).

Peeters and Gillberg (1999) suggest approximately 80% of children with autism score lower than 70 on IQ tests and as such demonstrate profound learning difficulties. Other studies report that 50–70% of children with ASD are reported to have an intellectual disability (Yeargin-Allsopp et al., 2003).

UK prevalence figures vary between studies, with some figures suggesting prevalence as high as 157 cases per 10,000 children (1.6%; Baron-Cohen et al., 2009) and other studies suggesting figures between 0.2 and 1% (Baird et al., 2006). Despite discrepancies in figures, UK prevalence clusters around 1% across studies (Green, McGinnity, Meltzer, Ford, & Goodman, 2005). US prevalence figures reflect those in the UK with ASD diagnosis estimations of 1 in 91 children (1%) in the early 21st century compared with 0.05% in the 1980s (Kogan et al., 2009). Increases in ASD diagnosis have been observed across many Western countries and whilst the reasons for such increases remain unclear, two suggestions are that either diagnosis has become better or public perception has become better and in turn more children are being diagnosed.

KEY STUDY

Autism: Harpreet

Harpreet is an 18-month-old boy living in Manchester. Harpreet has two brothers and a younger sister but he never wishes to play with any of them and his parents have become worried about him. Harpreet's mother has noticed that he does not respond to her touch and appears to be 'unloving', which she finds very upsetting. Harpreet spends a considerable amount of time flicking his fingers across his face and demonstrates a number of repetitive body movements. When Harpreet's father tries to engage in eye contact with his son, Harpreet tries to avoid his father's gaze and prefers to look beyond him. Harpreet's father has also noticed that on two occasions Harpreet has spoken back a phrase exactly as he said it to him but several days later. Harpreet's family are becoming increasingly concerned about his strange behaviour and are not sure what to do.

The case study reflects many of the social isolation, ritualistic acts and communication deficits present in ASDs. Many children with ASD demonstrate social isolation and are unlikely to engage in social activities with other children or their parents. When parents attempt to engage in eye contact, the child is unable to perceive any social message in the act (Ristic et al., 2005) and instead prefers to look away. Children with ASDs are more likely to engage in ritualistic behaviour and play rather than symbolic play and when disrupted from their pattern can demonstrate considerable distress. Repetition of previously spoken words or phrases is known as echolalia and is viewed as an attempt at communication. Children with ASDs may also demonstrate pronoun reversal and refer to themselves in the third person.

Test your knowledge

10.5 How is autism defined?

10.6 What is the difference between autism and autism spectrum disorders?

10.7 What communication deficits do children with ASDs experience?

Answers to the questions can be found on the companion website at:
www.pearsoned.co.uk/psychologyexpress

Causes of autism

A significant body of evidence suggests that autism is an organic disorder caused by prenatal, perinatal, postnatal or early childhood damage to the central nervous system (CNS). Baird et al. (2006) suggest that autism results from a variety of causal pathways. Furthermore, some individuals are more genetically susceptible to autism, suggesting a genetic link. Frith (1987), for example, demonstrated an autism concordance rate of 36% for monozygotic twins and 0% for dizygotic twins. Whilst the actual 'causes' of autism remain controversial a number of potential causes are reported (Table 10.5).

Table 10.5 Reported causes of autism

Reported causes of autism	Evidence
Metal metabolism disorder	Increase in heavy metals (e.g. zinc, copper and mercury), present in the blood and urine of individuals with autism (Walsh, Usman, & Tarpey, 2001), suggesting defective metallothionein in these individuals. Metallothioneins are metal-binding proteins and in individuals with autism these proteins are defective.
Measles mumps rubella (MMR) vaccine	A number of studies have not found an association between autism and the MMR vaccine (e.g. DeStefano, 2007), but a study by Goldman and Yazbak (2004) suggests a temporal association between the introduction of an MMR vaccine in Denmark and an increase in autism.
Genetics	Rodier (2000) argues that there is indisputable evidence for a genetic component to autism. Twin studies suggest different prevalence figures between monozygotic twins; however, DeFrancesco (2001) suggests that if one twin is autistic, there is a 90% chance the other will have some form of autism compared with 2–3% for dizygotic twins.
Genetic comorbidity	The FMR-1 gene associated with fragile X is associated with autism with a greater prosperity of children with fragile X being diagnosed with an ASD (Farzin et al., 2006).
Infections	The rubella virus was the first known cause of autism (Ziring, 2001) and additionally measles and mumps can result in encephalitis, which can result in autism at a later date.

▶

Table 10.5 Continued

Reported causes of autism	Evidence
Clinical comorbidity	Although not necessarily a cause of autism, Morgan, Roy and Chance (2003) report comorbidity between autism and a number of psychiatric disorders including: major depression, bipolar disorder, schizophrenia and hypertension.
Parental age	Increases in parental age have been tentatively linked to ASD (Parner, Baron-Cohen, & Lauritsen, 2012), although results are not fully conclusive.

A number of genetic causes and/or inflammation of the brain are well documented in respect of the causes of autism. However, Ratajczak (2011) suggests that inflammation could be attributed to a wide range of environmental toxins, e.g. metals, infections (e.g. rubella) and comorbidities in individuals genetically prone to the developmental disorder.

> **Further reading Parental age and autism spectrum disorders**
>
> *Key reading*
>
> Parner, E. T., Baron-Cohen, S., Lauritsen, M. B., Jorgensen, M., Schieve, L. A., Yeargin-Allsopp, M., & Obel, C. (2012). Parental age and autism spectrum disorders. *Annals of Epidemiology, 22*(3), 143–150.

Treatment approaches for autism

Neuroleptic drugs which block the effects of dopamine, e.g. Haloperidol, have been effective in treating the symptoms of autism such as stereotyped behaviour and withdrawal (Campbell, Adams, Perry, Spencer, & Overall, 1988). Risperidone (an antipsychotic drug more commonly associated with the treatment of schizophrenia and schizoaffective disorder) has also been reported as beneficial in reducing severe behavioural problems, aggression and self-inflicted injury behaviour in individuals with autism.

Behavioural treatment approaches focus on direct reinforcement of behaviours such as speech or pro-social behaviour, e.g. eye contact and symbolic play. In some treatment programmes inappropriate behaviours such as self-injury may be followed by an aversive stimulus including electric shocks or smell of ammonia (Koegel, Koegel, & McNerney, 2001).

Many individuals with ASDs experience social anxiety disorder, causing the individual to experience anxiety and psychological distress when faced with social situations. Since social anxiety is often integral to ASDs it is often under-diagnosed and under-treated (SIGN, 2007). McCorkindale (2011) suggests Cognitive Behavioural Therapy (CBT) is an effective treatment approach for individuals with ASDs who experience social anxiety.

Sensory-integration therapy (SIT) has been used as a treatment approach to help target the inefficient neurological processing of sensory information in children with autism. Watling, Deitz, Kanny and McLaughlin (1999) report that 82% of occupational therapists surveyed in their study use SIT with children with autism. SIT reports that individuals with autism may experience problems integrating information from the vestibular and tactile systems (Devlin, Healy, Leader, & Hughes, 2011). The vestibular system provides sensory input to the brain about the body's movement through space, and impairment results in poor posture and difficulties in planning motor actions. Tactile deficits are demonstrated as a lack of sensitivity or over-sensitivity to sensory stimuli. SIT provides sensory stimulation through activities such as jumping, rocking and trampolining. Additionally, weighted vests, oral motor exercises and body brushing are used to provide sensory stimulation and improve arousal states (Wilbarger, 1995).

The effectiveness of SIT remains inconclusive, despite numerous studies researching effectiveness. Vargas and Camili (1999), following a meta-analysis of 32 SIT studies, report that well-designed and rigorous studies did not benefit individuals receiving SIT intervention.

Test your knowledge

10.8 To what extent can autism and ASDs be attributed to generic factors?

10.9 To what extent does inflammation of the brain contribute towards autism and ASDs?

10.10 What treatment approaches are used in autism?

Answers to these questions can be found on the companion website at: www.pearsoned.co.uk/psychologyexpress

---

✳ Sample question   Essay

With reference to empirical evidence, critically consider the effectiveness of treatment approaches for ASDs.

Attention-deficit/hyperactivity disorder (ADHD)

DSM-IV-TR (APA, 2000) identifies three categories of attention-deficit/hyperactivity disorder (ADHD): problems of poor attention, hyperactive-impulsive behaviour and a combination of poor attention and hyperactive-impulsive behaviour. Although the behaviours can be viewed separately, most children demonstrate both and for a diagnosis of ADHD to be made, children should engage in at least six of the behaviours in Table 10.6 and for a duration of at least six months. The behaviours should occur at both home and school, and have an onset age of seven years and under, and should significantly impair the individual. Many children with ADHD fail to recognise that behaviour

Table 10.6 DSM-IV-TR (2000) ADHD diagnostic criteria

Inattention	Hyperactivity-impulsivity
Failure to pay close attention to details and makes careless errors at school and in other activities.	Rather than sitting still, squirms in seat and fidgets.
Difficulty paying attention during play or keeping to task.	Leaves seat inappropriately despite being told to stay seated.
Doesn't appear to listen when being told something or spoken to.	Experiences difficulties in playing quietly or engaging in leisurely activity.
Experiences difficulties in organising tasks or activities.	Appears continually driven and 'on the go'.
Appears routinely forgetful.	Talks excessively.
Easily distracted away from primary task.	Interrupts others and answers questions before they have been fully asked.
Dislikes tasks involving mental effort, e.g. homework.	Experiences difficulties in waiting turn.

is annoying, even though they may recognise this in hypothetical situations (Whalen, Henker, & Hinshaw, 1985).

ADHD is neither culturally nor socially bound, and occurs across all ethnic groups (Selikowitz, 2004). Prevalence figures vary by country and study, with US prevalence reported between 5 and 8% (Goldstein, 2006) and UK figures between 0.5 and 1% (Taylor & Hemsley, 1995). Prevalence figures may vary between countries as a result of ADHD being underdiagnosed or underreported in the UK (Kewley, 1995).

Dysfunction of the dopaminergic system resulting in low levels of dopamine has been associated with ADHD, and in particular, failure of activation of dopamine D4 and D5 receptors.

Castellanos et al. (1996, 2002) report smaller frontal lobes among children with ADHD than in control children. This suggests such children may experience problems associated with executive functioning and demonstrate deficits in decision-making and control of inappropriate behaviour.

Psychological explanations of ADHD suggest that children with ADHD are characterised by impulsivity rather than hyperactivity and simply act out and do what other children are thinking (Barkley, 1997). Barkley (1997) suggests ADHD is a failure to inhibit inappropriate responses to environmental acts.

> CRITICAL FOCUS

Is ADHD a series of psychosocial symptomatic behaviours?

The diagnostic terms used in classification, including forgetfulness, inattentiveness, hyperactivity and impulsivity, have led some researchers (e.g. Burton, 2011) to question whether such criteria are useful and whether ADHD is really a singular disorder or a series of psychosocial symptomatic behaviours. This assertion is made based on the lack of neuropsychological evidence suggesting a uniformly physiological pathology (Rosemond & Ravenel, 2009) or a unique aetiology for ADHD. Despite the lack of neuropsychological evidence, one of the predominant treatment approaches, particularly for boys, is stimulant medication (Burton, 2011), drawing into question whether such medication is truly effective.

Environmental risks have been tentatively associated with ADHD. However, as correlation does not equate to causation, Thapar, Cooper, Eyre and Langley (2013) advise caution when considering environmental risks since 'many observed associations could arise as a consequence of child and/or parent psychopathology or disposition (e.g. negative mother-child relationship)' (2013: 8).

Patterson, DeGarmo and Forgatch (2004) suggest a strong causal link between negative parenting, maltreatment and poverty, and ADHD. Other environmental risks are outlined in Table 10.7.

Table 10.7 Environmental risks associated with ADHD

Pre- and perinatal factors	Dietary factors	Psychosocial adversity
Maternal smoking, alcohol and substance misuse. *Risk but not proven causal risk factor.*	Nutritional deficiencies, e.g. zinc and magnesium. *Correlated risk although not proven risk factor.*	Family adversity and low income. *Correlated risk although not proven risk factor.*
Maternal stress. *Risk but not proven causal risk factor.*	Nutritional surpluses, e.g. sugar and food colouring. *Correlated risk although not proven risk factor.*	Conflict/parent–child hostility. *Correlated risk although not proven risk factor.*
Low birth weight and prematurity. *Risk but not proven risk factor.*		Severely early deprivation. *Risk and a likely causal risk factor.*

Source: adapted from Thapar et al. (2013).

The internal dialogue theory (Barkley, 1997; Barkley, Edwards, Laneri, Fletcher, & Metevia, 2001) proposes that at between three and four years of age children develop an internal dialogue and use this as they grow older as means of self-control. A characteristic of ADHD is that children experience disorganised internal dialogue; in turn this influences how they process external events, which are commonly also processed as disorganised. Instead of their dialogue focusing on planning for the future, it instead focuses on the present, e.g. here and now, rather than future planning. As a result children with ADHD experience difficulties in planning and abstract issues and never reach a point but instead talk around concepts. The lack of planning and poor organisation combined with limited self-control is reflective of frontal cortex deficit suggested by Castellanos et al. (1996, 2002).

The most widely prescribed pharmacological treatment for ADHD is Ritalin (methylphenidate), with reported effectiveness rates of approximately 60% in the prescribed condition compared with 10% in the control condition in one study (Wender, Wolf, & Wasserstein, 2001). The prescription of Ritalin, however, is not without controversy, partly because of the side effects, which include loss of appetite, weight loss, insomnia, increased heart rate and vomiting. The prescription of Ritalin is also controversial since Widener (1998) estimates that as many as 5 million US children are currently being medicated for ADHD with Ritalin and that many parents do not fully understand the requirement for more psychological rather than pharmacological treatment approaches.

Psychotherapies where children and adults are treated in parallel may be sufficient to address hyperactive behaviour without the need for medication (Pozzi-Monzo, 2012). In addition to psychotherapy, operant approaches such as token economies have also been used effectively with children with ADHD (Pelham et al., 1993). Collecting tokens in response to desired behaviour, e.g. sitting quietly, helps children to learn that desired behaviour is good and undesired behaviour will not be reinforced.

In educational settings many ADHD behaviours are an immediate response to environmental factors reflecting the bio-social relationship in ADHD. The Educational Resources Information Centre (ERIC) has developed a series of guidelines to help teachers manage children with ADHD:

- Seat students at the front of the class and with their backs to the remainder of the class to prevent distraction from other children.
- Provide role models to students with ADHD to demonstrate exemplary behaviour.
- Avoid placing distracting stimuli in the classroom.
- Provide stimuli-free or reduced stimuli areas for teaching and concentration.

Further reading	
Topic	*Key reading*
Causes of ADHD	Thapar, A., Cooper, M., Eyre, O., & Langley, K. (2013). Practitioner review: What have we learnt about the causes of ADHD? *The Journal of Child Psychology and Psychiatry*, *54*(1), 3–16.
ADHD treatment approaches and Ritalin	Pozzi-Monzo, M. (2012). Ritalin for whom? Revisited: Further thinking on ADHD. *Journal of Child Psychotherapy*, *38*(1), 49–60.

Chapter summary – pulling it all together

→ Can you tick all the points from the revision checklist at the beginning of this chapter?

→ Attempt the sample question from the beginning of this chapter using the answer guidelines below.

→ Go to the companion website at www.pearsoned.co.uk/psychologyexpress to access more revision support online, including interactive quizzes, flashcards, You be the marker exercises as well as answer guidance for the Test your knowledge and Sample questions from this chapter.

Answer guidelines

> **✱ Sample question**   **Essay**
>
> With reference to empirical evidence and at least *two* developmental disorders, critically discuss the role of IQ in those disorders.

Approaching the question

This question requires you to draw on empirical evidence to critically discuss whether IQ plays a role in the diagnosis, aetiology and treatment approach to any two developmental disorders. Although the question does not explicitly state that you should focus on the role of IQ in diagnosis, aetiology and treatment, since it requires you to fully consider and critically discuss the role of IQ, it is asking you to consider how IQ may influence all aspects of a developmental disorder.

It is important that you choose two developmental disorders and fully explain to the same extent the role that IQ plays. Importantly, you should choose two different disorders to demonstrate breadth of knowledge in addition to the depth of knowledge demonstrated through the critical discussion.

You should ensure that your answer contains research-based evidence and theoretical approaches to support the claims that you make and to help you construct an argument before reaching a reasoned conclusion.

Important points to include

- It is important to fully discuss the role of IQ in relation to two developmental disorders. In introducing developmental disorders you should show an appreciation of disorders as spectrum rather absolute disorders, and this is particularly important when considering ASDs and ADHD. Although children may demonstrate a particular series of behaviours it should be critically questioned whether the behaviours are truly reflective of an actual disorder (see Critical Focus box). You should carefully consider the usefulness of diagnostic criteria and pay particular reference to the role of IQ in such criteria, to question the extent to which criteria may result in both the over- and under-diagnosis of developmental disorders.

- In selecting two developmental disorders you should choose two disorders where IQ is strongly involved in the diagnosis and may impact on treatment approaches. If autism was selected as one of the disorders, you should critically consider the suggestion that approximately 80% of children with autism score lower than 70 on IQ tests (Peeters & Gillberg, 1999) and the extent to which children with ASD have an intellectual disability. You should compare and contrast the implications of a lower IQ in terms of cognitive and social functioning with another developmental disorder, e.g. fragile X or Down's syndrome.

- In treating developmental disorders you should consider the role of CBT and the applicability and successfulness of using such an approach with individuals with low IQs. You should also consider the role of medication in treating developmental disorders.

> **Make your answer stand out**
>
> *Whilst many developmental disorders are treated with CBT techniques some, such as ADHD, are treated with medication. Considering the limited neuropsychological evidence for ADHD as having a biological basis, combined with individuals with ADHD having on average an IQ nine points lower than the mean (Frazier, Demaree, & Youngstrom, 2004), you should carefully consider the ability of individuals to make choices about the treatment approach applicable to them.*

Explore the accompanying website at www.pearsoned.co.uk/psychologyexpress

→ Prepare more effectively for exams and assignments using the answer guidelines for questions from this chapter.

→ Test your knowledge using multiple choice questions and flashcards.

→ Improve your essay skills by exploring the You be the marker exercises.

Notes

Notes

And finally, before the exam . . .

How to approach revision from here

You should be now at a reasonable stage in your revision process – you should have developed your skills and knowledge base over your course and used this text judiciously during that period. Now, however, you have used the book to reflect on, remind yourself of and reinforce the material you have researched over the year/seminar. You will, of course, need to do additional reading and research to that included here (and appropriate directions are provided) but you will be well on your way with the material presented in this book.

It is important that in answering any question in psychology you take a research- and evidence-based approach to your response. For example, do not make generalised or sweeping statements that cannot be substantiated or supported by evidence from the literature. Remember as well that the evidence should not be anecdotal – it is of no use citing your mum, dad, best friend or the latest news from a celebrity website. After all, you are not writing an opinion piece – you are crafting an argument that is based on current scientific knowledge and understanding. You need to be careful about the evidence you present: do review the material and from where it was sourced.

Furthermore, whatever type of assessment you have to undertake, it is important to take an evaluative approach to the evidence. Whether you are writing an essay, sitting an exam or designing a webpage, the key advice is to avoid simply presenting a descriptive answer. Rather, it is necessary to think about the strength of the evidence in each area. One of the key skills for psychology students is critical thinking and for this reason the tasks featured in this series focus upon developing this way of thinking. Thus you are not expected to simply learn a set of facts and figures, but to think about the implications of what we know and how this might be applied in everyday life. The best assessment answers are the ones that take this critical approach.

It is also important to note that psychology is a theoretical subject: when answering any question about psychology, not only refer to the prevailing theories of the field, but outline the development of them as well. It is also important to evaluate these theories and models either through comparison with other models and theories or through the use of studies that have assessed them and highlighted their strengths and weaknesses. It is essential to read widely – within each section of this book there are directions to interesting and pertinent papers relating to the specific topic area. Find these papers, read these papers and make notes from these papers. But don't stop there. Let them lead you to other sources that may be important to the field. One thing that an examiner hates to see is the same old sources being cited all of the time: be innovative and, as well as reading the seminal works, find the more obscure and interesting sources as well – just make sure they're relevant to your answer!

How not to revise

Tips on what not to do when it comes to revision

- **Don't avoid revision.** This is the best tip ever. There is something on the TV, the pub is having a two-for-one offer, the fridge needs cleaning, your budgie looks lonely . . . You have all of these activities to do and they need doing now! Really . . . ? Do some revision!
- **Don't spend too long at each revision session.** Working all day and night is not the answer to revision. You do need to take breaks, so schedule your revision so you are not working from dawn until dusk. A break gives time for the information you have been revising to consolidate.
- **Don't worry.** Worrying will cause you to lose sleep, lose concentration and lose revision time by leaving it late and then later. When the exam comes, you will have no revision completed and will be tired and confused.
- **Don't cram.** This is the worst revision technique in the universe! You will not remember the majority of the information that you try to stuff into your skull, so why bother?
- **Don't read over old notes with no plan.** Your brain will take nothing in. If you wrote your lecture notes in September and the exam is in May is there any point in trying to decipher your scrawly handwriting now?
- **Don't write model answers and learn by rote.** When it comes to the exam you will simply regurgitate the model answer irrespective of the question – not a brilliant way to impress the examiner!

Tips for exam success

What you should do when it comes to revision

Exams are one form of assessment that students often worry about the most. The key to exam success, as with many other types of assessment, lies in good preparation and self-organisation. One of the most important things is knowing what to expect – this does not necessarily mean knowing what the questions will be on the exam paper, but rather what the structure of the paper is, how many questions you are expected to answer, how long the exam will last and so on.

To pass an exam you need a good grasp of the course material and, obvious as it may seem, to turn up for the exam itself. It is important to remember that you aren't expected to know or remember everything in the course, but you should be able to show your understanding of what you have studied. Remember as well that examiners are interested in what you know, not what you don't know. They try to write exam questions that give you a good chance of passing – not ones to catch you out or trick you in any way. You may want to consider some of these top exam tips.

- Start your revision in plenty of time.
- Make a revision timetable and stick to it.
- Practise jotting down answers and making essay plans.
- Practise writing against the clock using past exam papers.
- Check that you have really answered the question and have not strayed off the point.
- Review a recent past paper and check the marking structure.
- Carefully select the topics you are going to revise.
- Use your lecture/study notes and refine them further, if possible, into lists or diagrams and transfer them on to index cards/Post-it notes. Mind maps are a good way of making links between topics and ideas.
- Practise your handwriting – make sure it's neat and legible.

One to two days before the exam
- Recheck times, dates and venue.
- Actively review your notes and key facts.
- Exercise, eat sensibly and get a few good nights' sleep.

On the day
- Get a good night's sleep.
- Have a good meal, two to three hours before the start time.
- Arrive in good time.
- Spend a few minutes calming and focussing.

In the exam room
- Keep calm.
- Take a few minutes to read each question carefully. Don't jump to conclusions – think calmly about what each question means and the area it is focussed on.
- Start with the question you feel most confident about. This helps your morale.
- By the same token, don't expend all your efforts on that one question – if you are expected to answer three questions then don't just answer two.
- Keep to time and spread your effort evenly on all opportunities to score marks.
- Once you have chosen a question, jot down any salient facts or key points. Then take five minutes to plan your answer – a spider diagram or a few notes may be enough to focus your ideas. Try to think in terms of 'why and how' not just 'facts'.

- You might find it useful to create a visual plan or map before writing your answer to help you remember to cover everything you need to address.
- Keep reminding yourself of the question and try not to wander off the point.
- Remember that quality of argument is more important than quantity of facts.
- Take 30–60-second breaks whenever you find your focus slipping (typically every 20 minutes).
- Make sure you reference properly – according to your university requirements.
- Watch your spelling and grammar – you could lose marks if you make too many errors.

> ### → Final revision checklist
>
> ❏ Have you revised the topics highlighted in the revision checklists?
> ❏ Have you attended revision classes and taken note of and/or followed up on your lecturers' advice about the exams or assessment process at your university?
> ❏ Can you answer the questions posed in this text satisfactorily? Don't forget to check sample answers on the website too.
> ❏ Have you read the additional material to make your answer stand out?
> ❏ Remember to criticise appropriately – based on evidence.

Test your knowledge by using the material presented in this text or on the website: **www.pearsoned.co.uk/psychologyexpress**.

Glossary

ABC model Describes how our beliefs about particular events can influence our emotional reactions to them. For example, someone who sees a friend in the street but is ignored (A = Activating event) may believe (B = Belief about the event) that their friend no longer likes them and may become depressed as a result (C = Consequence of the belief).

aetiology The cause or origin of a clinical disorder.

amenorrhea Absence of menstrual period in a woman of reproductive age.

amygdala A brain area within the limbic system which plays an important role in emotion.

androgen deprivation therapy Chemical suppression of the production or action of androgens to reduce the male libido.

anorexia nervosa Characterised by a desire to keep the body as thin as possible, resulting in the individual being significantly underweight combined with an intense fear of weight gain. Body weight is maintained below 85% expected for age and height.

anterograde amnesia Inability to lay down new memory traces following the onset of amnesia.

antidepressant medication Medications to treat depression which act by altering levels of neurotransmitter systems.

antipsychotic A class of medication which is used to treat psychotic symptoms.

anxiolytic medication Medication which is used to reduce anxiety.

applied relaxation A treatment used with anxiety disorders where the individual is taught relaxation techniques.

attention deficit-hyperactivity disorder (ADHD) A developmental disorder characterised by problems of poor attention and hyperactive-impulsive behaviour.

autism Characterised as a pervasive developmental disorder with impairments most notably in social interaction and communication skills.

aversion therapy Exposure to undesirable stimulus followed by aversive stimulus.

behavioural activation therapy A treatment for depression with a focus on getting the individual more involved in pleasurable activities.

biopsychosocial The idea that mental illness stems from a combination of biological, psychological and social factors.

blood alcohol content The level of alcohol circulating in the bloodstream at a particular point in time.

borderline personality disorder Characterised by extreme mood variability accompanied with feelings of emptiness or anger and difficulties in making and maintaining relationships due to instability of self-identity and self-harming behaviours.

bulimia nervosa Characterised by recurrent binge eating, recurrent and inappropriate use of compensatory behaviours, including vomiting after eating (to control weight gain), high frequency of eating binges and compensatory behaviour and self-evaluation unduly influenced by body weight and shape.

catalepsy Muscular rigidity where limbs remain fixed in certain positions and there is a lack of response to external stimuli.

catastrophic thinking The belief that the worst will always happen. It typifies the thinking patterns in several anxiety disorders. For example, if someone is late for work they may believe that as a consequence they will get fired and end up living on the street.

circadian rhythms Daily and regular changes in physiological activity which includes the sleep/wake cycle.

cognitive behavioural therapy (CBT) An therapeutic technique widely used in clinical psychology where there is a focus on changing maladaptive behaviour and dysfunctional thought patterns.

cognitive therapy Treatment approach seeking to identify and modify the cognitions and underlying schema driving inappropriate behaviour.

comorbidity The presence of one or more disorders at the same time. Depression and alcohol problems (abuse/dependence) are well documented in terms of comorbidity with alcohol problems in depressed patients recorded at around 16% as opposed to 7% in the general population (Sullivan, Fiellin, & O'Connor, 2005). Disorder comorbidity is particularly problematic in the assessment and treatment of disorders, as major depression, for example, cannot be adequately treated if substance abuse is also present, therefore requiring initial treatment of the substance abuse ahead of treatment for the depressive disorder.

cortisol A hormone released by the adrenal gland in response to stress.

delta 9 tetrahydrocannabinol (THC) The primary psychoactive ingredient in cannabis which increases cerebral dopamine activity.

delusion An irrational belief which is held despite disconfirming evidence.

dopamine Neurotransmitter involved in the control of the brain's reward and pleasure centres.

dopamine hypothesis An influential theory which proposes that schizophrenia is caused by an excess of the neurotransmitter dopamine.

Down's syndrome/trisomy-21 A developmental disorder characterised by the full or part presence of a third 21st chromosome.

drug Any biologically active chemical that does not occur naturally in the human body.

DSM This is the Diagnostic and Statistical Manual for mental disorders, which is the handbook used by clinicians to guide their diagnosis of mental health problems. The DSM-IV TR (Text Revision) was replaced by the DSM-5 in 2013.

Electra complex The neo-Freudian idea that girls desire their fathers and see their mothers as competitors for their father's love.

electroconvulsive therapy (ECT) The administration of an electric current to the brain which is mainly used in depression where other treatments have been ineffective.

emotional awareness training Structured training programme used with individuals with borderline personality disorder to increase levels of self-awareness.

emotion dysregulation Difficulties experienced in the self-regulation of emotions.

encephalitis Inflammation of the brain resulting in altered mental states including confusion, drowsiness, disorientation, seizures and personality changes.

epidemiology A branch of medicine interested in mapping the pattern, causes, distribution and control of diseases.

exposure-based treatment Treatment for phobia which involves exposing the phobic to the feared object or situation.

expressed emotion Emotionally loaded communication patterns between family members which is of a hostile nature and associated with increased relapse rates in schizophrenia.

eye movement desensitisation and reprocessing (EMDR) A treatment sometimes used in post-traumatic stress disorder where the client focusses on the traumatic event whilst engaging in therapist-directed eye movements.

family-focussed therapy (FFT) A psychological treatment for bipolar disorder which focuses on enhancing positive communication patterns between family members.

family intervention Treatment approach involving the familial system with focuses on parenting skills, support and reduction of stress in the family environment.

faulty thinking Maladaptive thinking patterns which play a role in mental health problems.

flashback The sudden reoccurrence of a vivid memory where the individual may believe they are reliving a past event. In post-traumatic stress disorder these flashbacks relate to a traumatic experience and involve extreme feelings of fear.

hallucination A perception of a sensory event (e.g. voice) which has no basis in reality.

heterogeneity The diverse nature and non-comparable aspects of disorders. In relation to eating disorders some individuals may present with partial aspects of anorexia nervosa (extreme fear of weight gain despite being underweight) and partial aspects of bulimia nervosa (purging following eating) and as such prevent a single diagnosis being made.

humours Fluids which were thought to be present in the body in differing quantities; Black Bile, Yellow Bile, Blood and Phlegm. An imbalance of humours was thought to cause madness.

hypomania Symptoms are similar to those in mania, i.e. elevated mood, grandiose ideas and decreased need for sleep. However, unlike during a manic episode, these symptoms are not severe enough to impair functioning. Hypomania can therefore be described as a less severe form of mania.

hysteria Emotional stress which is manifested in physical symptoms.

interoceptive conditioning A type of classical conditioning where changes in bodily state, such as an increase in heart rate, result in feelings of fear and panic so that someone may think they are about to have a heart attack. The change in bodily sensation becomes the conditioned stimulus leading to fear and panic which are the conditioned response.

IQ A mathematical equation measuring the levels of a person's intelligence quotient (IQ).

Korsakoff's syndrome An organic amnesia associated with chronic alcoholism and characterised predominately by anterograde amnesia.

law of effect Thorndike's proposal that any behaviour that is rewarded will be repeated and any behaviour that is followed by negative consequences will not be repeated.

learned helplessness An explanation for depression where an individual believes that they have no control over their environment.

learning difficulty Individuals with an IQ score falling at least two standard deviations below the population mean.

libido The extent of an individual's sexual desire or drive.

masturbatory reconditioning Masturbation to climax following exposure to desirable stimuli.

monoamine neurotransmitters This class of neurotransmitter appears to play a role in emotional regulation, arousal and cognition. A depletion of monoamine neurotransmitters is one of the biological explanations for depression, as medications that increase these neurotransmitter levels also improve mood. They include serotonin, dopamine and norepinephrine.

monozygotic twins Identical twins who share 100% of their genes.

mood-stabilising drugs Medication which is used to treat the symptoms of both mania and depression in bipolar disorder.

negative symptoms A cluster of symptoms seen in schizophrenia including an inability to display the usual range of emotions.

neurotransmitter Chemical enabling the transmission of signals from one neuron to the next via synapses.

Oedipal conflict The Freudian idea where boys desire their mothers and see their fathers as competitors for their mothers love.

paedophilia Intense and recurrent sexual urges, sexually arousing fantasies and sexual activity with a prepubescent child or children.

paraphilia Branch of sexual disorders characterised by reoccurring and intense sexual fantasies, sexual urges or behaviours involving nonhuman objects, humiliation or non-consenting partners.

pharmacological treatment The use of medication to treat the symptoms of mental illness.

pharmacology A branch of medicine focusing on the use, effects and actions of drugs.

polydrug Consumption of more than one drug at the same time.

positive symptoms A cluster of symptoms seen in schizophrenia including hallucinations and delusions.

prefrontal lobotomy A neurosurgical technique where the frontal area of the brain is deliberately damaged in order to produce changes in thought and behaviour.

preparedness theory Suggests that humans have an innate tendency to be afraid of certain objects or situations that could potentially cause us harm, e.g. snakes or heights. By avoiding these things, we have a better chance of survival. This theory is one explanation for the acquisition of phobias and contrasts with other theories which suggest phobias can be learnt.

prevalence The proportion of the population displaying a disorder.

prodromal phase The gradual build-up of schizophrenic symptoms prior to the onset of the full disorder. For example, the individual may start to express odd ideas, have trouble concentrating and become withdrawn.

psychoactive A drug altering mood, cognition and behavioural responses.

psychodynamic approach Explaining mental health problems as being due to dysfunctional childhood experiences and conflicts between different aspects of the personality.

psychoeducation The provision of knowledge and training about a particular disorder in order to facilitate better understanding and recovery. For example, clients may be taught to recognise symptoms indicative of a reoccurrence of an illness, or how to reduce stress.

psychopathy Characterised by a cluster of psychological, interpersonal and neurological features resulting in antisocial behaviours, limited capacity for remorse and poor behavioural regulation.

psychopharmacology The use of prescribed drugs to alter neurotransmitter systems in order to treat mental health problems. These include antidepressant, antianxiety and antipsychotic medications.

psychosexual stages The Freudian idea that children pass through a series of psychological stages of development.

psychotic disorders A disorder where the main characteristic is a loss of contact with reality.

purging Self-induced vomiting, laxative or diuretic use to control weight.

rapid cycling Extreme fluctuations in mood over a period of days which is sometimes seen in mood disorders.

recidivism Whether an individual will repeat an undesirable behaviour following a previous negative outcome or experience.

reductionism The idea that complex mental and behavioural phenomena can be explained by looking at their most basic elements, e.g. genes.

retrograde amnesia Inability to recall existing memory traces following the onset of amnesia.

Ritalin Commercial name of methylphenidate, a pharmacological treatment prescribed for the control of attention-deficit hyperactivity disorder.

safety behaviours Behaviours that reduce anxiety in those with social phobia.

schizoid personality disorder Less extreme form of schizotypal personality disorder characterised by patterns of reduced attachment from social relationships and a restricted range of emotional expression.

schizophrenia An episodic psychotic-based disorder characterised by impairments in emotional response and thought processes. Schizophrenia is a 'split' from reality disorder rather than 'split personality disorder' since fantasy and reality are not disentangled.

schizotypal personality disorder Long-term and stable development of personality whereby long-term symptoms, including odd beliefs and magical thinking inconsistent with subcultural norms, unusual perceptions and experiences, odd thinking and speech, and odd behaviour or appearance amongst others, are consistently presented.

schizotypy Group of personality traits leaving the individual susceptible to delusional-like beliefs, awkward social interactions and demonstrating impaired behaviour and language.

seasonal affective disorder (SAD) Depressive symptoms which usually occur with the onset of autumn or winter.

selective serotonin reuptake inhibitors (SSRIs) A class of antidepressant medication which increases the availability of serotonin by inhibiting its absorption. A depletion of serotonin is one of the biological theories of depression, and thereby by increasing the availability of this neurotransmitter it is believed that depression can be treated.

serotonin transporter gene A gene which plays a key role in the availability of serotonin and may be dysfunctional in depression.

sexual dysfunction Problems of sexual response including aversion to sexual activity and problems associated with reaching orgasm.

sexual fantasy Fleeting or reoccurring sexual thoughts and feelings that are recalled, rehearsed, manipulated and abandoned as the individual chooses.

sexual scripts Distorted and deviant patterns of sexual arousal, inappropriate emotional experience and cognitive distortions relating to sexual behaviour.

Social approach (to madness) This approach to madness was prominent in the USA in the 19th century and considered madness to derive from a range of social factors such as poor parenting and social deprivation. Treatment using this approach focused on promoting order, structure and responsibility.

social constructionist approach The idea that what constitutes a mental illness is determined by social and cultural factors.

striatum Subcortical (inside) area of the forebrain.

thalamus Part of the forebrain. It plays an important role in relaying sensory information from the sense organs to the cortex.

theory of mind An influential theory which explains some of the schizophrenic symptoms as being due to a mistaken assumption that internal thoughts are externally generated.

therapeutic community Intensive intervention programme whereby each individual is responsible for the physical and emotional care of others in a community environment.

token economy Behavioural adaptation technique designed to reward for appropriate behaviour through the use of token collection when a desired behaviour is demonstrated.

tolerance The extent to which an individual needs to increase the level of a substance to produce the desired effect.

trauma-focused cognitive behavioural therapy (TFCBT) A treatment sometimes used in post-traumatic stress disorder where the client uses their imagination to relive the traumatic event.

trepanning The practice of removing parts of the skull through surgery for supposed therapeutic benfit.

(the) unconscious According to Freud, the unconscious mind is the place where all our hidden desires are held, and if these desires were allowed into our conscious minds then they would cause us anxiety and distress. For example, Freud said boys have an aggressive impulse towards their fathers which is held within the unconscious.

ventricles Cavities within the brain containing cerebrospinal fluid which are enlarged in some people with schizophrenia.

vicarious conditioning Learning that occurs through the observation of others. For example, a child who sees his mother panicking at the sight of a spider may learn to be afraid of spiders.

References

Abramson, L. Y., Seligman, M. E., & Teasdale, J. D. (1978). Learned helplessness in humans: Critique and reformulation. *Journal of Abnormal Psychology, 87,* 49–74.

Adegunloye, O. A., & Ezeoke, G. G. (2011). Sexual dysfunction – a silent hurt: Issues on treatment awareness. *Journal of Sexual Medicine, 8*(5), 1332–1329.

Agras, W. S., Walsh, T., Fairburn, C. G., Wilson, G. T., & Kraemer, H. C. (2000). A multicenter comparison of cognitive behavioral therapy and interpersonal psychotherapy for bulimia nervosa. *Archives of General Psychiatry, 57,* 459–466.

Allan, A., Roberts, M. C., Allan, M. M., Pienaar, W. P., & Stein, D. J. (2001). Intoxication, criminal offences and suicide attempts in a group of South African problem drinkers. *South African Medical Journal, 91,* 145–150.

Alloway, T. P. (2009). Working memory, but not IQ predicts subsequent learning in children with learning difficulties. *European Journal of Psychological Assessment, 25*(2), 92–98.

Alloway, T. P., Gathercole, S. E., Willis, C., & Adams, A. M. (2005). Working memory and special educational needs. *Educational and Child Psychology, 22,* 56–67.

Anderson, D. A., & Maloney, K. C. (2001). The efficacy of cognitive-behavioral therapy on the core symptoms of bulimia nervosa. *Clinical Psychology Review, 21,* 971–988.

Andrèasson, S., Allebeck, P., Engstrom, A., & Ryldberg, U. (1987). Cannabis and schizophrenia: A longitudinal study of Swedish conscripts. *Lancet, 26,* 1483–1486.

Angst, J., & Sellaro, R. (2000). Historical perspectives and natural history of bipolar disorder. *Biological Psychiatry, 48*(6), 445–457.

Annis, H. M., Graham, J. M., & Davis, C. S. (1987). *Inventory of Drinking Situations (IDS). User's Guide.* Toronto: Addiction Research Foundation.

APA. (1974). *Diagnostic and Statistical Manual of Mental Disorders* (DSM-II; 2nd ed., 7th printing). Washington, DC: American Psychiatric Association.

APA. (1987). *Diagnostic and Statistical Manual of Mental Disorders* (DSM-III; 3rd ed., text rev.). Washington, DC: American Psychiatric Association.

APA. (1994). *Diagnostic and Statistical Manual of Mental Disorders* (DSM-IV; 4th ed.). Washington, DC: American Psychiatric Association.

APA. (2000). *The Diagnostic and Statistical Manual of Mental Disorders* (DSM-IV-TR; 4th ed., text rev.). Washington, DC: American Psychiatric Association.

APA. (2011). American Psychiatric Association home page. http://www.psych.org/ (accessed 2011).

APA. (2013). *Diagnostic and Statistical Manual of Mental Disorders* (DSM-5; 5th ed.). Washington, DC: American Psychiatric Association.

Arnone, D., Cavanagh, J., Gerber, D., Lawrie, S. M., Ebmeier, K. P., & McIntosh, A. M. (2009). Magnetic resonance imaging studies in bipolar disorder and schizophrenia: Meta-analysis. *British Journal of Psychiatry, 195*(3), 194–201.

Arnsten, A. F. T. (2009). Stress signaling pathways that impair prefrontal cortex structure and function. *Nature Reviews Neuroscience, 10,* 410–422.

Arntz, A. (2003). Cognitive therapy versus applied relaxation as treatment of generalized anxiety disorder. *Behaviour Research and Therapy, 41*(6), 633–646.

Arseneault, L., Cannon, M., Fisher, H. L., Polancyk, G., Moffitt, T. E., & Caspi, A. (2011). Childhood trauma and children's emerging psychotic symptoms: A genetically sensitive longitudinal cohort study. *American Journal of Psychiatry, 168,* 65–72.

Attia, E., & Schroeder, L. (2005). Pharmacologic treatment of anorexia nervosa: Where do we go from here? *International Journal of Eating Disorders, 37,* S60–63.

References

Ayllon, T., & Azrin, N. H. (1964). Reinforcement and instructions with mental patients. *Journal of the Experimental Analysis of Behaviour, 7*(4) 327–331.

Babiss, L. A., & Gangwisch, J. E. (2009). Sports participation as a protective factor against depression and suicidal ideation in adolescents as mediated by self-esteem and social support. *Journal of Developmental and Behavioral Pediatrics, 30*, 376–384.

Bagby, E. (1922). The etiology of phobias. *The Journal of Abnormal and Social Psychology, 17* (1), 16–18.

Baird, G., Simonoff, E., Pickles, A., Chander, S., Loucas, T., Meldrum, D., & Charman, T. (2006). Prevalence of disorders of the autism spectrum in a population cohort of children in South Thames: the Special Needs and Autism Project (SNAP). *Lancet, 368*, 210–215.

Baldaçara, L., Nery-Fernandes F., Rocha, M., Quarantini, L. C., Rocha, G. G., Guimarães, J. L., Araújo, C., Oliveira, I., Miranda-Scippa, A., & Jackowski, A. (2011). Is cerebellar volume related to bipolar disorder. *Journal of Affective Disorders, 135*(1–3), 305–309.

Bandura, A., Roth, D., & Ross, S. (1963). Imitation of film-mediated aggressive models. *Journal of Abnormal & Social Psychology, 66*, 3–11.

Barbaree, H. E. (1990). Denial and minimization among sex offenders: Five distinct age preference profiles. *Canadian Journal of Behavioural Science, 21*, 70–82.

Barbaree, H. E., & Seto, M. C. (1997). Pedophilia: Assessment and treatment. In D. R. Laws & W. O'Donohue (Eds.), *Sexual deviance: Theory, assessment, and treatment.* New York: Guildford.

Barkley, A. (1997). Behavioral inhibition, sustained attention and executive functions: constructing a unifying theory of ADHD. *Psychological Bulletin, 121*, 65–94.

Barkley, R. A., Edwards, G., Laneri, M., Fletcher, K., & Metevia, L. (2001). The efficacy of problem solving communication training alone, behavior management training alone, and their combination for parent–adolescent conflict in teenagers with ADHD and ODD. *Journal of Consulting and Clinical Psychology, 69*, 926–41.

Baron-Cohen, S., Scott, F. J., Allison, C., Bolton, P., Matthews, F. E., & Brayne, C. (2009). Prevalence of autism-spectrum conditions: UK school-based population study. *The British Journal of Psychiatry, 194*, 500–509.

Bartholow, B. D., Sher, K. J., & Krull, J. L. (2003). Changes in heavy drinking over the third decade as a function of collegiate fraternity and sorority involvement: A prospective, multilevel analysis. *Health Psychology, 22*, 616–626.

Bartol, C. R., & Bartol, A. M. (2011). *Introduction to forensic psychology: Research and application.* Thousand Oaks, CA: Sage.

Bauer, M., Beaulieu, S., Dunner, D. L., Lafer, B., & Kupka, R. (2008). Rapid cycling bipolar disorder – diagnostic concepts. *Bipolar Disorders,10*, 153–162.

Baum, M., & Poser, E. G. (1971). Comparison of flooding procedures in animals and man. *Behaviour Research and Therapy, 9*, 249–254.

Bayes, A., & Madden, S. (2011). Early onset eating disorders in male adolescents: A series of 10 inpatients. *Child and Adolescent Psychiatry, 19*(6), 1–6.

Beck, A. T. (1977). *Cognitive therapy of depression.* New York: Guildford

Beck, A. T. (1997). Cognitive therapy: reflections. In J. K. Zeig (Ed.). *The evolution of psychotherapy: the Third conference.* New York: Brunner/Mazel.

Beck, A. T., & Weishaar, M. E. (2010). Cognitive therapy. In R. J. Corsini & D. Wedding (Eds.), *Current Psychotherapies* (9th ed., pp. 301–322). Belmont, CA: Brooks/Cole.

Beck, A. T., Emery, G., & Greenberg, R. L. (1985). *Anxiety disorders and phobias: A cognitive perspective.* New York: Basic Books.

Beck, A. T., Rush, A. J., Shaw, B. F., & Emery, G. (1987). *Cognitive therapy of depression* (Guilford Clinical Psychology and Psychopathology). New York: Guilford Press.

Becker, A. E., Grinspoon, S. K., Kilbanski, A., & Herzog, D. B. (1999). Eating disorders. *New England Journal of Medicine, 340*, 1092–1098.

Beech, A., Fisher, D., & Beckett, R. (1999). *STEP 3: An evaluation of the Prison Sex Offender Treatment Programme; A report for the Home Office by the STEP team.* London: The Home Office.

Beinart, H., Kennedy, P., & Llewelyn, S. (Eds.). (2009). *Clinical psychology in practice*. Chichester: BPS Blackwell.

Belenko, S., Sprott, J. B., & Peterson, C. (2004). Drug and alcohol involvement among minority and female juvenile offenders: Treatment and policy issues. *Criminal Justice Policy Review, 15*, 3–36.

Benazzi, F. (2004). Depressive mixed state: A feature of the natural course of bipolar II (and major depressive) disorder. *Psychopathology, 37*(5), 207–212.

Bennett, P. (2006). *Abnormal and clinical psychology: An introductory textbook*. Maidenhead, UK. Open University Press.

Bennett, P. (2011). *Abnormal and clinical psychology – An introductory textbook* (3rd ed.). Maidenhead: McGraw Hill.

Bentall, R. P., Claridge, G. S., & Slade, P. D. (1989). The multidimensional nature of schizotypal traits: A factor analytic study with normal subjects. *British Journal of Clinical Psychology, 28*(4), 363–375.

Bentall, R. P., Corcoran, R., Howard, R., Blackwood, N., & Kinderman, P. (2001). Persecutory delusions: A review and theoretical integration. *Clinical Psychology Review, 21*, 1143–1192.

Bergman, A. J., Harvey, P. D., Mitropoulou, V., Aronson, A., Marder, D., Silverman, J., Trestman, R., & Siever, L. J. (1996). The factor structure of schizotypal symptoms in a clinical population. *Schizophrenia Bulletin, 22*(3), 501–509.

Bergman, A. J., Wolfson, M. A., & Walker, E. F. (1997). Neuromotor functioning and behavior problems in children at risk for psychopathology. *Journal of Abnormal Child Psychology, 25*(3), 229–237.

Berlin, F. S., & Meinecke, C. F. (1981). Treatment of sex offenders with antiandrogenic medication: Conceptualization, review of treatment modalities, and preliminary findings. *American Journal of Psychiatry, 138*, 601–607.

Berridge, V. (1978). Victorian opium eating: Responses to opiate use in nineteenth-century England. *Victorian Studies*, 437–461.

Bickley, J. A., & Beech, A. R. (2002). An investigation of the Ward and Hudson Pathways Model of the Sexual Offence Process with Child Abusers. *Journal of Interpersonal Violence, 17*(4), 371–393.

Birmingham, C. L., Su, J., Hlynsky, J. A., Goldner, E. M., & Gao, M. (2005). The mortality rate from anorexia nervosa. *International Journal of Eating Disorders, 38*, 143–146.

Bisson, J. I., Ehlers, A., Matthews, R., Pilling, S., Richards, D., & Turner, S. (2007). Psychological treatments for chronic post-traumatic stress disorder: Systematic review and meta-analysis. *British Journal of Psychiatry, 190*, 97–104.

Blanchard, E. B. (1970). Relative contributions of modeling, informational influences, and physical contact in extinction of phobic behavior. *Journal of Abnormal Psychology, 76*(1), 55–61.

Blanchard, R. (2009). DSM-5 options: Paraphilias and paraphilic disorders, pedohebephilic disorder, and transvestic disorder. Paper presented at the 28th Annual Meeting of the Association for the Treatment of Sexual Abusers, October 1, 2009, Dallas, TX.

Blaney, P. H. (1977). Contemporary theories of depression: Critique and comparison. *Journal of Abnormal Psychology, 86*, 203–223.

Bonn, J. A., Readhead, C. P., & Timmons, B. H. (1984). Enhanced adaptive behavioural response in agoraphobic patients pretreated with breathing retraining. Lancet, 22(2), 665–669.

Borduin, C. M. (1999). Multisystemic treatment of criminality and violence in adolescents, *Journal of the Academy of Child and Adolescent Psychiatry, 38*, 242–249.

Bowman, M. L. (1998). Bulimia: From syncope to obsession. *Psychology of Addictive Behaviors, 12*(2), 83–92.

Bradvik, L., & Berglund, M. (2006). Long-term treatment and suicidal behavior in severe depression: ECT and antidepressant pharmacotherapy may have different effects on the occurrence and seriousness of suicide attempts. *Depression and Anxiety, 23*, 34–41.

Breitborde, N. J .K., Lopez, S. R., & Nuechterlien, K. H. (2009). Expressed emotion, human agency, and schizophrenia: Towards a new model for the EE-relapse association. *Cultural and Medical Psychiatry, 33*, 41–60.

Breuer, J., & Freud, S. (1895). *Studien über Hysterie (Studies on Hysteria)* (Standard Edition, vol. II). Leipzig and Vienna: Franz Deuticke.

Broeren, S., Lester, K. J., Muris, P., & Field, A. P. (2011). They are afraid of the animal, so therefore I am too: Influence of peer modeling on fear beliefs and approach-avoidance behaviors towards animals in typically developing children. *Behaviour Research and Therapy, 49*(1), 50–57.

Brooks, S. J., O'Daly, O., Uher, R., Friederich, H-C., Giampietro, V., Brammer, M….Campbell, I. C. (2012). Thinking about eating food activates visual cortex with reduced bilateral cerebellar activation in females with anorexia nervosa: An fMRI study. *Neural Responses in Anorexia Nervosa, 7*(3), 1–11.

Brown, S. A., Tate, S. R., Vik, P. W., Haas, A. L., & Aarons, G. A. (1999). Modeling of alcohol use mediates the effect of family history of alcoholism on adolescent alcohol expectancies. *Experimental and Clinical Psychopharmacology, 7*(1), 20–27.

Brysbaert, M., & Rastle, K. (2009). *Historical and conceptual issues in psychology*. Harlow: Pearson Education.

Bulik, C. M., Reba, L., Siega-Riz, A-M., & Reichborn-Kjennerud, T. (2005). Anorexia nervosa: Definition, epidemiology, and cycle of risk. *International Journal of Eating Disorders, 37*, 2–9.

Burcusa, S. L., & Iacono, W. G. (2007). Risk for recurrence in depression. *Clinical Psychology Review, 27*(8), 959–985.

Burstein, M. A., & Ginsburg, G. S. (2010). The effect of parental modelling of anxious behaviours and cognitions in school-aged children: An experimental pilot study. *Behaviour Research and Therapy, 48*(6), 506–515.

Burstein, M. A., Ginsburg, G. S., & Tein, J. Y. (2010). Parental anxiety and child symptomatology: An examination of additive and interactive effects of parent psychopathology. *Journal of Abnormal Child Psychology, 38*(7), 897–909.

Burton, N. S. (2011). Is ADHD a real neurological disorder or collection of psychosocial symptomatic behaviors? Implications for treatment in the Case of Randall E. *Journal of Infant, Child, and Adolescent Psychotherapy, 10*, 116–129.

Bussy, G., Charrin, E., Brun, A., Curie, A., & des Portes, V. (2011). Implicit procedural learning in fragile X and Down Syndrome. *Journal of Intellectual Disability Research, 55*(5), 521–528.

Button, E., Aldridge, S., & Palmer, R. (2008). Males assessed by a specialized adult eating disorders service. Patterns over time and comparisons with females. *International Journal of Eating Disorders, 41*(8), 758–761.

Cachelin, F. M., Striegel-Moore, R. H., & Regan, P. C. (2006). Factors associated with treatment seeking in a community sample of European American and Mexican American women with eating disorders. *European Eating Disorders Review, 14*, 422–429.

Campbell, M., Adams, P., Perry, R., Spencer, E. K., & Overall, J. E. (1988). Tardive and withdrawal dyskinesias in autistic children: A prospective study. *Psychopharmacology Bulletin, 24*, 251–255.

Campbell, S., & MacQueen, G. (2004). The role of the hippocampus in the pathophysiology of major depression. *Journal of Psychiatry & Neuroscience, 29*(6), 417–426.

Campo, J. A., Frederikx, M., Nijman, H., & Merckelback, H. (1998). Schizophrenia and changes in physical appearance. *Journal of Clinical Psychiatry, 59*, 197–198.

Cannon, D. S., & Baker, T. B. (1981). Emetic and electric shock alcohol aversion therapy: Assessment of conditioning. *Journal of Consulting and Clinical Psychology, 49*(1), 20–33.

Cannon, M., Jones, P. B., & Murray, R. M. (2002). Obstetric complications and schizophrenia: Historical and meta-analytic review. *American Journal of Psychiatry, 159*, 1080–1092.

Cao, G., & Prior, L. (2000). Red wine in moderation: potential health benefits independent of alcohol. *Nutrition in Clinical Care, 3*(2), 76–82.

Capone, C., & Wood, M. D. (2008). Density of familial alcoholism and its effects on alcohol use and problems in college students. *Alcoholism: Clinical and Experimental Research, 32,* 1451–1458.

Carr, J. (2012), Six weeks to 45 years: A longitudinal study of a population with Down Syndrome. *Journal of Applied Research in Intellectual Disabilities, 25,* 414–422.

Castellanos, F. X., Giedd, J. N., Marsh, W. L., Hamburger, S. D., Vaituzis, A. C., Dickstein, D. P....Rapoport, J. L. (1996). Quantitative brain magnetic resonance imaging in attention-deficit hyperactivity disorder. *Archives of General Psychiatry, 53,* 607–616.

Castellanos, F. X., Xavier, L., Sharp, P. P., Greenstein, D. K., Clasen, L. S., Blumenthal, J. D.... Rapoport, J. L. (2002). Developmental trajectories of brain volume abnormalities in children and adolescents with attention-deficit/hyperactivity disorder. *Journal of the American Medical Association, 288,* 1740–1748.

Chen, S. H., & Johnson, S. L. (2012). Family influences on mania-relevant cognitions and beliefs: A cognitive model of mania and reward. *Journal of Clinical Psychology, 68*(7), 829–842.

Chen, Y. C., O'Brien, M. S., & Anthony, J. C. (2005). Who becomes cannabis dependent soon after onset of use? Epidemiological evidence from the United States 2001. *Drug and Alcohol Dependence, 79,* 11–22.

Chen, W. J., Hsiao, C. K., & Lin, C. C. (1997). Schizotypy in community samples: The three-factor structure and correlation with sustained attention. *Journal of Abnormal Psychology, 106*(4), 649.

Childs, K., Dembo, R., Belenko, S., Wareham, J., & Schmeidler, J. (2011). A comparison of individual-level and community-level predictors of marijuana and cocaine use among a sample of newly arrested juvenile offenders. *Journal of Child and Adolescent Substance Abuse, 20,* 114–134.

Chopra, M. P., Landes, R. D., Gatchalian, K. M. J., Jackson, L. C., Buchhalter, A. R., Stitzer, M. L....Bickel, W. K. (2009). Buprenorphine medication versus voucher contingencies in promoting abstinence from opioids and cocaine. *Experimental and Clinical Psychopharmacology, 17*(4), 226–236.

Claridge, G. S. (1988). Schizotypy and schizophrenia. In P. Bebbington & P. McGuffin (Eds.), *Schizophrenia: The major issues* (pp. 187–200). Oxford: Heinemann Professional.

Claridge, G. S., & Brooks, P. (1984). Schizotypy and hemisphere function: I. Theoretical considerations and the measurement of schizotypy. *Personality and Individual Differences, 5,* 633– 648.

Claridge, G. S., McCreery, C., Mason, O., Bentall, R., Boyle, G., Slade, P., & Popplewell, D. (1996). The factor structure of 'schizotypal 'traits: A large replication study. *British Journal of Clinical Psychology, 35*(1), 103–115.

Clark, D. A., & Beck, A. T. (2009). *Cognitive therapy of anxiety disorders: Science and practice.* New York: Guilford Press.

Coelho, C. M., & Purkis, H. (2009). The origins of specific phobias: Influential theories and current perspectives. *Review of General Psychology, 13*(4), 335–348.

Cohen, L. J., McGeoch, P. G., Gans, S. W., Nikiforov, K., Cullen, K., & Galynker, I. (2002). Childhood sexual history of 20 male pedophiles vs. 24 healthy control subjects. *Journal of Nervous and Mental Diseases, 190,* 757–766.

Coid, J. (1998). The management of dangerous psychopaths in prison. *Psychopathy: Antisocial, Criminal and Violent Behavior,* 431–457.

Conley, R. R., & Buchanan, R. W. (1997). Evaluation of treatment resistant schizophrenia. *Schizophrenia Bulletin, 23*(4), 663–674.

Conrad, P., & Schneider, J. W. (1992). *Deviance and medicalization: From badness to sickness.* Philadelphia: Temple University Press.

Cook, C. C. H. (2012). Psychiatry in scripture: Sacred texts and psychopathology. *The Psychiatrist, 36*(6), 225–229.

Cornblatt, B. A., Lencz, T., Smith, C. W., Correll, C. U., Auther, A. M., & Nakayama, E. (2003). The schizophrenia prodrome revisited: A neurodevelopmental perspective. *Schizophrenia Bulletin, 29*(4), 633–651.

References

Cornic, F., Consoli, A., & Cohen, D. (2007). Catatonia in children and adolescents. *Psychiatric Annals, 37*, 19–26.

Costa Jr, P. T., & McCrae, R. R. (1995). Domains and facets: Hierarchical personality assessment using the Revised NEO Personality Inventory. *Journal of Personality Assessment, 64*(1), 21–50.

Cox, J. M. (1813). *Practical observations on insanity*. London: Baldwin and Underwood.

Craig, L. A., & Campbell-Fuller, N. (2009). The use of olfactory aversion and directed masturbation in modifying deviant sexual interest: A case study. *Journal of Sexual Aggression, 15*(2), 179–191.

Craig, L. A., Beech, A., & Browne, K. D. (2006). Sexual recidivism: Advances in actuarial estimates. *Forensic Updates, 85*, 13–18.

Craig, L. A., Browne, K. D., & Stringer, I. (2003). Risk scales and factors predictive of sexual offence recidivism. *Trauma, Violence, and Abuse, 4*, 45–69.

Dalle Grave, R., Bohn, K., Hawker, D., & Fairburn, C. G. (2008). Inpatient, day patient and two forms of outpatient CBT-E. In C. G. Fairburn (Ed.), *Cognitive behavior therapy and eating disorders* (pp. 231–244). New York: Guilford Press.

Dandescu, A., & Wolfe, R. (2003). Considerations on fantasy use by child molesters and exhibitionists. *Sexual Abuse: Journal of Research and Treatment, 15*(4), 297–305.

Davidson, J. R., Tupler, L. A., & Potts, N. L. (1994) Treatment of social phobia with benzodiazepines. *Journal of Clinical Psychiatry, 55*, 28–32.

Davidson, R. J., Pizzagalli, D., Nitschke, J. B., & Putnam, K. (2002). Depression: Perspectives from affective neuroscience. *Annual Review of Psychology, 53*, 545–574.

Davison, K. (2006). Historical aspects of mood disorders. *Psychiatry, 5*(4), 115–118.

de Graff, G., Vis, J. C., Haveman, M., van Hove, G., de Graaf, E. A. B., Tijssen, J. G. P., & Mulder, B. J. M. (2011). Assessment of prevalence of persons with Down Syndrome: A theory-based demographic model. *Journal of Applied Research in Intellectual Disabilities, 24*, 247–262.

DeFrancesco, L. (2001). Scientists question rise in autism. *Nature Medicine, 7*, 645.

Del Boca, F. K., & Darkes, J. (2003). The validity of self-reports of alcohol consumption: State of the science and challenges for research. *Addiction, 98* (Suppl. 2), 1–12.

Dembo, R., Wareham, J., & Schmeidler, J. (2007). Drug use and delinquent involvement: A growth model of parallel processes among high risk youths. *Criminal Justice & Behavior, 34*, 680–696.

Depla, M. F., ten Have, M. L., van Balkom, A. J., & de Graaf, R. (2008). Specific fears and phobias in the general population: Results from the Netherlands Mental Health Survey and Incidence Study (NEMESIS). *Social Psychiatry and Psychiatric Epidemiology, 43*(3), 200–208.

DeStefano, F. (2007). Vaccines and autism: Evidence does not support a causal association. *Clinical Pharmacology and Therapeutics, 82*(6), 756–759.

Devlin, S., Healy, O., Leader, G., & Hughes, B. M. (2011). Comparison of behavioral intervention and sensory-integration therapy in the treatment of challenging behaviour. *Journal of Autism Development Disorder, 41*, 1303–1320.

Dobson, K. S. (1989). A meta-analysis of the efficacy of cognitive therapy for depression. *Journal of Consulting and Clinical Psychology, 57*(3), 414–419.

Dolk, H., Loane, M., Garne, E., De Walle, H., Queisser-Luft, A., De Vigan, C. . . . Bianchi, F. (2005). Trends and geographic inequalities in the prevalence of Down Syndrome in Europe, 1980–1999. *Revue d'Epidémiologie et de Santé Publique, 53*(2), S87–95.

Doll, E. (1953). *Measurement of social competence: A manual for the Vineland Social Maturity Scale*. Minneapolis: Educational Publishers.

Donohew, L., Hoyle, R., Clayton, R., Skinner, W., Rice, S., & Colon, R. E. (1999). Sensation seeking and drug use by adolescents and their friends: Models for marijuana and alcohol. *Journal of Studies on Alcohol, 60*(5), 622–631.

Doskoch, P. (1995). The darker side of fantasies. *Psychology Today, 33*, 1.

Dozois, D. J. A. (2000). Influences on Freud's *Mourning and melancholia* and its contextual validity. *Journal of Theoretical and Philosophical Psychology, 20*(2), 167–195.

Dugas, M. J., & Robichaud, M. (2007). *Cognitive-behavioral treatment for generalized anxiety disorder: From science to practice*. New York: Routledge.

Dyer, C. (2012). Anorexic woman cannot be force fed, judge rules. *British Medical Journal (News)*, 1.

Eastman, C. (1976). Behavioral formulations of depression. *Psychological Review, 83* (4), 277–291.

Eaton, W. W., Kramer, M., Anthony, J. C., Dryman, A., Shapiro, S., & Locke, B. Z. (1989). The incidence of specific DIS/DSM-III mental disorders: Data from the NIMH Epidemiologic Catchment Area Program. *Acta Psychiatrica Scandinavica, 79*, 163–178.

Eddy, K. T., Celio Doyle, A., Hoste, R., Herzog, D. B., & le Grange, D. (2008). Eating disorder not otherwise specified in adolescents. *Journal of the American Academy of Child and Adolescent Psychiatry, 47*(2), 156–164.

Ehlers, A., & Clark, D. M. (2000). A cognitive model of posttraumatic stress disorder. *Behaviour Research and Therapy, 38*, 319–345.

Ellis, A. (1977). The basic clinical theory of rational-emotive therapy. In A. Ellis & R. Grieger (Eds.), *Handbook of rational-emotional therapy*. New York: Springer.

Ellis, A. (1993). Reflections on rational-emotive therapy. *Journal of Consulting and Clinical Psychology, 61*(2), 199–201.

Ellison-Wright, I., & Bullmore, E. (2010). Anatomy of bipolar disorder and schizophrenia: A meta-analysis. *Schizophrenia Research, 117*(1), 1–12.

EMCDDA. (2003). The state of the drugs problem in the acceding and candidate countries to the European Union. Portugal: European Monitoring Centre for Drugs and Drug Addiction.

Eysenck, H. J., & Eysenck, S. B. G. (1975). *Manual of the Eysenck Personality Questionnaire (junior and adult)*. Hodder and Stoughton.

Fagan, P. J., Wise, T. N., Schmidt, C. W. Jr., & Berline, F. S. (2002). Pedophilia. *Journal of the American Medical Association, 288*, 2458–2465.

Fairburn, C. G., & Harrison, P. J. (2003). Eating disorders. *The Lancet, 361*, 407–416.

Fairburn, C. G., Cooper, Z., & Shafran, R. (2003). Cognitive behaviour therapy for eating disorders: A 'transdiagnostic' theory and treatment. *Behaviour Research and Therapy, 41*, 509–528.

Fairburn, C. G., Cooper, Z., Doll, H. A., O'Connor, M. E., Bohn, K., Hawker, D. M.....Palmer, R. L. (2009). Transdiagnostic cognitive-behavioral therapy for patients with eating disorders: A two-site trial with 60-week follow-up. *American Journal of Psychiatry, 166*, 311–319.

Fairburn, C. G., Norman, P. A., Welch, S. L., O'Connor, M. E., Doll, H. A., & Peveler, R. C. (1995). A prospective study of outcome in bulimia nervosa and the long-term effects of three psychological treatments. *Archives of General Psychiatry, 52*(4), 304–312.

Farrell, J. M., & Shaw, I. A. (1994). Emotional awareness training: A prerequisite to effective cognitive-behavioral treatment of borderline personality disorder. *Cognitive and Behavioral Practice, 1*(1), 71–91.

Farzin, F., Perry, H., Hessl, D., Loesch, D., Cohen, J., Bacalman, S.....Hagerman, R. (2006). Autism spectrum disorders and attention-deficit/hyperactivity disorder in boys with the fragile X premutation. *Journal of Developmental Behavior Pediatr, 27*, S137–144.

Fassino, S., Piero, A., Gramaglia, C., Daga, G. A., Gandione, M., Rovera, G. G., & Bartocci, G. (2006). Clinical, psychological and personality correlates of asceticism in anorexia nervosa: From Saint Anorexia to pathologic perfectionism. *Transcultural Psychiatry, 43*(4), 600–614.

Fazio, A. F., & Erck, T. W. (1973). Components in a treatment of insect phobias. *Journal of Abnormal Psychology, 82*(3), 463–468.

Feighner, J. P., Robins, E., Guze, S. B., Woodruff, R. A. Jr, Winokur, G., & Munoz, R. (1972). Diagnostic criteria for use in psychiatric research. *Archives of General Psychiatry, 26*, 57–63.

Fennell, M. J. V. (1998). Depression. In K. Hawton, P. M. Salkovskis, J. Kirk & D. M. Clark (Eds), *Cognitive behaviour therapy for psychiatric problems: A practical guide*. Oxford: Oxford University Press.

Fenske, J. N., & Schwenk, T. L. (2009). Obsessive compulsive disorder: Diagnosis and management. *American Family Physician, 80*, 239–245.

Finger, S., & Clower, W. T. (2003). On the birth of trepanation: The thoughts of Paul Broca and Victor Horsley. In: R. Arnott, S. Finger, & C. U. M. Smith (Eds.), *Trepanation: History, discovery, theory*. Lisse: Swets & Zeitlinger.

Finkelhor, D. (1984). *Child sexual abuse*. New York: The Free Press.

Fisher, H. L., Jones, P. B., Fearon, P., Craig, T. K., Dazzan, P. ... Morgan, C. (2010). The varying impact of type, timing and frequency of exposure to childhood adversity on its association with adult psychotic disorder. *Psychological Medicine, 40*, 1967–1978.

Foa, E. B., Dancu, C. V., Hembree, E. A., Jaycox, L. H., Meadows, E. A., & Street, G. P. (1999). A comparison of exposure therapy, stress inoculation training, and their combination for reducing posttraumatic stress disorder in female assault victims. *Journal of Consulting and Clinical Psychology, 67*(2), 194–200.

Frazier, T. W., Demaree, H. A., & Youngstrom, E. A. (2004). Meta-analysis of intellectual and neuropsychological test performance in attention-deficit/hyperactivity disorder. *Neuropsychology, 18*, 543–555.

Fredrikson, M., Annas, P., Fischer, H., & Wik, G. (1996). Gender and age differences in the prevalence of specific fears and phobias. *Behaviour Research and Therapy, 34* (1) 33–39.

Freud, S. (1913). *The interpretation of dreams* (3rd ed). Trans. by A. A. Brill. New York: The Macmillan Company.

Freud, S. (1971). *Mourning and melancholia* (J. Riviere, Trans.). In M. Khan (Ed.), *Collected papers* (Vol. 4, pp. 152–170). London: Hogarth Press. (Original work published in 1917.)

Frid, C., Drott, P., Lundell, B., Rasmussen, F., & Annerne, G. (1999). Mortality in Down's syndrome in relation to congenital malformations. *Journal of Intellectual Disability Research, 43*, 234–241.

Friederich, H. C., & Herzog, W. (2011). Cognitive-behavioral flexibility in anorerxia nervosa. *Current Topics in Behavioral Neuroscience, 6*, 111–123.

Frieling, H., Romer, K. D., Scholz, S., Mittelbach, F., Wilhelm, J., De Zwaan, M. ... Bleich, S. (2010). Epigenetic dysregulation of dopaminergic genes in eating disorders. *International Journal of Eating Disorders, 43*(7), 577–583.

Frith, C. D. (1992). *The cognitive neuropsychology of schizophrenia*. Hove: Lawrence Erlbaum.

Frith, U. (1987). A developmental model for autism. In F. Grémy, S. Tomkiewicz, P. Ferrari, & G. Lelord, G. (Eds.), *Autisme infantile* (pp. 175–184). Colloque INSERM, vol. 146.

Fullana, M. A., Vilaqut, G., Rojas-Farreras, S., Mataix-Cols, D., de Graaf, R., Demyttenaere, K. ... ESEMeD/MHEDEA 2000 investigators. (2010). Obsessive-compulsive symptom dimensions in the general population: Results from an epidemiological study in six European countries. *Journal of Affective Disorders, 124*, 291–299.

Furnham, A., Ingle, H., Gunter, B., & McClelland, A. (1997). A content analysis of alcohol portrayal and drinking in British television soap operas. *Health Education Research, 12*, 519–529.

Furukawa, T. A., Watanabe, N., & Churchill, R. (2006). Psychotherapy plus antidepressant for panic disorder with or without agoraphobia: Systematic review. *British Journal of Psychiatry, 188*, 305–312.

Galbraith, N., Manktelow, K., & Morris, N. (2008). Subclinical delusional ideation and a self-reference bias in everyday reasoning. *British Journal of Psychology, 99*(1), 29–44.

Galbraith, N. D., Manktelow, K. I., & Morris, N. G. (2010). Subclinical delusional ideation and appreciation of sample size and heterogeneity in statistical judgment. *British Journal of Psychology, 101*(4), 621–635.

Galderisi, S., Quarantelli, M., Volpe, U., Mucci, A., Cassano, G. B., Invernizzi, G. ... Maj, M. (2008). Patterns of structural abnormalities in deficit and non-deficit schizophrenia. *Schizophrenia Bulletin, 34*, 393–401.

Garlipp, P., Gödecke-Koch, T., Dietrich, D. E., & Haltenhof, H. (2004). Lycanthropy – psychopathological and psychodynamical aspects. *Acta Psychiatrica Scandinavica, 109*, 19–22.

Geddes, J. R., Verdoux, H., Takei, N. Lawrie, S. M., Bovet, P., Eagles, J. M. . . . Murray, R. M. (1999) Schizophrenia and complications of pregnancy and labor: An individual patient data meta-analysis. *Schizophrenia Bulletin, 25*, 413–23.

Germain, A., & Kupfer, D. J. (2008). Circadian rhythm disturbances in depression. *Human Psychopharmacology: Clinical and Experimental, 23*, 571–585.

Goldman, G. S., & Yazbak, F. E. (2004). An investigation of the association between MMR and autism in Denmark. *Journal of American Physicians and Surgeons, 9*(3), 70–75.

Goldman-Rakic, P., & Selemon, L. D. (1997). Functional and anatomical aspects of prefrontal pathology in schizophrenia. *Schizophrenia Bulletin, 23* (3), 437–458.

Goldstein, I., Lue, T. F., Padma-Nathan, H., Rosen, Steers, & Wicker, P. A. (1998). Oral sildenafil in the treatment of erectile dysfunction: Sildenafil Study Group. *New England Journal of Medicine, 338*, 1397–1404.

Goldstein, S. (2006). ADHD Throughout the lifespan. In T. Fitzner, C. Nauhaus, & M. Townson (Eds.), *International Conference on ADHD.* Bad Boll, Germany: Evangelische Akademie Press.

Gorman, J. M., Kent, J. M., Sullivan, G. M., & Coplan, J. D. (2000). Neuroanatomical hypothesis of panic disorder, revised. *American Journal of Psychiatry, 157*, 493–505.

Gotlib, I., & Joormann, J. (2010). Cognition and depression: Current status and future directions. *Annual Review of Clinical Psychology, 6*, 285–312.

Gottesman, I. I. (1991). *Schizophrenia genesis: The origins of madness.* New York: Freeman.

Grant, B. F., Dawson, D. A., Stinson, F. S., Chou, S. P., Dufour, M. C., & Pickering, R. P. (2004). The 12-month prevalence and trends in DSM-IV alcohol abuse and dependence: United States, 1991–1992 and 2001–2002. *Drug and Alcohol Dependence, 74*, 223–234.

Gratacòs, M., Sahún, I., Gallego, X., Amador-Arjona, A., Estivill, X., & Dierssen, M. (2007). Candidate genes for panic disorder: Insight from human and mouse genetic studies. *Genes, Brain & Behavior, 6*(Suppl. 1), 2–23.

Green, H., McGinnity, A., Meltzer, H., Ford, T., & Goodman, R. (2005). Mental health of children and young people in Great Britain, 2004. Basingstoke: Palgrave Macmillan. Available to download at http://www.esds.ac.uk/doc/5269/mrdoc/pdf/5269technicalreport.pdf [accessed 22 July 2013].

Green, R. (2001). (Serious) Sadomasochism: A protected right of privacy? *Archives of Sexual Behaviour, 30*, 543–550.

Grilo, C. M., Crosby, R. D., Wilson, G. T., & Masheb, R. M. (2012). 12-month follow-up of fluoxetine and cognitive behavioral therapy for binge eating disorder. *Journal of Consulting and Clinical Psychology, 80*(6), 1108–1113.

Gross, C. G. (1999). A hole in the head. *The Neuroscientist, 5*(4), 263–269.

Gruzelier, J. H. (1996). The factorial structure of schizotypy: I. Affinities with syndromes of schizophrenia. *Schizophrenia Bulletin, 22*(4), 611–620

Gupta, M. A., & Johnson, A. M. (2000). Nonweight-related body image concerns among female eating-disordered patients and nonclinical controls: some preliminary observations. *International Journal of Eating Disorders, 27*, 304–309.

Hall, G. C. N., & Hirschman, R. (1992). Sexual aggression against children: A conceptual perspective on etiology. *Criminal Justice and Behaviour, 19*, 8–23.

Hall, W., & Acula, R. L. (2003). *Cannabis use and dependence: Public health and public policy.* Cambridge: Cambridge University Press.

Halmi, K. A., Sunday, S. R., Strober, M., Kaplan, A., Woodside, D. B., Fichter, M. . . . Kaye, W. H. (2000). Perfectionism in anorexia nervosa: Variation by clinical subtype, obsessionality, and pathological eating behavior. *American Journal of Psychiatry, 157*(11), 1799–1805.

Ham, L. S., Casner, H. G., Bacon, A. K., & Shaver, J. A. (2011). Speeches, strangers and alcohol use: The role of context in social stress response dampening. *Journal of Behaviour Therapy and Experimental Psychiatry, 42*, 462–472.

Hammen, C., Kim, E. Y., Eberhart, N. K., & Brennan, P. A. (2009). Chronic and acute stress and the prediction of major depression in women. *Depression and Anxiety, 26*, 718–723.

Hanson, R. K., & Slater, S. (1988). Sexual victimization in the history of child sexual abusers: A review. *Annals of Sex Research, 1,* 485–499.

Hare, R. D. (1980). A research scale for the assessment of psychopathy in criminal populations. *Personality and Individual Differences, 1,* 111–119.

Hare, R. D. (1991). *The Hare psychopathy checklist-revised (PCL-R).* Toronto, Ontario: Multi-Health Systems.

Hare, R. D. (1993). *Without conscience: The disturbing world of the psychopaths among us.* New York: Pocket Books.

Hare, R. D., Clark, D., Grann, M., & Thornton, D. (2000). Psychopathy and the predictive validity of the PCL-R: An international perspective. *Behavioral Sciences and the Law, 18*(5), 623–645.

Hare, R. D., & Vertommen, H. (2003). *The Hare psychopathy checklist – revised.* Toronto, Ontario: Multi-Health Systems, Incorporated.

Harris, D., & Bakti, S. L. (2000). Stimulant psychosis: Symptom profile and acute clinical course. *American Journal on Addictions, 9,* 28–37.

Harris, E. C., & Barraclough, B. (1998). Excess mortality of mental disorder. *The British Journal of Psychiatry, 173,* 11–53.

Hasin, D. S., Goodwin, R. D., Stinson, F. S., & Grabt, B. F. (2005). Epidemiology of major depressive disorder: Results from the National Epidemiologic Survey on Alcoholism and Related Conditions. *Archives of General Psychiatry, 62,* 1097–1106.

Hausenblas, H. A., & Symons Downs, D. (2002). Relationship among sex, imagery, and exercise dependence symptoms. *Psychology of Addictive Behaviors, 16*(2), 169–172.

Haworth-Hoeppner, S. (2000). The critical shapes of body image: The role of culture and family in the production of eating disorders. *Journal of Marriage and the Family, 62,* 212–227.

Hemmingsson, T., Lundberg, I., Romelsjö, A., & Alfredsson, L. (1997). Alcoholism in social classes and occupations in Sweden. *International Journal of Epidemiology, 26,* 584–591.

Hemsley, D. R. (1996). Schizophrenia: A cognitive model and its implications for psychological intervention, *Behaviour Modification, 20,* 139–169.

Henggeler, S. W., Melton, G. B., & Smith, L. A. (1992). Family preservation using multisystemic therapy: An effective alternative to incarcerating serious juvenile offenders. *Journal of Consulting and Clinical Psychology, 60*(6), 953.

Henquet, C., Di Forti, M., Morrison, P., Kuepper, R., & Murray, R. M. (2008). Gene–environment interplay between cannabis and psychosis. *Schizophrenia Bulletin, 34*(6), 1111–1121.

Henquet, C., Murray, R., Linszen, D., & van Os, J. (2005). The environment and schizophrenia: The role of cannabis use. *Schizophrenia Bulletin, 31,* 608–612.

Hettema, J. M. (2010). Genetics of depression. *Focus: The Journal of Lifelong Learning in Psychiatry, 8*(3), 316–322.

Hettema, J. M., Annas, P., Neale, M. C., Kendler, K. S., & Fredrikson, M. (2003). A twin study of the genetics of fear conditioning. *Archives of General Psychiatry, 60*(7), 702–728.

Hettema, J. M., Neale, M. C., & Kendler, K. S. (2001). A review and meta-analysis of the genetic epidemiology of anxiety disorders. *American Journal of Psychiatry, 158,* 1568–1578.

Heumann, K. A., & Morey, L. C. (1990). Reliability of categorical and dimensional judgments. *American Journal of Psychiatry, 147*(4), 498–500.

Hibell, B., Andersson, B., Bjarnasson, T., Kokkevi, A., Morgan, M., & Narusk, A. (1997). *The 1995 ESPAD Report: Alcohol and other drug use among Students in 26 European Countries.* Stockholm: Council of Europe Pompidou Group.

Hicks, T. V., & Leitenberg, H. (2001). Sexual fantasies about one's partner versus someone else: Gender differences in incidence and frequency. *Journal of Sex Research, 38,* 43–51.

Hicks, T. V., Leitenberg, H., Barlow, D. H., Gorman, J. M., Shear, M. K., & Woods, S. W. (2005). Physical, mental, and social catastrophic cognitions as prognostic factors in cognitive-behavioural and pharmacological treatments for panic disorder. *Journal of Consulting and Clinical Psychology, 7*(3), 506–514.

Highet, G. (2004). The role of cannabis in supporting young people's cigarette smoking: A qualitative exploration. *Health Education Research, 19,* 635–643.

Hirschfield, R. M. (2000). History and evolution of the monoamine hypothesis of depression. *Journal of Clinical Psychiatry, 61*(6), 4–6.

Hodapp, R., & Dykens, E. (1996). Mental retardation. In E. Mash & R. Barkley (Eds.), *Child psychopathology* (pp. 362–369). New York: Guilford.

Hogan, R. A., & Kirchner, J. H. (1968). Implosive, eclectic verbal and bibliotherapy in the treatment of fears of snakes. *Behaviour Research and Therapy, 6*, 167–171.

Houlihan, D. D., & Jones, R. N. (1989). Treatment of a boy's school phobia with *in vivo* systematic desensitization. *Professional School Psychology, 4*(4), 285–293.

Hoyer, J., Becker, E. S., & Roth, W. T. (2001). Characteristics of worry in GAD patients, social phobics and controls. *Depression and Anxiety, 13*(2), 89–96.

Hudson, J. L., Hiripi, E., Pope, H. G., & Kessler, R. C. (2007). The prevalence and correlates of eating disorders in the National Comorbidity Survey Replication. *Biological Psychiatry, 61*, 348–358.

Huprich, S. K. (2003). Evaluating facet-level predictions and construct validity of depressive personality disorder. *Journal of Personality Disorders 17*(3), 219–232.

Inglis, P. A., & Swain, J. (2012). Men with learning difficulties doing research: Challenging views of learning difficulties. *Disability and Society, 27*(3), 339–352.

Irani, F., & Siegal, S. J. (2006). Predicting outcome in schizophrenia. *Psychiatric Times, 23*, 69–71.

Jackson, P. M. (1978). Another case of lycanthropy. *American Journal of Psychiatry, 135*, 134–135.

Jacobson, P. B., Bovberg, D. H., Schwartz, M. D., Hudis, C. A., Gilewski, T. A., & Norton, L. (1995). Conditioned emotional distress in women receiving chemotherapy for breast cancer. *Journal of Consulting and Clinical Psychology, 63*(1), 108–114.

Jaskiw, G. E., & Popli, A. P. (2004). A meta-analysis of the response to chronic L-dopa in patients with schizophrenia: Therapeutic and heuristic implications. *Psychopharmacology, 171*, 365–374.

Jaspers, K. (1951). Der Prophet Ezechiel. Eine pathographische Studie. In *Rechenschaft und Ausblick: Reden und Aufsätze* (Trans. S. Keen). Munich: R. Piper & Co.

Jimerson, D. C., Lesem, M. D., Kaye, W. H., & Brewerton, T. D. (1992). Low serotonin and dopamine metabolite concentrations in cerebrospinal fluid from bulimic patients with frequent bulimic episodes. *Archives of General Psychiatry, 49*, 132–138.

Jobe, T. H., & Harrow, M. (2005). Long-term outcome of patients with schizophrenia: A review. *Canadian Journal of Psychiatry, 50*(14), 892–900.

Johnson, S. L., & Jones, S. (2009). Cognitive correlates of mania risk: Are responses to success, positive moods, and manic symptoms distinct or overlapping? *Journal of Clinical Psychology, 65*(9), 891–905.

Jones, M. K., & Menzies, R. G. (2000). Danger expectancies, self-efficacy and insight in spider phobia. *Behaviour Research and Therapy, 38*, 585–600.

Jones, P., & Cannon, M. (1998). The new epidemiology of schizophrenia. *Psychiatric Clinics of North America, 21*, 1–25.

Jones, T., & Wilson, D. (2008). Thinking & doing; fantasy & reality: An analysis of convicted paedophiles. In P. Birch, C. Ireland, & J. Ireland (Eds.), *The assessment, treatment and management of violent and sexual offenders*. London: Willan.

Jónsson, H., Hougaard, E., & Bennedsen, B. E. (2011). Randomized comparative study of group versus individual cognitive behavioural therapy for obsessive compulsive disorder. *Acta Psychiatrica Scandinavica, 123*, 387–397.

Joughin, N. A., Crisp, A. H., Gowers, S. G., & Bhat, A. V. (1991). The clinical features of late onset anorexia nervosa. *Postgraduate Medical Journal, 67*(793), 973–977.

Kamphuis, J. H., & Telch, M. J. (2000). Effects of distraction and guided threat reappraisal on fear reduction during exposure-based treatments for specific fears. *Behaviour Research and Therapy, 38*, 1163–1181.

Kapur, S., Mizrahi, R., & Li, M. (2005). From dopamine salience to psychosis – linking biology, pharmacology and phenomenology of psychosis. *Schizophrenia Research, 79*, 59–68.

References

Karg, K., Burmeister, M., Shedden, K., & Sen, S. (2011). The serotonin transporter promotor variant (5-HTTLPR), stress, and depression meta-analysis revisited: Evidence of genetic moderation. *Archives of General Psychiatry, 68*(5), 444–454.

Karpowicz, E., Skarsater, I., & Nevonen, L. (2009). Self-esteem in patients treated for anorexia nervosa. *International Journal of Mental Health Nursing, 18*, 318–325.

Kato, T. (2007). Molecular genetics of bipolar disorder and depression. *Psychiatry and Clinical Neurosciences, 61*, 3–19.

Kavale, K. A., Spaulding, L. S., & Beam, A. P. (2009). Time to define: Making the specific learning disability definition prescribe specific learning disability. *Learning Disability Quarterly, 32*, 39–49.

Kaye, W. H., Klump, K. L., Frank, G. K., & Strober, M. (2001). Anorexia and bulimia nervosa. *Annual Review of Medicine, 51*, 299–313.

Kearney, C. A., & Trull, T. J. (2012). *Abnormal psychology and life: A dimensional approach.* Belmont, CA: Cengage Learning/Wadsworth.

Keel, P. K., Brown, T. A., Holm-Denoma, J., & Bodell, L. P. (2011). Comparison of DSM-IV versus proposed DSM-5 diagnostic criteria for eating disorders: reduction of eating disorder not otherwise specified and validity. *International Journal of Eating Disorders, 44*, 553–560.

Keel, P. K., Heathertom, T. F., Dorer, D. J., Joiner, T. E., & Zalta, A. K. (2002). Point prevalance of bulimia nervosa in 1982, 1992, and 2002. *Psychological Medicine, 36*, 119–127.

Kendler, K. S. (1985). Diagnostic approaches to schizotypal personality disorder: A historical perspective. *Schizophrenia Bulletin, 11*, 538–553.

Kendler, K. S., Hettema, J. M., Butera, F., Gardner, C. O., & Prescott, C. A. (2003). Life event dimensions of loss, humiliation, entrapment and danger in the prediction of onsets of major depression and generalised anxiety. *Archives of General Psychiatry, 60*, 789–796.

Keski-Rahkonen, A., Hoek, H. W., Linna, M. S., Raevuori, A., Sihvola, E., Bulik, C. M. . . . Kaprio, J. (2009). Incidence and outcomes of bulimia nervosa: A nationwide population-based study. *Psychological Medicine, 39*(5), 23–31.

Kessler, R. C., Berglund, P., Demler, O., Jin, R., Koretz, D., Merikangas, K. R. … Wang, P. S. (2003). The epidemiology of major depressive disorder: Results from the National Comorbidity Survey Replication (NCS-R). *Journal of the American Medical Association, 289*, 3095–3105.

Kessler, R. C., Berglund, P., Demler, O., Jin, R., Merikangas, K. R., & Walters, E. E. (2005). Lifetime prevalence and age-of-onset distributions of DSM-IV disorders in the National Comorbidity Survey Replication. *Archives of General Psychiatry, 62*, 593–602.

Kessler, R. C., Chiu, W. T., Jin, R., Ruscio, A. M., Shear, K., & Walters, E. E. (2006). The epidemiology of panic attacks, panic disorder, and agoraphobia in the National Comorbidity Survey Replication. *Archives of General Psychiatry, 63*, 415–424.

Kewley, G. D. (1995). Personal paper: Attention deficit hyperactivity disorder is underdiagnosed and undertreated in Britain. *British Medical Journal, 23*(316), 1594–1596.

Kidd, G. E. (1946). Trepanation among the early Indians of British Columbia. *Canadian Medical Association Journal, 55*, 513–516.

Kimura, H., Tonoike, T., Muroya, T., Yoshida, K., & Ozaki, N. (2007). Age of onset has limited association with body mass index at time of presentation for anorexia nervosa: Comparison of peak-onset and late-onset anorexia nervosa groups. *Psychiatry and Clinical Neurosciences, 61*, 646–650.

King, B., State, M., Shah, B., Davanzo, P., & Dykens, E. (1997). Mental retardation: A review of the past 10 years. Part I. *Journal of the American Academy of Child and Adolescent Psychiatry, 36*(12), 1656–1683.

Klauke, B., Deckert, J., Reif, A., Pauli, P., & Domschke, K. (2010). Life events in panic disorder – an update on 'candidate stressors'. *Depression and Anxiety, 27*, 716–730.

Klein, M. (1940). Mourning and its relation to manic-depressive states. *The International Journal of Psychoanalysis, 21*, 125–153.

Klonoff, H. (1974). Marijuana and driving in real-life situations. *Science, 186*(4161), 317–324.

Knowlton, A. R., & Latkin, C. A. (2007). Network financial support and conflict as predictors of depressive symptoms among a disadvantaged population. *Journal of Community Psychology, 35*, 13–28.

Koegel, R. L., Koegel, L. K., & McNerney, E. K. (2001). Pivotal areas in intervention for autism. *Journal of Clinical Child Psychology, 30*, 19–32.

Koenen, K. C., Nugent, N. R., & Amstadter, A. B. (2008). Gene–environment interaction in posttraumatic stress disorder: Review, strategy and new directions for future research. *European Archives of Psychiatry and Clinical Neuroscience, 258*, 82–96.

Kogan, M. D., Blumberg, S. J., Schieve, L. A., Boyle, C. A., Perrin, J. M., Ghandour, R. M. . . . van Dyck, P. C. (2009). Prevalence of parent-reported diagnosis of autism spectrum disorder among children in the US, 2007. *Pediatrics, 124*(50), 1395–403.

Krabbendam, L., & van Os, J. (2005) Schizophrenia and urbanicity: A major environmental influence-conditional on genetic risk. *Schizophrenia Bulletin, 31*(4), 795–799.

Kraepelin, E. ([1883], 1981). *Clinical psychiatry* (trans A. R. Diefendorf). New York: Scholar's Facsimiles and Reprints.

Kurtz, P. F., Chin, M. D., Huete, J. M., Tarbox, R. S., O'Conner, J. T., Paclawskyj, T. R., & Rush, K. S. (2003). Functional analysis and treatment of self-injurious behavior in young children: A summary of 30 cases. *Journal of Applied Behavior Analysis, 36*(2), 205–219.

Lang, P. J., & Lazovik, D. A. (1963). Experimental desensitization of a phobia. *Journal of Abnormal and Social Psychology, 66*(6), 519–525.

Lara, M. E., Klein, D. N., & Kasch, K. L. (2000). Psychosocial predictors of the short-term course and outcome of major depression: A longitudinal study of a nonclinical sample with recent-onset episodes. *Journal of Abnormal Psychology, 109*, 644–650.

Laumann, E. O., Palik, A., & Rosen, R. (1999). Sexual dysfunction in the United States: Prevalence and predictors. *Journal of the American Medical Association, 21*, 547–544.

Lawford, B. R., Young, R., Rowell, J. A., Gibson, J. N., Feeney, G. F., Ritchie. T. L. . . . Noble, E. P. (1997). Association of the D2 dopamine receptor A1 allele with alcoholism: Medical severity of alcoholism and type of controls. *Biological Psychiatry, 41*, 386–393.

Lawrie, S. M., McIntosh, A. M., Hall, J., Owens, D. G. C., & Johnstone, E. C. (2008). Brain structure and function changes during the development of schizophrenia: The evidence from studies of subjects at increased genetic risk. *Schizophrenia Bulletin, 34*, 330–340.

Laws, R., & Marshall, W. L. (1991). Masturbatory reconditioning with sexual deviates: An evaluative review. *Advances in Behavioral Research and Therapy, 13*, 13–25.

Le Grange, D., & Lock, J. (2005). The dearth of psychological treatment studies for anorexia nervosa. *International Journal of Eating Disorders, 37*, 79–91.

Leahy, R. L. (Ed) (2004). *Contemporary cognitive therapy: Theory, research, and practice.* New York: Guilford Press.

Lee, J., Jackson, H., Pattison, P., & Ward, T. (2002). Developmental risk factors for sexual offending. *Child Abuse & Neglect, 26*, 73–92.

Lejeune, J., Gautier, M., & Turpin, R. (1959). Les chromosomes humains en culture de tissues. *Academic Sciences, 248*(4), 602–603.

Lenzenweger, M. F., & Korfine, L. (1994). Perceptual aberrations, schizotypy, and the Wisconsin card sorting test. *Schizophrenia Bulletin, 20*(2), 345–357.

Leonard, B. E. (2010). The concept of depression as a dysfunction of the immune system. *Current Immunology Review, 6*(3), 205–212.

Levy, K. N., & Scala, J. W. (2012). Transference, transference interpretations, and transference-focused psychotherapies. *Psychotherapy, 49*(3), 391–403.

Lewinsohn, P. M. (1974). A behavioural approach to depression. In R. J. Friedman & M. M. Katz (Eds.), *The psychology of depression: Contemporary theory and research.* New York: Wiley.

Lewinsohn, P. M., Munoz, R. F., Youngren, M. A., & Zeiss, A. M. (1994). *Control your depression* (revised ed.) New York: Fireside.

Licata, A., Taylor, S., Berman, M., & Cranston, J. (1993). Effects of cocaine on human aggression. *Pharmacology Biochemistry and Behavior, 45*(3), 549–552.

References

Liddle, P. F. (1987). The symptoms of chronic schizophrenia. A re-examination of the positive-negative dichotomy. *The British Journal of Psychiatry, 151*(2), 145–151.

Lieberman, J. A., Kinon, B. J., & Loebel, A. D. (1990). Dopaminergic mechanisms in idiopathic and drug-induced psychoses. *Schizophrenia Bulletin, 16*, 97–109.

Lieberman, J., Chakos, M., Wu, H., Alvir, J., Hoffman, E., Robinson, D. & Bilder, R. (2001). Longitudinal study of brain morphology in first episode schizophrenia. *Biological Psychiatry, 49*, 487–499.

Lillie, M. C. (1998). Cranial surgery dates back to the Mesolithic. *Nature, 391*, 854.

Linszen, D. H., Dingemans, P. M., & Lenoir, M. E. (1994). Cannabis abuse and the course of recent onset schizophrenic disorders. *Archives of General Psychiatry, 51*, 273–279.

Livesley, W. J. (2006). The Dimensional Assessment of Personality Pathology (DAPP) approach to personality disorder. In Stephen Strack (ed), (2006). *Differentiating normal and abnormal personality* (2nd ed.). New York: Springer.

Loranger, A. W., Sartorius, N., Andreoli, A., Berger, P., Buchheim, P., & Channabasavanna, S. M. (1994). The International Personality Disorder Examination (IPDE). The World Health Organization/Alcohol, Drug Abuse, and Mental Health Administration International Pilot Study of Personality Disorders. *Archives of General Psychiatry, 51*, 215–224.

Losel, F., & Schmucker, M. (2005). The effectiveness of treatment for sexual offenders: A comprehensive meta-analysis. *Journal of Experimental Criminology, 1*, 117–146.

Lundgren, J., Carlsson, S. G., & Berggren, U. (2006). Relaxation versus cognitive therapies for dental fear – a psychophysiological approach. *Health Psychology, 25*(3), 267–273.

Lynam, D. R., & Gudonis, L. (2005). The development of psychopathy. *Annual Review of Clinical Psychology, 1*, 381–407.

Lynch, D., Laws, K. R., & McKenna, P. J. (2010). Cognitive behavioural treatment for major psychiatric disorder: Does it really work? A meta-analytical review of well-controlled trials. *Psychological Medicine, 40*(1), 9–24.

MacKay, T. (2009). Severe and complex learning difficulties: Issues of definition, classification and prevalence. *Educational and Child Psychology, 26*(4), 9–18.

MacMahon, B., & Trichopoulos, D. (1996). *Epidemiology: Principles and methods* (2nd ed.). Boston, MA: Little Brown.

Malhi, G. S., & Lagopoulos, J. (2008) Making sense of neuroimaging in psychiatry. *Acta Psychiatrica Scandinavica, 117*, 100–117.

Maltby, N., Kirsch, I., Mayers, M., & Allen, G. J. (2002). Virtual reality exposure therapy for the treatment of fear of flying: A controlled investigation. *Journal of Consulting and Clinical Psychology, 70*, 1112–1118.

Marjoram, D., Tansley, H., Miller, P., MacIntyre, D., Owens, D. G. C., Johnstone, E. C., & Lawrie, S. (2005) A theory of mind investigation into the appreciation of visual jokes in schizophrenia. *BMC Psychiatry, 5*, 12.

Markarian, Y., Larson, M. J., Aldea, M. A., Baldwin, S. A., Good, D., Berkeljon, A....McKay, D. (2010). Multiple pathways to functional impairment in obsessive-compulsive disorder. *Clinical Psychology Review, 30*, 78–88.

Maron, E., & Shlik, J. (2006). Serotonin function in panic disorder: Important, but why? *Neurosychopharmacology, 31*, 1–11.

Marques, J. K., Nelson, C., Alaarcon, J-M., & Day, D. M. (2000). Preventing relapse in sex offenders: What we learned from SOTEP's experimental treatment program. In D. R. Laws, S. M. Hudson, & T. Ward (Eds.), *Remaking relapse prevention with sex offenders: A sourcebook*. Thousand Oaks, CA: Sage.

Marshall, W. L., & Marshall, L. E. (2000). The origins of sex offending. *Trauma Violence and Abuse, 1*(3), 250–263.

Martin, S. E., Maxwell, C. D., White, H. R., & Zhang, Y. (2004). Trends in alcohol use, cocaine use and crime: 1989–1998, *Journal of Drug Issues*, 333–360.

Mason, A., Hawkins, J., Kosterman, R., McCarty, C. A., Herrenkohl, T. I., & Hawkins, J. D. (2010). Growth in adolescent delinquency and alcohol use in relation to young adult crime, alcohol use disorders, and risky sex: A comparison of youth from low- versus middle-income backgrounds. *Journal of Child Psychology and Psychiatry and Allied Disciplines, 51*(2), 1377–1385.

Masters, W. H., & Johnson, V. E. (1970). *Human sexual inadequacy.* Toronto; New York: Bantam Books.

McCarthy, E., & Petrakis, I. (2010). Epidemiology and management of alcohol dependence in individuals with post-traumatic stress disorder. *Central Nervous System Drugs, 24*(12), 997–1007.

McClure, E. B., Monk, C. S., Nelson, E. E., Parrish, J. M., Adler, A., Blair, R .J. R. ... Pine, D. S. (2007). Abnormal attention modulation of fear circuit function in pediatric generalized anxiety disorder. *Archives of General Psychiatry, 64*, 97–106.

McConaghy, N., Armstrong, M. S., Blaszczynski, A., & Allcock, C. (1983). Controlled comparison of aversive therapy and imaginal desensitization in compulsive gambling. *British Journal of Psychiatry, 142*, 366–372.

McCorkindale, S. (2011), Cognitive behaviour therapy for children with social anxiety. *Learning Disability Practice, 14*(7), 20–22.

McCrady, B. S. (2004). To have but one true friend: Implications for practice of research on alcohol use disorders and social network. *Psychology of Addictive Behavior, 18*(2), 113–121.

McCrystal, P., Higgins, K., Percy, A., & Thornton, M. (2005). Adolescent substance abuse among young people excluded from school in Belfast. *Drugs: Education, Prevention and Policy, 12*, 101–113.

McIntosh, J., MacDonald, F., & McKeganey, N. (2003). Knowledge and perception of illegal drugs in a sample of pre-teenage children. *Drugs: Education, Prevention and Policy, 10*, 331–344.

McKenzie, S. J., Williamson, D. A., & Cubic, B. A. (1993). Stable and reactive body image disturbances in bulimia nervosa. *Behavior Therapy, 24*, 195–207.

McLellan, A. T., Lewis, D. C., O'Brien, C. P., & Kleber, H. D. (2000). Drug dependence, a chronic medical illness: Implications for treatment, insurance, and outcomes evaluation. *The Journal of the American Medical Association, 284*(13), 1689–1695.

McWilliams, N. (1994). *Psychoanalytic diagnosis: Understanding personality structure in the clinical process.* New York: Guilford Press.

Melnik, T., Soares, B. G., & Nasello, A. G. (2008). The effectiveness of psychological interventions for the treatment of erectile dysfunction: Systematic review and meta-analysis, including comparisons to sildenafil treatment, intracavernosal injection, and vacuum devices. *Journal of Sex Medicine, 5*(11), 2562–2574.

Merikangas, K. R., Jin, R., He, J. P., Kessler, R. C., Lee, S ... Zarkov, Z. (2011). Prevalence and correlates of bipolar spectrum disorder in the world mental health survey initiative. *Archives of General Psychiatry, 68*, 241–51.

Messer, S. B. (2002). A psychodynamic perspective on resistance in psychotherapy: *Vive la résistance. Journal of Clinical Psychology, 58*(2), 157–163.

Mihalopoulus, C., Harris, M., Henry, L., Harrigan, S., & McGorry, P. (2009). Is early intervention in psychosis cost-effective over the long term? *Schizophrenia Bulletin, 35*, 909–918.

Miller, P., & Plant, M. (2002). Heavy cannabis use among UK teenagers: An exploration. *Drug and Alcohol Dependence, 65*, 235–242.

Miller, W. R., & Wilbourne, P. L. (2002). Mesa Grande: A methodological analysis of clinical trials of treatments for alcohol use disorders. *Addiction, 97*, 265–277.

Mineka, S., & Cook, M. (1986). Immunization against the observational conditioning of snake fear in rhesus monkeys. *Journal of Abnormal Psychology, 95*, 307–318.

Minuchin, S., Rosman, B., & Baker, L. (1978). *Psychosomatic families: Anorexia nervosa in context.* Cambridge, MA: Harvard University Press.

Mogg, K., & Bradley, B. P. (2006). Time course of attentional bias for fear-relevant pictures in spider-fearful individuals. *Behaviour Research and Therapy, 44*, 1241–1250.

Monshouwer, K., Smit, F., de Graaf, R., van Os, J., & Vollebergh, W. (2005). First cannabis use: Does onset shift to younger ages? Findings from 1988 to 2003 from the Dutch National School Survey on Substance Use. *Addiction, 100*, 963–970.

Moos, R. H., Cronkite, R. C., & Moos, B. S. (1998) Family and extra family resources and the ten-year course of treated depression. *Journal of Abnormal Psychology, 107*, 450–460.

Moreira, E. D., Glasser, D. B., Nicolosi, A., Duarte, F. G., & Gigell, C. (2008). Sexual problems and help-seeking behaviour in adults in the United Kingdom and continental Europe. *BJU International, 101*(8), 1005–1011.

Morgan, C. N., Roy, M., & Chance, P. (2003). Psychiatric comorbidity and medication use in autism: A community survey. *The Psychiatrist, 27*, 378–381.

Muris, P., van Zwol, L., Huijding, J., & Mayer, B. (2010). Mom told me scary things about this animal: Parents installing fear beliefs in their children via the verbal information pathway. *Behaviour Research and Therapy, 48*(4), 341–346.

Murphy, C. J. A., & Rose, S. (2007). Drug misuse declared: Findings from the 2006/07 British crime survey. London: Home Office Statistical Bulletin. www.homeoffice.gov.uk (accessed 29 November 2012).

Murray, J. B. (2000). Psychological profile of pedophiles and child molesters. *Journal of Psychology, 134*(2), 211–224.

Murray, J., Ehlers, A., & Mayou, R. A. (2002). Dissociation and post-traumatic stress disorder: Two prospective studies of road traffic accident survivors. *British Journal of Psychiatry, 180*, 363–368.

Nazareth, I., Boynton, P., & King, M. (2003). Problems with sexual function in people attending London general practitioners: A cross sectional study. *Canadian Journal of Human Sexuality, 12*(1), 423–428.

Neal, D. J., & Fromme, K. (2007). Event-level covariation of alcohol intoxication and behavioral risks during the first year of college. *Journal of Consulting and Clinical Psychology, 75*, 294–306.

Nee, C., & Farman, S. (2005). Female prisoners with borderline personality disorder: Some promising treatment developments. *Criminal Behaviour and Mental Health, 15*(1), 2–16.

Neff, J. L., & Waite, D. E. (2007). Male versus female substance abuse patterns among incarcerated juvenile offenders: Comparing strain and social learning variables. *Justice Quarterly, 24*, 106–132.

Nikolaus, S., Hautzel, H., Heinzel, A., & Müller, H. W. (2012). Key players in major and bipolar depression – a retrospective analysis of *in vivo* imaging studies. *Behavioural Brain Research, 232*(2), 358–390.

Norbeck, E. (1961). *Religion in primitive society.* New York: Harper & Row.

O'Brien, M. P., Gordon, J. L., Bearden, C. E., Lopez, S. R., Kopelowicz, A., & Cannon, T. D. (2006). Positive family environment predicts improvement in symptoms and social functioning among adolescents at imminent risk for onset of psychosis. *Schizophrenia Research, 81*, 269–275.

O'Carroll, R. (2000). Cognitive impairment in schizophrenia. *Advances in Psychiatric Treatment, 6*, 161–168.

Obsessive Compulsive Cognitions Working Group (1997). Cognitive assessment of obsessive–compulsive disorder. *Behaviour Research and Therapy, 35*, 667–681.

O'Farrell, A., Allwright, S., Downey, J., Bedford, D., & Howell, F. (2004), The burden of alcohol misuse on emergency in-patient hospital admissions among residents from a health board region in Ireland. *Addiction, 99*, 1279–1285.

Öhman, A., & Mineka, S. (2001). Fears, phobias, and preparedness: Toward an evolved module of fear and fear learning. *Psychological Review, 108*(3), 483–522.

Olatunji, B. O., Davis, M. L., Powers, M. B., & Smits, J. A. (2011). Cognitive-behavioural therapy for obsessive-compulsive disorder: A meta-analysis of treatment outcome and moderators. *Journal of Psychiatric Research, 47*(1), 33–41.

Ollendick, T. H., & King, N. J. (1991). Origins of childhood fears: An evaluation of Rachman's theory of fear acquisition. *Behaviour Research and Therapy, 29*, 117–123.

Olszewski, D., Matias, J., Monshouwer, K., & Kokkevi, A. (2010). Polydrug use among 15- to 16-year olds: Similarities and differences in Europe. *Drugs: Education, Prevention and Policy, 17*(4), 287–302.

ONS. (2009). *Statistics on alcohol: England, 2009.* The Health and Social Care Information Centre. London: Office for National Statistics.

Oosterink, F. M., de Jongh, A., & Hoogstraten J. (2009). Prevalence of dental fear and phobia relative to other fear and phobia subtypes. *European Journal of Oral Sciences, 117*(2), 135–143.

Öst, L. G. (1987). Age of onset in different phobias. *Journal of Abnormal Psychology, 96*(3), 223–229.

Öst, L. G., & Breitholtz, E. (2000). Applied relaxation vs. cognitive therapy in the treatment of generalized anxiety disorder. *Behaviour Research & Therapy, 38*(8), 777–790.

Ougrin, D. (2011). Efficacy of exposure versus cognitive therapy in anxiety disorders: Systematic review and meta-analysis. *Psychiatry, 11,* 200.

Park, M.S., Sohn, S., Park, J.E., Kim, S.H., Yu, I.K., & Sohn, J.H.(2011). Brain functions associated with verbal working memory tasks among young males with alcohol use disorders. *Scand.J.Psychol.52*(1), 1–7

Pagnin, D., de Queiroz, V., Pini, S., & Cassano, G. B. (2004). Efficacy of ECT in depression: A meta-analytic review. *Journal of ECT, 20*(1), 13–20.

Parner, E. T., Baron-Cohen, S., & Lauritsen, M. B. (2012). Parental age and autism spectrum disorders. *Annals of Epidemiology, 22*(3), 143–150.

Parrott, A., Morinan, A., Moss, M., & Scholey, A. (2005). *Understanding drugs and behaviour.* Chichester: John Wiley & Sons.

Patterson, G. R., DeGarmo, D., & Forgatch, M. S. (2004). Systematic changes in families following prevention trials. *Journal of Abnormal Child Psychology, 32,* 621–633.

Pauls, D. L. (2010) The genetics of obsessive-compulsive disorder: A review. *Dialogues in Clinical Neuroscience, 12*(2), 149–163.

Peeters, T., & Gillberg, C. (1999). *Autism: Medical and educational aspects.* Oxford: WileyBlackwell.

Peters, E., Joseph, S., Day, S., & Garety, P. (2004). Measuring delusional ideation. *Schizophrenia Bulletin, 30*(4), 1005–1022.

Pelham, W. E., Carlson, C., Sams, S. E., Vallano, G., Dixon, M. J., & Hoza, B. (1993). Separate and combined effectis of methylphenidate and behavior modification on boys with attention deficit/hyperactivity in the classroom. *Journal of Consulting and Clinical Psychology, 61,* 506–515.

Peri, T., Ben-Shakhar, G., Orr, S. P., & Shalev, A. Y. (2000). Psychophysiological assessment of aversive conditioning in posttraumatic stress disorder. *Biological Psychiatry, 47,* 512–519.

Perugi, G., Frare, F., & Toni, C. (2007). Diagnosis and treatment of agoraphobia with panic disorder. *CNS Drugs, 21*(9), 741–764.

Pharoah, F., Mari, J., Rathbone, J., & Wong, W. (2010). Family intervention for schizophrenia. *Cochrane Database Systematic Review,* Dec 8: (12): CD000088.

Pike, K. M. (1998). Long-term course of anorexia nervosa: response, relapse, remission and recovery. *Clinical Psychology Review, 18,* 447–475.

Pinel, J. P. (2008). *Biopsychology.* New York: Allyn & Bacon.

Polcin, D. L. (1997). The etiology and diagnosis of alcohol dependence: Differences in the professional literature. *Psychotherapy, 34*(3), 297–306.

Poreh, A. M., Ross, T. P., & Whitman, R. D. (1995). Reexamination of executive functions in psychosis-prone college students. *Personality and Individual Differences, 18*(4), 535–539.

Pozzi-Monzo, M. (2012). Ritalin for whom? Revisited: Further thinking on ADHD. *Journal of Child Psychotherapy, 38*(1), 46–90.

Prochaska, J. O., DiClemente, C. C., & Norcross, J. C. (1992). In search of how people change. *American Journal of Psychology, 47,* 1102–1114.

Purdon, C. (2004). Cognitive-behavioural treatment of repugnant obsessions. *Journal of Clinical Psychology, 60*(11), 1169–1180.

Pusey, E. B. (1865). *Daniel The prophet: Nine lectures.* New York: Funk & Wagnalls.

QAA (2010).

Quayle, E., & Taylor, M. (2003). Model of problematic Internet use in people with a sexual interest in children. *CyberPsychology & Behaviour, 6*(1), 93–106.

Quinsey, V. L., & Lalumière, M. L. (1995). Evolutionary perspectives on sexual offending. *Sexual Abuse, 7*, 301–315.

Rachman, S. (2002). Fears born and bred: Non-associative fear acquisition? *Behaviour Research and Therapy, 40*(2), 212–216.

Radomsky, A. S., & Rachman, S. (2004). Symmetry, ordering and arranging compulsive behavior. *Behaviour Research and Therapy, 42*, 893–913.

Raine, A., Reynolds, C., Lencz, T., & Scerbo, A. (1994). Cognitive-perceptual, interpersonal, and disorganized features of schizotypal personality. *Schizophrenia Bulletin, 20*(1), 191.

Ralph, D. J., & McNicholas, T. (2000). UK management guidelines for erectile dysfunction. *British Medical Journal, 321*, 499–503.

Ramchand, R., Schell, T. L., Karney, B. R., Osilla, K. C., Burns, R. M., & Caldarone, L. B. (2010). Disparate prevalence estimates of PTSD among service members who served in Iraq and Afghanistan: Possible explanations. *Journal of Traumatic Stress, 23*(1), 59–68.

Ratajczak, H. V. (2011). Theoretical aspects of autism: Causes – A review. *Journal of Immunotoxicology, 8*(1), 68–79.

Reinecke, A., Becker, E. S., Hoyer, J., & Rinck, M. (2010). Generalized implicit fear associations in generalized anxiety disorder. *Depression and Anxiety, 27*(3), 252–259.

Remmerswaal, D., Muris, P., Mayer, B., & Smeets, G. (2010). 'Will a Cuscus bite you, if he shows his teeth?' Inducing a fear-related confirmation bias in children by providing verbal threat information to their mothers. *Journal of Anxiety Disorders, 24*(5), 540–546.

Renner, F., Lobbestael, J., Peeters, F., Arntz, A., & Huibers, M. (2012). Early maladaptive schemas in depressed patients: Stability and relation with depressive symptoms over the course of treatment. *Journal of Affective Disorders, 136*(3), 581–590.

Ressler, K. J. (2010). Amygdala activity, fear, and anxiety: Modulation by stress. *Biological Psychiatry, 67*(12), 1117–1119.

Reynolds, C. A., Raine, A., Mellingen, K., Venables, P. H., & Mednick, S. A. (2000). Three-factor model of schizotypal personality. *Schizophrenia Bulletin, 26*(3), 603–618.

Rice, M. E., & Harris, G. T. (2011). Is androgen deprivation therapy effective in the treatment of sex offenders? *Psychology, Public Policy and Law, 17*(2), 315–332.

Rice, M. E., Harris, G. T., & Cormier, C. A. (1992). An evaluation of a maximum security therapeutic community for psychopaths and other mentally disordered offenders. *Law and Human Behavior, 16*(4), 399–412.

Rickels, K., & Rynn, M. (2002). Pharmacotherapy of generalized anxiety disorder. *Journal of Clinical Psychiatry, 63*(Suppl. 14), 9–16.

Ristic, J., Mottron, L, Friesen, C. K., Iarocci, G., Burack, J. A., & Kingstone, A. (2005). Eyes are special but not for everyone: The case of autism. *Cognitive Brain Research, 24*, 715–718.

Robb, H. W. J., & O'Hanlon, J. F. (1993). Marijuana's effect on actual driving: Summary of a 3-year experimental program. In H. D. Utzelmann, G. Berghaus, and G. Kroj (Eds.), *Alcohol, drugs and traffic safety.* Cologne: Verlag TUV.

Rodier, P. M. (2000). The early origins of autism. *Scientific American, 282*(2), 56–63.

Roitman, S. E. L., Cornblatt, A. C., Bergman, A., Obuchowski, M., Mitropoulou, V., Keefe, R. S. E., Silverman, J. M., & Siever, L. J. (1997). Attentional functioning in Schizotypal Personality Disorder. *American Journal of Psychiatry, 154*, 655–660.

Romme, M. A.. & Escher, A. D. (1989). Hearing voices. *Schizophrenia Bulletin, 15*, 209–216.

Rooney, B., McClelland, L., Crisp, A. H., & Sedgwick, P. M. (1995). The incidence and prevalence of anorexia nervosa in three suburban health districts in south-west London, UK. *International Journal of Eating Disorders, 18*, 299–307.

Rosemond, J., & Ravenel, B. (2009). *The diseasing of America's children*. Boston, MA: Thomas Nelson.

Rosen, G. (1968). *Madness in society: Chapters in the historical sociology of mental illness*. Chicago, IL: The University of Chicago Press

Roth, A., & Fonagy, P. (1998). *What works for whom? A critical review of psychotherapy research*. New York: Guildford.

Roth, A., & Fonagy, P. (2005). *What works for whom: A critical review of psychotherapy research* (2nd ed.). New York: Guilford Press.

Rothblum, E. D. (2000). 'Somewhere on Des Moines or San Antonio': Historical perspectives on lesbian, gay and bisexual health. In R. M. Perez, K. A. DeBord, & K. J. Bieschke (Eds.), *Handbook of counselling and psychotherapy with lesbian, gay and bisexual clients* (pp. 57–80), Washington, DC: American Psychological Association.

Roy-Byrne, P. P., Craske, M. G., & Stein, M. B. (2006). Panic disorder. *The Lancet, 368*, 1023–1032.

Russel, C., & Keel, P. (2002). Homosexuality as a specific risk factor for eating disorders in men *International Journal of Eating Disorders, 3*, 300–306.

Ryle, A. (1975). *Cognitive analytic therapy: Developments in theory and practice*. Chichester: Wiley.

Sadock, B., & Sadock, V. (2007). *Kaplan & Sadock's synopsis of psychiatry: Behavioural sciences/ clinical psychiatry* (10th ed.). Philadelphia, PA: Lippincott Williams & Wilkins.

Sameroff A. J., & Fiese, B. H. (2000). Models of development and developmental risk. In C. H. Zeanah, Jr. (Ed.), *Handbook of infant mental health* (2nd ed., pp. 3–13). New York: Guilford Press.

Sanders, A. R., Duan, J., Levinson, D. F., Shi, J., He, D., Hou, C. . . . Gejman, P. V. (2008). No significant association of 14 candidate genes with schizophrenia in a large European ancestry sample: Implications for psychiatric genetics. *American Journal of Psychiatry, 165*, 497–506.

Saulsman, L. M., & Page, A. C. (2004). The five-factor model and personality disorder empirical literature: A meta-analytic review. *Clinical Psychology Review, 23*(8), 1055–1085.

Schmidt, N. B., Keough, M. E., Mitchell, M., Reynolds, E. K., MacPherson, L., Zvolensky, M. J., & Lejuez, C. W. (2010). Anxiety sensitivity: Prospective prediction of anxiety among early adolescents. *Journal of Anxiety Disorders, 24*(5), 503–508.

Schneier, F. R. (2001). Treatment of social phobia with antidepressants. *Journal of Clinical Psychiatry, 62*(Suppl 1), 43–48.

Schreier, A., Wolke, D., Thomas, K., Horwood, J., Hollis, C., Gunnell, D. . . . Harrison, G. (2009). Prospective study of peer victimisation in childhood and psychotic symptoms in a nonclinical population at age 12 years. *Archives of General Psychiatry, 66*, 527–536.

Schweckendiek, J., Klucken, T., Merz, C. J., Tabbert, K., Walter, B., Ambach, W. . . . Stark, R. (2011). Weaving the (neuronal) web: Fear learning in spider phobia. *Neuroimage, 54*(1), 681–688.

Seeber, K., & Cadenhead, K. S. (2005). How does studying schizotypal personality disorder inform us about the prodrome of schizophrenia? *Current Psychiatry Reports, 7*(1), 41–50.

Seligman, M. E. P. (1975). *Helplessness*. San Francisco, CA: Freeman.

Selikowitz, M. (2004). *ADHD: The facts*. Oxford: Oxford University Press.

Sellen, J. L., Oaksford, M., & Gray, N. S. (2005). Schizotypy and conditional reasoning. *Schizophrenia Bulletin, 31*(1), 105–116.

Serfaty, M. A., Turkington, D., Heap, M., Ledsham, L., & Jolley, E. (1999). Cognitive therapy versus dietary counseling in the outpatient treatment of anorexia nervosa: Effects of the treatment phase. *European Eating Disorders Review, 7*(5), 334–350.

Sharpley, C. F. (2010). A review of the neurobiological effects of psychotherapy for depression. *Psychotherapy Theory, Research, Practice, Training, 47*(4), 603–615.

Shaw, D. W., & Thoresen, C. E. (1974). Effects of modeling and desensitization in reducing dentist phobia. *Journal of Counseling Psychology, 21*(5), 415–420.

Sheikh, J. I., Leskin, G. A., & Klein, D. F. (2002). Gender differences in panic disorder: Findings from the National Comorbidity Survey. *American Journal of Psychiatry, 159*, 55–58.

Shibasaki, M., & Kawai, N. (2009). Rapid detection of snakes by Japanese monkeys (*Macacafuscata*): An evolutionary predisposed visual system. *Journal of Comparative Psychology, 123*(2), 131–135.

Shih, R. A., Belmonte, P. L., & Zandi, P. P. (2004) A review of the evidence from family, twin and adoption studies for a genetic contribution to adult psychiatric disorders. *International Review of Psychiatry, 16*(4), 260–283.

Shine, J., & Hobson, J. (1997). Construct validity of the Hare Psychopathy Checklist, Revised, on a UK prison population. *Journal of Forensic Psychiatry, 8*(3), 546–561.

Shrivastava, A., Shah, N., Johnston, M., Stitt, L., & Thakar, M. (2010). Predictors of long-term outcome of first episode schizophrenia: A ten year follow-up study. *Indian Journal of Psychiatry, 52*, 320–326.

SIGN. (2007). *Autism spectrum disorders: Booklet for parents and carers.* Scotland: Scottish Intercollegiate Guidelines Network.

Silverstein, C. (2009). Letter to the Editor: The implications of removing homosexuality as a mental disorder. *Archives of Sex Behavior, 38*(2), 1–3.

Simons, J., & Carey, M. P. (2001). Prevalence of sexual dysfunctions: Results from a decade of research. *Archives of Sexual Behavior, 30*, 177–219.

Simpson, H. B. (2010). Pharmacological treatment of obsessive-compulsive disorder. *Current Topics in Behavioral Neurosciences, 2*, 527–543.

Simpson, H. B., Hubbert, J. D., Petkova, E., Foa, E. B., & Liebowitz, M. R. (2006). Response versus remission in obsessive-compulsive disorder. *Journal of Clinical Psychiatry, 67*(2), 269–276.

Skinner, B. F. (1990) Can psychology be a science of mind? *American Psychologist, 45*, 1206–1210.

Slade, P. D., & Brodie, D. (1994). Body image distortion and eating disorder: A reconceptualisation based on the recent literature. *European Eating Disorders Review, 2*, 32–46.

Slattery, D. A., Hudson, A. L., & Nutt, D. J. (2004). The evolution of antidepressant mechanisms. *Fundamental & Clinical Pharmacology, 18*, 1–21.

Slavich, G. M., Way, B. M., Eisenberger, N. I., & Taylor, S. E. (2010). Neural sensitivity to social rejection is associated with inflammatory responses to social stress. *Proceedings of the National Academy of Science USA, 107*, 14817–14822.

Smink, F. R. E., van Hoeken, D., & Hoek, H. W. (2012). Epidemiology of eating disorders: Incidence, prevalence and mortality rates. *Current Psychiatry Reports, 14*, 406–414.

Smith, A., & Cook-Cottone, C. (2011). A review of family therapy as an effective intervention for anorexia nervosa in adolescents. *Journal of Clinical Psychological Medicine, 18*, 323–334.

Smith, R. E., & Sharpe, T. M. (1970). Treatment of a school phobia with implosive therapy. *Journal of Consulting and Clinical Psychology, 35*(2), 239–243.

Soares, S. C., Esteves, F., Lundqvist, D., & Öhman, A. (2009). Some animal specific fears are more specific than others: Evidence from attention and emotion measures. *Behaviour Research and Therapy, 47*(12), 1032–1042.

Sobell, L. C., Agrawal, S., Annis, H., Ayala-Velazquez, H., Echeverria, L., Leo, G. I....Ziólkowski, M. (2001). Cross-cultural evaluation of two drinking assessment instruments: Alcohol timeline followback and inventory of drinking situations. *Substance Use and Misuse, 36*(3), 313–331.

Soloff, P. H., Cornelius, J. R., George, A., Nathan, S., Perel, J. M., & Ulrich, R. E. (1993). Efficacy of ohenelzine and haloperidol in borderline personality disorder. *Archives of General Psychiatry, 50*, 377–385.

Solomon, A. H., & Chung, B. (2012). Understanding autism: How family therapists can support parents of children with autism spectrum disorders. *Family Process, 51*(2), 250–264.

Soria, V., Martínez-Amorós, E., Escaramís, G., Valero, J., Pérez-Egea, R., García, C.... Urretavizcaya, M. (2010). Differential association of circadian genes with mood disorders: CRY1 and NPAS2 are associated with unipolar major depression and CLOCK and VIP with bipolar disorder. *Neuropsychopharmacology, 35*(6), 1279–89.

Spindler, K. A., Sullivan, E. V., Menon, V., Lim, K. O., & Pfefferbaum, A. (1997). Deficits in multiple systems of working memory in schizophrenia. *Schizophrenia Research, 27,* 1–10.

Sprong, M., Schothorst, P., Vos, E., Hox, J., & Van Engeland, H. (2007). Theory of mind in schizophrenia: Meta-analysis. *British Journal of Psychiatry, 191,* 5–13.

Stahl, S. M. (1996). *Essential psychopharmacology: Neuroscientific basis and practical applications.* Cambridge: Cambridge University Press.

Steffen, K. J., Mitchell, J. E., Roerig, J. L., & Lancaster, K. L. (2007). The eating disorders medicine cabinet revisited: A clinician's guide to ipecac and laxatives. *International Journal of Eating Disorders, 40,* 360–368.

Stein, D. J., Ipser, J. C., & Seedat, S. (2009). Pharmacotherapy for post traumatic stress disorder. *The Cochrane Collaboration,* 1.

Stein, D. J., & Stahl, S. (2000). Serotonin and anxiety: Current models. *International Clinical Psychopharmacology, 15*(Suppl 2), S1–6.

Stein, G. (2010). The voices that Ezekial hears. *British Journal of Psychiatry, 196,* 101.

Steiner, H., & Lock, J. (1998). Anorexia nervosa and bulimia nervosa in children and adolescents: A review of the past 10 years. *Journal of the American Academy of Child and Adolescent Psychiatry, 37*(4), 352–359.

Stevens, R. (1983). *Freud and psychoanalysis.* Milton Keynes: Open University Press.

Stice, E., Marti, C. N., & Rohde, P. (2012). Prevalence, incidence, impairment, and course of the proposed DSM-5 eating disorder diagnoses in an 8-year prospective community study of young women. *Journal of Abnormal Psychology,* 1–13.

Stickgold, R. (2002). EMDR: A putative neurobiological mechanism of action. *Journal of Clinical Psychology, 58*(1), 61–75.

Stirling, J., Hellewell, J. S. E., & Ndlovu, D. (2001). Self-monitoring dysfunction and the positive symptoms of schizophrenia. *Psychopathology, 34,* 198–202.

Stone, M. H. (1998). *Healing the mind: A history of psychiatry from antiquity to the present.* London: Pimlico.

Stone, M. H., & Thompson, E. H. (2001). Executive function impairment in sexual offenders. *Journal of Individual Psychology, 57,* 51–59.

Strack, S., Lorr, M., & Campbell, L. (1990). An evaluation of Millon's circular model of personality disorders. *Journal of Personality Disorders, 4*(4), 353–361.

Striegel Moore, R. H., DeBar, L., Wilson, G., Dickerson, J., Rosselli, F., Perrin, N. … Kraemer, H. C. (2008). Health services use in eating disorders. *Psychological Medicine, 38*(10), 1465–1474.

Striegel-Moore, R. H., Garvin, V., Dohm, F. A., & Rosenheck, R. A. (1999). Psychiatric comorbidity of eating disorders in men: a national study of hospitalized veterans. *International Journal of Eating Disorders, 25*(4), 399–404.

Student-Pavlovich, D., & Elliott, M. A. (2001). Eating disorders in women's oral health. *Dental Clinics of North America, 45*(3), 491–511.

Sue, D., Sue, D. W., Sue, D., & Sue, S. (2010). *Foundations of abnormal behavior.* Boston, MA: Wadsworth, Cengage Learning.

Suhr, J. A. (1997). Executive functioning deficits in hypothetically psychosis-prone college students. *Schizophrenia Research, 27,* 29–35.

Sullivan, J. T., Sykora, K., Schneiderman, J., Naranjo, C. A., & Sellers, E. M. (1989). Assessment of alcohol withdrawal: The revised clinical institute withdrawal assessment for alcohol scale (CIWA-Ar). *British Journal of Addiction, 84*(11), 1353–1357.

Sullivan, L. E., Fiellin, D. A., & O'Connor, P. G. (2005). The prevalence and impact of alcohol problems in major depression: A systematic review. *American Journal of Medicine, 118,* 330–341.

Swann, A. C., Moeller, F. G., Steinberg, J. L. Schneider, L., Barratt, E. S., & Dougherty, D. M. (2007). Manic symptoms and impulsivity during bipolar depressive episodes. *Bipolar Disorders, 9,* 206–212.

Swedo, S. (2009). Report of the DSM-5 Neurodevelopmental Disorders Work Group. American Psychiatric Association: http://www.dsm5.org/progressreports/pages/0904reportofthedsm-vneurodevelopmentaldisorderswrkgroup.aspx [accessed: 22 July 2013].

Tai, S., & Turkington, D. (2009). The evolution of cognitive behaviour therapy for schizophrenia: Current practice and recent developments. *Schizophrenia Bulletin, 35*(5), 865–873.

Takei, N., van Os, J., & Murray, R. M. (1995) Maternal exposure to influenza and risk of schizophrenia: A 22-year study from the Netherlands, *Journal of Psychiatric Research, 29*, 435–45.

Tasca, G. A., Ritchie, K., & Balfour, L. (2011). Implications of attachment thory and research for the assessment and treatment of eating disorders. *Psychotherapy, 48*(3), 249–259.

Taylor, E., & Hemsley, R. (1995). Treating hyperkinetic disorders in childhood. *British Medical Journal, 24*(310), 1617–1618.

Thapar, A., Cooper, M., Eyre, O., & Langley, K. (2013). Practitioner review: What have we learnt about the causes of ADHD? *Journal of Child Psychology and Psychiatry, 54*(1), 3–16.

Thibaut, F., De La Barra, F., Gordon, H., Cosyns, P., Bradford, J. M./WFSBP Task Force on Sexual Disorders (2010). The World Federation of Societies of Biological Psychiatry (WFSBP) guidelines for the biological treatment of paraphilias. *World Journal of Biological Psychiatry, 11*(40), 604–655.

Thom, A., Sartory, G., & Jöhren, P. (2000). Comparison between one-session psychological treatment and benzodiazepine in dental phobia. *Journal of Consulting and Clinical Psychology, 68*(3), 378–387.

Thomas, T. (2000). *Sex crime: Sex offending and society*. Cullompton: Willan.

Thompson, P. M., Vidal, C., Giedd, J. N., Gochman, P., Blumenthal, J., Nicolson, R.... Rapoport, J. L. (2001). Mapping adolescent brain change reveals dynamic wave of accelerated gray matter loss in very early onset schizophrenia. *Proceedings of the National Academy of Sciences USA, 98*, 11650–11655.

Tienari, P., Wynne, L. C., Moring, J., Laksy, K., Nieminen, P., & Sorri, A. (2000). Finnish adoptive family study: Sample selection and adoptee DSM III R diagnoses. *Acta Psychiatrica Scandinavica, 101*, 433–443.

Treasure, J., Sepulveda, A., MacDonald, P., Whitaker, W., Lopez, C., Zabala, M....Todd, G. (2008). The assessment of the family of people with eating disorders. *European Eating Disorders Review, 16*(4), 247–255.

Treasure, T. (2001). *The Mental Health Act and eating disorders*. London: Institute of Psychiatry, Division of Psychological Medicine, Eating Disorders Research Unit.

True, W. R., Rice, J., Eisen, S. A., Heath, A. C., Goldberg, J., Lyons, M. J., & Novak, J. (1993). A twin study of genetic and environmental contributions to liability for posttraumatic stress symptoms. *Archives of General Psychiatry, 50*(4), 257–264.

Tsakanikos, E. (2004) Logical reasoning in schizotypal personality. *Personality and Individual Differences, 37*, 1717–1726.

Tsakanikos, E., & Reed, P. (2003). Visuo-spatial processing and dimensions of schizotypy: Figure–ground segregation as a function of psychotic-like features. *Personality and Individual Differences, 35*(3), 703–712.

Turkington, D., Kingdon, D., & Weiden, P. J. (2006). Cognitive behaviour therapy for schizophrenia. *American Journal of Psychiatry, 163*, 365–373.

Turner, J., Batik, M., Palmer, L. J., Forbes, D., & McDermott, B. M. (2000). Detection and importance of laxative use in adolescents with anorexia nervosa. *Journal of American Academy of Child and Adolescent Psychiatry, 39*(3), 378–385.

Tyrer, P., & Baldwin, D. (2006) Generalised anxiety disorder.*The Lancet, 368*, 2156–2166.

Tyson, P. (2011). Psychology, intelligence and I.Q. In: P. J. Tyson, D. Jones, & J. Elcock (Eds.), *Psychology in social context: Issues and debates*. Chichester: BPS Blackwell.

Tyson, P. (2011). Psychology and mental health. In P.J. Tyson, D. Jones, & J. Elcock, *Psychology in social context: Issues and Debates*. BPS Blackwell, Chichester, UK.

Ullrich, S., Borkenau, P., & Marneros, A. (2001). Personality disorder in offenders: Categorical versus dimensional approaches, *Journal of Personality Disorders, 15*, 442–449.

Vahabzadeh, A. B. N., Delaffon, V., Abbas, M., & Biswass, A. B. (2011). Severe learning disability. *InnovAiT, 4*(2), 91–97.

Vaillant, G. E. (1995). *The natural history of alcoholism revisited.* Cambridge, MA: Harvard University Press.

VanDeventer, A. D., & Laws, D. R. (1978). Orgasmic reconditioning to redirect sexual arousal in pedophiles. *Behavior Therapy, 9*(5), 748–765.

van Os J., Hanssen M., Bijl R. V. & Ravelli A. (2000). Strauss (1969) revisited: A psychosis continuum in the general population? *Schizophrenia Research, 45,* 11–20.

Vargas, S., & Camilli, G. (1999). A meta-analysis of research on sensory integration therapy. *American Journal of Occupational Therapy, 53,* 189–198.

Volkow, N. D., Fowler, J. S., Wang, G. J., & Swanson, J. M. (2004). Dopamine in drug abuse and addiction: Results from imaging studies and treatment implications. *Psychiatry, 9*(6), 557–569.

Vollema, M. G., & van den Bosch, R. J. (1995). The multidimensionality of schizotypy. *Schizophrenia Bulletin, 21*(1), 19–31.

Vollmer, T. R., Marcus, B. A., & Ringdahl, J. E. (1995). Noncontingent escape as treatment for self-injurious behavior maintained by negative reinforcement. *Journal of Applied Behavior Analysis, 28*(1), 15–26.

Voruganti, L. N., Slomka, P., Zabel, P., Mattar, A., & Awad, A. G. (2001). Cannabis-induced dopamine release: An *in vivo* SPECT study. *Psychiatry Research, 107,* 173–1777.

Walker, E. F., & Diforio, D. (1997). Schizophrenia: A neural diathesis-stress model. *Psychological Review, 4,* 667–685.

Walsh, W. J., Usman, A., & Tarpey, J. (2001). Disordered metal metabolism in a large autism population. American Psychiatric Association Meeting May, New Orleans.

Ward, T., & Hudson, S. M. (1998). A model of the relapse process in sexual offenders. *Journal of Interpersonal Violence, 13,* 700–725.

Ward, T., & Hudson, S. M. (2000). A self-regulation model of relapse prevention. In D. R. Laws, S. M. Hudson & T. Ward (Eds.), *Remaking relapse prevention with sex offenders: A sourcebook* (pp. 79–101). Thousand Oaks, CA: Sage Publications.

Ward, T., & Siegert, R. J. (2002). Towards a comprehensive theory of child sexual abuse: A theory knitting perspective. *Psychology, Crime and Law, 8,* 319–351.

Warner, R. (2009). Recovery from schizophrenia and the recovery model. *Current Opinions in Psychiatry, 22,* 374–380.

Watling, R., Deitz, J., Kanny, E. M., & McLaughlin, J. F. (1999). Current practice of occupational therapy for children with autism. *American Journal of Occupational Therapy, 53,* 489–497.

Watson, J. B., & Rayner, R. (1920). Conditioned emotional reactions. *Journal of Experimental Psychology, 3*(1), 1–14.

Watson, T. L., & Andersen, A. E. (2003). A critical examination of the amenorrhea and weight criteria for diagnosing anorexia nervosa. *Acta Psychiatrica Scandanavica, 108*(3), 175–182.

Wells, A. (2005). The metacognitive model of GAD: Assessment of meta-worry and relationship with DSM-IV generalized anxiety disorder. *Cognitive Therapy and Research, 29,* 107–121.

Wells, A. (2009). *Metacognitive therapy for anxiety and depression.* New York: Guilford Press.

Wells, A., Clark, D. M., Salkovskis, P., Ludgate, J., Hackmann, A., & Gelder, M. (1995). Social phobia: The role of in-situation safety behaviors in maintaining anxiety and negative beliefs. *Behavior Therapy, 26*(1), 153–161.

Weltzin, T. E., Cornella-Carlson, T, Fitzpatrick, M. E., Kennington, B., Bean, P., & Jefferies, C. (2012). Treatment issues and outcomes for males with eating disorders. *Eating Disorders, 20,* 444–459.

Wender, P. H., Wolf, L. E., & Wasserstein, J. (2001). Adults with ADHD: An overview. *Annals of the New York Academy of Science, 931,* 1–16.

Westrin, A., & Lam, R. W. (2007). Seasonal affective disorder: A clinical update. *Annals of Clinical Psychiatry, 19*(4), 239–246.

Whalen, C. K., Henker, B., & Hinshaw, S. P. (1985). Cognitive-behavioral therapies for hyperactive children: Premises, problems, and prospects. *Journal of Abnormal Child Psychology, 13,* 391–409.

Whitaker, S. (2004) Hidden learning disability. *British Journal of Learning Disabilities, 32,* 139–143.

Whitaker, S., & Porter, J. (2002) Letter to the editor: Valuing people: a new strategy for learning disability for the 21st century. *British Journal of Learning Disabilities, 30*(3), 133.

Whiteside, S. P., Port, J. D., & Abramowitz, J. S. (2004). A meta-analysis of functional neuroimaging in obsessive-compulsive disorder. *Psychiatry Research: Neuroimaging, 132,* 69–79.

Widener, A. J. (1998), Beyond Ritalin: The importance of therapeutic work with parents and children diagnosed ADD/ADHD. *Journal of Child Psychotherapy, 24*(2), 267–281.

Widiger, T. A., & Samuel, D. B. (2005). Diagnostic categories or dimensions? A question for the Diagnostic and statistical manual of mental disorders. *Journal of Abnormal Psychology, 114*(4), 494.

Widiger, T. A., & Sanderson, C. J. (1995). Towards a dimensional model of personality disorders in DSM-IV and DSM-V. In W. J. Livesley (Ed.), *The DSM-IV personality disorders* (pp. 433–458). NY: Guilford Press.

Widiger, T. A., & Simonsen, E. (2005). Alternative dimensional models of personality disorder: Finding a common ground. *Journal of Personality Disorders, 19*(2), 110–130.

Widiger, T. A., Trull, T. J., Clarkin, J. F., Sanderson, C., & Costa Jr, P. T. (2002). A description of the DSM-IV personality disorders with the five-factor model of personality. In P. T. Costa & T. A. Widiger (Eds.), *Personality disorders and the five-factor model of personality* (2nd ed., pp. 89–99). Washington, DC: American Psychological Association.

Wiersma, D., Nienhuis, F. J., & Slooff, C. J. (1998). Natural course of schizophrenic disorders: 15 year follow-up of a Dutch incidence cohort. *Schizophrenia. Bulletin. 24,* 75–85.

Wiggins, J. S., & Pincus, A. L. (1994). Personality structure and the structure of personality disorders. In P. T. Costa & T. A. Widiger (Eds.), *Personality disorders and the five-factor model of personality* (pp. 73–93). Washington, DC: American Psychological Association.

Wilbarger, P. (1995). The sensory diet: Activity programs based on sensory processing theory. *Sensory Integration: Special Interest Section Newsletter, 18*(2), 1–4.

Williams, M. T., Farris, S. G., Turkheimer, E., Pinto, A., Ozanick, K., Franklin, M. F....Foa, E. B. (2011). Myth of the pure obsessional type in obsessive-compulsive disorder. *Depression and Anxiety, 28,* 495–500.

Wilson, D. (1997). Gender differences in sexual fantasy: An evolutionary analysis. *Personality and Individual Differences, 22,* 27–31.

Wilson, D. (2007). Is seeing doing? http://www.martinfrost.ws/htmlfiles/feb2007/crimes_seedo.html [accessed: 1 March 2007].

Wilson, D., & Jones, T. (2008). 'In my own world': A case study of a paedophile's thinking and doing and his use of the Internet. *The Howard Journal of Criminal Justice, 47*(3), 1–14.

Witmer, L. (1907). Clinical psychology. *Psychological Clinic, 1,* 1–9.

Wolfensberger, W. (1972). *The principle of normalization in human services.* Toronto: National Institutes of Mental Retardation.

Wolitzky-Taylor, K. B., Horowitz, J. D., Powers, M. B., & Telch, M. J. (2008). Psychological approaches in the treatment of specific phobias: A meta-analysis. *Clinical Psychology Review, 28,* 1021–1037.

World Health Organization. (1994) *ICD-10 Classifications of Mental and Behavioural Disorder: Clinical Descriptions and Diagnostic Guidelines.* Geneva: WHO.

World Health Organization. (1994). *International Statistical Classification of Diseases & Related Health Problems; V. 3: Alphabetical Index.* Geneva: WHO.

Wright, I. C., Rabe-Hesketh, S., Woodruff, P. W., David, A..S., & Murray, R. M. (2000). Meta-analysis of regional brain volumes in schizophrenia. *American Journal of Psychiatry, 157,* 16–25.

Wyre, R. (1992). Pornography and sexual violence: Working with sex offenders. In C. Itzin (eds), *Pornography: Women, violence and civil liberties.* Oxford: Oxford University Press.

Xing, J. H., & Soffer, E. E. (2001). Adverse effects of laxatives. *Diseases of the Colon & Rectum, 44*(8), 1201–1209.

Yeargin-Allsopp, M., Rice, C., Karapurkar, T., Doernberg, N., Boyle, C., & Murphy, C. (2003). Prevalence of autism in a US metropolitan area. *Journal of the American Medical Association, 289*(1), 49–55.

Yehuda, R., Halligan, S. L., & Bierer, L. M. (2001). Relationship of parental trauma exposure and PTSD to PTSD, depressive and anxiety disorders in offspring. *Journal of Psychiatric Research, 35*, 261–270.

Yoon, S. A., Kang, D. H., & Kwon, J. S. (2008). The emotional characteristics of schizotypy. *Psychiatry Investigation, 5*, 148–154.

Young, A. H. (2004). Cortisol in mood disorders. *Stress, 7*(4) 205–208.

Zakhari, S., & Gordis, E. (1998). Moderate drinking and cardiovascular health. *Proceedings of the Association of American Physicians, 111*, 148–158.

Zanarini, M. C., Frankenburg, F. R., Hennen, J., Reich, B., & Silk, K. R. (2005). The McLean study of adult development (MSAD): Overview and implications of the first six years of prospective follow-up. *Journal of Personality Disorders, 19*, 505–523.

Zilbergeld, B. (1992). *The new male sexuality.* New York: Random House Publishing.

Zilboorg, G. (1941). *A history of medical psychology.* New York: W.W. Norton & Co.

Ziring, P. (2001). Committee on Children with Disabilities: The pediatrician's role in the diagnosis and management of autistic spectrum disorder in children. *Pediatrics, 107*, 1221–1226.

Index

Note: Note page entries in **bold** refer to glossary definitions